Guardian of the Wall

Photo courtesy of Susan Pfeffer.

Guardian of the Wall

Leo Pfeffer and the Religion Clauses of the First Amendment

J. David Holcomb

LEXINGTON BOOKS
Lanham • Boulder • New York • London

Published by Lexington Books
An imprint of The Rowman & Littlefield Publishing Group, Inc.
4501 Forbes Boulevard, Suite 200, Lanham, Maryland 20706
www.rowman.com

6 Tinworth Street, London SE11 5AL, United Kingdom

British Library Cataloguing in Publication Information Available

Library of Congress Cataloging-in-Publication Data Available

ISBN 978-0-7391-4901-0 (cloth)
ISBN 978-0-7391-4903-4 (electronic)

Contents

Acknowledgments

I write these acknowledgments in June of 2020, more than three months into the COVID-19 pandemic that has caused illness, death, and economic destruction around the globe. In the United States alone, the virus has claimed over 120,000 lives and put more than 35 million Americans out of work. At universities around the country, the Spring semester came to an abrupt halt as states imposed lockdowns and other social distancing measures in order to "flatten the curve" of the pandemic's impact. Professors like me were forced to shift their courses to an online learning format for the remainder of the semester as students and faculty alike were cloistered in their homes. The transition to online learning was labor intensive, and the stress and uncertainty about what the future holds has been unusually distracting. If there is a silver lining to the pandemic, though, it is that the extended home stay has provided me blocks of time to complete final revisions and editorial corrections on this long overdue manuscript. It has also given me the opportunity to reflect on those who have provided assistance and encouragement along the way.

James E. Wood, Jr., who passed away last year at age ninty-six, was my mentor for two graduate degrees in the J.M. Dawson Institute of Church-State Studies at Baylor University. His profound influence on me included his suggestion that I examine the thought of Leo Pfeffer for my dissertation. While this book is a substantial revision and expansion of the dissertation, Dr. Wood's influence can undoubtedly been seen in the manuscript. I am also thankful to Dr. Wood for securing copies of most all of Leo Pfeffer's publications, briefs, and unpublished writings for what was the Institute's research center. I've been very fortunate to have a treasure trove of primary sources at my fingertips. Dr. Wood's successor as director of the Institute and later my dean at the University of Mary Hardin-Baylor, Derek Davis, has encouraged my scholarship, supported my professional aspirations, and has been a good friend and colleague.

This book would not have come to fruition without the support of the University of Mary Hardin-Baylor. I am thankful for being awarded two summer development leaves and a semester-long sabbatical that allowed me to give sustained attention to the project. My colleagues in the Department of History and Political Science, Janet Adamski, David Chrisman, Rebecca Peterson, and Claire Phelan, have been sources of encouragement and a fun group to work with over the years.

I owe a special word of thanks to several people who reviewed individual chapters or complete drafts of the manuscript. John Blakeman, Steve Green, Melissa Rogers, and Doug Weaver have all provided insightful comments. While their recommendations have helped strengthen the work, any errors or limitations of the book are my own.

The editors at Lexington Books have been exceedingly patient and helpful. This project has dragged on for a long time, so I appreciate their willingness to stick with me. While I've worked with several editors, Becca Breuer has been especially helpful in answering questions during the latter stages of the publication process.

My deepest gratitude goes out to my family for their support. My late mother was a high-school science teacher and my father served as a college and seminary professor for more than fifty years. Both of my parents unfailingly encouraged my professional pursuits and modeled for me the important balance between academic and family life. My wife Carol and I have enjoyed having all three of our sons home during the Coronavirus pandemic. Ben, Andrew, and Daniel have handled the disruption to their high school and college careers with amazing patience and good humor and have given me space to finish my book. Most of all, I am thankful for the love and support of my wife Carol. This work would not have come to fruition without her constant encouragement and support. She has read each chapter carefully and made invaluable recommendations and editorial corrections. I am very fortunate to have a wife who is also my colleague and best friend. There is no one else I'd rather shelter-in-place with during a pandemic.

Introduction

In the years following World War II, a host of cases flooded the courts that transformed church-state relations in the United States. These legal disputes flourished in the context of a post–War religious revival as well as a battle with "atheistic Communism" that spawned renewed interest in religion in public life.[1] Religious exercises in the public schools, such as teacher-led prayers and Bible reading, led to some of the most controversial First Amendment battles in American history. A massive Catholic parochial school system in desperate need of funds provided still another battleground as proponents and opponents of public funds for religious schools faced off in the courts. An ever expanding federal government blurred the lines between the sacred and the secular, while minority and nonconventional faiths sought protection from discriminatory laws. And with the incorporation of the Free Exercise and Establishment Clauses of the First Amendment of the Constitution to the states, the U.S. Supreme Court increasingly became the final arbiter of these legal contests.[2]

These church-state confrontations forced lawyers, judges, scholars, and advocates to reflect on the meaning and proper application of the religion clauses of the First Amendment. The Establishment Clause's ban on laws "respecting an establishment of religion" generated multiple interpretations; however, generally speaking, two approaches prevailed. The first, often called the separationist position, held that the church and the state should have, in Thomas Jefferson's words, "a wall of separation" between the two. Also known as the "no-aid" interpretation, advocates of this approach believed that the Establishment Clause prohibited the government from providing any financial aid or other support of religion or religious institutions. In this schema, the state was to be secular or neutral with regard to religious matters. The second interpretation held that the framers of the U.S. Constitution never intended to create a secular state. Rather, a single established church was to be avoided, but government could assist religion as long as it was done on a "nonpreferential" basis. These "accommodationists" argued that the Establishment Clause allowed greater cooperation between church and state.

This book is about how Leo Pfeffer, the most influential and articulate advocate, scholar, and jurist of the separationist position in the twentieth century, interpreted the religion clauses of the First Amendment and influenced the U.S. Supreme Court's First Amendment jurisprudence. Hungarian born and the son of an Orthodox Jewish Rabbi, Pfeffer was brought to the United States at the age of two by his parents. Raised in New York City, Pfeffer was educated at the City College of New York and New York University Law School, and in 1945, he began work for the Commission on Law and Social Action of the American Jewish Congress.[3] It was in this position, where he eventually served as director, general counsel, and special counsel, that Pfeffer quickly became recognized as an expert in church-state relations. Pfeffer likewise devoted a significant amount of time to issues of religion and public education in his role as counsel for the New York Committee for Public Education and Religious Liberty (PEARL) and the National Coalition for PEARL. In addition to his legal advocacy, Pfeffer served as professor and chair of political science at Long Island University from 1964 to 1979.

During his career, Pfeffer's contributions to law and religion were unmatched. As one scholar noted, he "probably argued more church-state cases before the United States Supreme Court than anyone else in American history, serving as counsel in almost 50 percent of all the cases on the Establishment Clause to be litigated in the United States Supreme Court."[4] Pfeffer's involvement was not limited to Establishment Clause issues. In many of his more than 120 briefs in religious liberty cases, Pfeffer defended the free exercise rights of conscientious objectors, sabbatarians, and religious groups such as the Amish and the Unification Church. When not serving as counsel to a party in a case, he utilized the amicus curiae, or friend-of-the-court, brief as an effective tool in influencing the Court's decisions.[5] Moreover, Pfeffer's role in these cases often was much more significant than the filing of a brief. He frequently influenced the litigation process by providing legal strategy and tactics. Organizations other than the American Jewish Congress often called upon Pfeffer to draft their amicus curiae briefs or to provide other legal expertise as well.

Pfeffer's involvement in the field was not limited to legal advocacy. A prolific author, Pfeffer published eight books and more than 250 articles and reviews, as well as having written scores of unpublished documents and manuscripts. His seminal work, *Church, State, and Freedom*[6] is considered a classic in the field and continues to be cited in scholarly literature, legal briefs, and court opinions.[7] A work of over 700 pages, *Church, State, and*

Freedom traced the historical development as well as constitutional debates surrounding religious freedom and church-state separation.

Individual scholars have frequently honored Pfeffer for his achievements. Constitutional scholar Samuel Krislov stated, "Leo Pfeffer is probably *sui generis*. . . . No one comes to mind, however, to rival Pfeffer's intellectual dominance over so vital an area of constitutional law for so extensive a period in his combination of pleading and intellectualizing."[8] "It is no exaggeration," David Fellman similarly argued, "that he [Pfeffer] is one of the principal architects of church-state law in our time."[9] And Gregg Ivers concluded that Pfeffer "was beyond doubt the most dominant and influential advocate of his generation (and quite possibly of all time) in the field of church-state law."[10] In a tribute to Pfeffer, who died in 1993, one scholar declared, "It may well be said that the United States has lost its greatest champion of religious liberty in this century."[11]

The purpose of this study is to provide an overview and analysis of Leo Pfeffer's church-state thought and its influence on the U.S. Supreme Court. I will argue that Pfeffer's understanding of the First Amendment's religion clauses, shaped as it was by his historical and religious context, led him to advocate a separationist historical narrative and absolutist application of the Establishment and Free Exercise Clauses that in large measure shaped the U.S. Supreme Court's interpretation of the First Amendment for much of the mid-to-late twentieth-century. In doing so, this work challenges a popular contention that Pfeffer's separationist philosophy was hostile to religion and sought to remove religion from the public square. Instead, this book illustrates how Pfeffer believed a broad reading of both religion clauses sought to protect religious freedom, secure equality, and level the playing field among religious participants in public life. As Pfeffer frequently stated his position, the separation of church and state was "best for church, best for the state and secures freedom for both."

Despite Pfeffer's profound impact on such a controversial area of the law, surprisingly little scholarship has been devoted exclusively to Pfeffer's thought and influence on the U.S. Supreme Court. In the early 1990s, Joseph Preville published articles in *Church History*, *The Catholic Historical Review*, and *The Journal of Church and State* focusing on Pfeffer's conflicts with Catholic institutions in the battles over aid to parochial schools.[12] Frank Sorauf's *The Wall of Separation: The Constitutional Politics of Church and State* devoted attention to Pfeffer in his study of church-state litigation over a twenty-year period.[13] It is a work of public law concerned primarily with the judicial process and the politics of litigation. Gregg Ivers completed a similar study in his *To Build a Wall: American Jews and the Separation of Church and State*.[14] Ivers gave significant attention to Leo Pfeffer while examining the relationship between the major Jewish lobbies and their approaches to church-state issues. Iver's utilization of the Pfeffer papers gives needed insight into Pfeffer's personality and relationship with the Jewish community. Nonetheless, both of these works are concerned more with Pfeffer's influence on public law and interest group litigation as opposed to Pfeffer's jurisprudence, his broader impact on church-state law, and his contributions to the debates over religion in public life. Naomi Cohen's *Jews in Christian America: The Pursuit of Religious Equality*[15] provides an invaluable historical narrative of how American Jews embraced the separation of church and state in their pursuit of equality in American society. She gives careful attention to Pfeffer in her chapters that focus on the shift of Jewish defense agencies to litigation to challenge Christian majoritarian practices and symbols in public institutions. To be sure, this book has benefited greatly from these studies. Yet no scholarly work dedicated exclusively to Pfeffer's thought and contribution to church-state law has been published.

This study is a broad overview of Pfeffer's historical context, intellectual contributions, and legal advocacy and is intended for a general academic readership. The goal was not to write a biography per se, but rather provide a synthesis of his legal philosophy that will be of interest to students of law, history, political science, and religious studies. Drawing Pfeffer's scholarly writings, legal briefs, oral arguments, Congressional testimony, correspondence, and a variety of other unpublished sources, this work not only examines his Establishment Clause advocacy but also his efforts to protect the free exercise rights of religious minorities.

Pfeffer's commitment to the separation of church and state was influenced by his Jewish identity and historical context. Chapter 1 describes the religious, political, and social factors that shaped his philosophy of church and state. Raised in an Orthodox Jewish home and the son of a Rabbi, Pfeffer was exposed to the messages of the Hebrew prophets and their calls for social justice. Moreover, his commitment to his faith was lifelong as he regularly attended synagogue, observed Jewish dietary laws, and maintained a keen interest in biblical study. Pfeffer's experiences as a child in public schools presaged his future battles over religion and public schools. The Holocaust and anti-Semitism compelled his commitment to religious liberty as well. Like many Jews, Pfeffer was very cognizant of the vulnerability of Jews in a Christian majority state which enhanced his commitment to church-state separation. Pfeffer's career as an attorney for the American Jewish Congress took place during a time when church-state relations was a burgeoning field due in part to the growth of the welfare state, the litigiousness of marginalized religious groups, religio-political battles over religion and education, and the increasing willingness of the U.S. Supreme Court to apply the Bill of Right's guarantees to the states. All of these factors set the stage for Pfeffer's scholarship and advocacy.

Chapter 2 explores Pfeffer's understanding of the relationship of religious freedom and church-state separation. For Pfeffer, the First Amendment of the U.S. Constitution was the embodiment of these two principles creating, what he would consistently argue to be, a unitary guarantee. As Pfeffer frequently stated it: "Notwithstanding occasional instances of apparent conflict, separation guarantees freedom, and freedom requires separation."[16] In defending his interpretation of the religion clauses, Pfeffer articulated what might be called the classic separationist historical narrative as he drew upon the writings of Roger Williams, James Madison, and Thomas Jefferson to bolster his broad reading of the First Amendment. While the U.S. Supreme Court largely adopted Pfeffer's reading of the history of the religion clauses, it was not without its critics. James M. O'Neill and later Robert Cord criticized Pfeffer for engaging in selective or "law office history" that was not consistent with the "original intent" of the Framers of the U.S. Constitution.[17] A more accurate reading, these scholars contended, was that the religion clauses merely banned the establishment of a single national church and thus countenanced government support of religion on a nonpreferential basis. Nonetheless, Pfeffer countered in his legal briefs and academic writings that the religious, social, and economic context, as well as the events surrounding the drafting of the First Amendment, compelled a broad reading of the First Amendment's religion clauses. History was central to Pfeffer's church-state jurisprudence and invariably was the starting point for his legal strategy.

Chapter 3 analyzes Pfeffer's application of the separationist principle, embodied in the Establishment Clause of the First Amendment. The relationship of religion and education has been fertile ground for church-state controversy and thus provides an appropriate context for understanding Pfeffer's interpretation of the Establishment Clause. Often called an absolutist, Pfeffer was unequivocal in his belief that the Establishment Clause forbade aid from the government to religion. In doing so, Pfeffer opposed not only public school sponsored religious exercises but also public aid to private religious schools. It was in the area of aid to religious institutions that Pfeffer was most actively involved and had his greatest influence on the Court. This chapter takes a careful look at Pfeffer's briefs and oral arguments to catalog his influence on the Court's opinions during this period. The Court frequently utilized Pfeffer's arguments and constitutional tests and, as one Court observer concluded: "It was hard to determine where Pfeffer's words ended and the Court's began."[18]

Pfeffer's Free Exercise Clause advocacy is examined in chapter 4. In the "clash of conflicting interests" between the state and the individual's conscience, Pfeffer would place a heavy burden on the state before justifying any restrictions on the free exercise of religion. Rejecting the notion that religious exemptions from otherwise neutral and generally applicable laws were not required by the Free Exercise Clause, Pfeffer supported the compelling state interest test adopted by the Court in the 1963 decision of *Sherbert v. Verner*. Pfeffer argued for an expansive view of the Free Exercise Clause defending nonmainstream religions such as "cults," sabbatarians, and conscientious objectors, while also advocating for abortion rights on the basis of religious conscience. Pfeffer's broad reading of the Free Exercise Clause made him vulnerable to criticism that his reading of the two clauses set them up for inevitable conflict. For Pfeffer, though, the conflict between the two clauses was "more apparent than real," arguing that typically a law that violated one clause violated the other as well.[19]

Chapter 5 examines Pfeffer's understanding of the role of religion in public life. Some Jewish scholars have been quite critical of the widespread support for separationism on the part of the American Jewish community. They argue that the strict adherence to separation has, in the words of Noah Pickus, "prevented them (American Jews) from recognizing that the moral decline resulting from the exclusion of religiously-grounded values" in public life.[20] Concern about the increasing secularization of society also motivated critiques of Pfeffer's separationism by Catholic scholar Richard John Neuhaus. Neuhaus contended that religious freedom has been "turned on its head" with the "Pfefferian" interpretation that the Establishment and Free Exercise Clauses had to be balanced against each other, rather than, as Neuhaus argued, that the Establishment Clause was to be subordinate to, and in the service of, the Free Exercise Clause. The result, Neuhaus argued, was that the emphasis placed on the Establishment Clause has led to a separation of religion from public life, creating a "naked public square."[21] Pfeffer, however, did not see a conflict between a high wall of separation between church and state and a robust role of religion in the public square. For him, commitment to a high wall of separation was not *intended* to marginalize religion from the public square, but rather to create a level playing field among the various religious participants in public debate and to preserve the integrity of both church and state. Moreover, the notion that Pfeffer's absolutism with regard to the separation of church had the *effect* of creating a naked public square is difficult to reconcile with the continued vitality and political influence of religion in America.

The conclusion reflects upon Pfeffer's legacy on American church-state relations in light of current trends on the Court and in First Amendment scholarship. Unquestionably, the evidence reveals that Pfeffer had a profound impact on the Court, particularly its Establishment Clause decisions during the "separationist era." His effective use of history and persistent advocacy of the unitary nature of freedom and separation influenced how the Court understood the role and relationship of the religion clauses. Pfeffer's commitment to a high wall of separation was in the interest of religious freedom and the belief that religion was a private matter, though by private, Pfeffer meant that religion's role in public life should be voluntary, not government sponsored. These commitments counter the claims that strict separation was rooted in hostility to religion.

Nonetheless, Pfeffer's legacy might rightly be questioned in light of the trajectory of the U.S. Supreme Court's religion clause decisions over the last thirty years. While the Court continues to find state-sponsored school prayer, Bible reading, and other religious exercises difficult to reconcile with the Establishment Clause, it has largely embraced an equal treatment approach in government aid cases. The product of a changing Court personnel, a changing religious and political landscape, and a growing embrace in both the legal and scholarly communities for a revised notion of government neutrality, the equal treatment approach has led the U.S. Supreme Court to reverse several of the Pfeffer-inspired separationist decisions of the 1970s and has allowed for greater public aid to religious institutions.

The more dynamic First Amendment battles in the last two decades have involved the Free Exercise Clause. Here, too, the broad reading of the Free Exercise Clause has been challenged. In the 1990 *Oregon v. Smith* decision, a plurality of the Court dispensed with the compelling state interest requiring strict scrutiny of laws that burdened free exercise. *Smith* was met with widespread criticism leading Congress to restore the compelling interest inquiry by passing the Religious Freedom Restoration Act in 1993. Yet RFRAs impact was limited by the *City of Boerne v. Flores* decision determining that it was unconstitutional as it was applied to the states. The debate over whether religious exemptions should be granted from neutral and generally applicable laws continues, but has shifted ideologically. No longer are exemptions sought primarily by Jehovah's Witnesses, Seventh Day Adventists, and other nonmainstream faiths from burdensome laws, but also by Christian business owners seeking to avoid federal health-care mandates, as well as anti-discrimination laws they say violate their consciences.[22]

Despite these trends, the Court remains divided on how best to interpret both religion clauses with a minority of justices still committed, albeit to varying degrees, to the broad reading Pfeffer advocated. Lower courts continue to articulate separationist principles and utilize the Lemon Test in their Establishment Clause opinions, and some influential scholars continue to advocate a broad reading of the religion clauses. Despite vigorous debate over religious exemptions, they retain widespread support among scholars and jurists alike. Religion clause jurisprudence remains fluid with justices and legal scholars continuing to grapple with many of the constitutional arguments articulated over a half-century ago by Leo Pfeffer.

NOTES

1. See Sydney E. Ahlstrom, *A Religious History of the American People* 2nd ed. (New Haven: Yale University Press, 2004), 949–63; see also Edwin Gaustad and Leigh E. Schmidt, *The Religious History of America*, Rev. ed. (New York: HarperSanFrancisco, 2002), 441–48; Keven Kruse has more recently argued that the post-War revival was fostered by conservative business leaders who sought to supplant Franklin Roosevelt's New Deal with a "Christian libertarianism." See Kevin M. Kruse, *One Nation Under God: How Corporate America Invented Christian America* (New York: Basic Books, 2015).

2. *Cantwell v. Connecticut*, 310 U.S. 296 (1940); *Everson v. Board of Education*, 330 U.S. 1 (1947).

3. See Leo Pfeffer, "An Autobiographical Sketch," in *Religion and the State: Essays in Honor of Leo Pfeffer*, ed. James E. Wood, Jr. (Waco, TX: Baylor University Press, 1984), 487–88.

4. James E. Wood, Jr., "A Tribute to Leo Pfeffer (1909–1993)," *Journal of Church and State* 35 (Summer 1993): 605.

5. Leo Pfeffer, "Amici in Church-State Litigation," *Law and Contemporary Problems* 44 (Winter 1984): 83–110.

6. Leo Pfeffer, *Church, State, and Freedom* (Boston: Beacon Press, 1953; rev. ed. 1967).

7. For a complete bibliography of Pfeffer's writings, see "The Writings of Leo Pfeffer: Prepared by Freda Pfeffer," in *Religion and the State: Essays in Honor of Leo Pfeffer*, ed. James E. Wood, Jr. (Waco, TX: Baylor University Press, 1984), 535–68.

8. Samuel Krislov, "Alternatives to Separation of Church and State in Countries Outside the United States," in *Religion and the State: Essays in Honor of Leo Pfeffer*, ed. James E. Wood, Jr. (Waco, TX: Baylor University Press, 1984), 421.

9. David Fellman, "How High the Wall of Separation? Pfeffer on Religion and the State," *American Bar Foundation Research Journal* 1 (1986): 123.

10. Gregg Ivers, *To Build a Wall: American Jews and the Separation of Church and State* (Charlottesville: University Press of Virginia, 1995), 193.

11. Wood, "A Tribute," 606.

12. See Joseph R. Preville, "Leo Pfeffer and the American Church-State Debate: A Confrontation with Catholicism," *Journal of Church and State* 33 (Winter 1991): 37–53; "Catholic Colleges, the Courts, and the Constitution: A Tale of Two Cases," *Church History* 58 (June 1989): 197–210; "Catholic Colleges and the Supreme Court: The Case of *Tilton* v. *Richardson*," *Journal of Church and State* 30 (Spring 1988): 291–307.

13. Frank Sorauf, *The Wall of Separation: The Constitutional Politics of Church and State* (Princeton, NJ: Princeton University Press, 1976).

14. Ivers, *To Build a Wall.*

15. Cohen Naomi, *Jews in Christian America*: *The Pursuit of Religious Equality* (New York: Oxford University Press, 1992).

16. Pfeffer, *Church, State, and Freedom*, 727.

17. James M. O'Neill, "Nonpreferential Aid to Religion is Not an Establishment of Religion," *Buffalo Law Review* 2 (Spring 1953): 18–52; Robert L. Cord, *Separation of Church and State: Historical Fact and Current Fiction* (New York: Lambeth Press, 1982).

18. Daniel L. Dreisbach, *Real Threat and Mere Shadow: Religious Liberty and the First Amendment* (Westchester, IL: Crossway Books, 1987), xvi.

19. See Leo Pfeffer, "The Legitimation of Marginal Religions in the United States," in *Religious Movements in Contemporary America*, eds. Irving I. Zaretsky and Mark P. Leone (Princeton, NJ: Princeton University Press, 1974), 14–15; "Religious Freedom and the American Community," *Judaism* 28 (Spring 1979): 137–46.

20. Noah Pickus, "'Before I Built a Wall'—Jews, Religion and American Public Life," *This World* 15 (1986): 29; see also David G. Dalin, ed. *American Jews and the Separationist Faith: The New Debate on Religion in Public Life* (Washington, DC: Ethics and Public Policy Center, 1993); and Alan Mittleman, et al., eds., *Jews and the American Public Square: Debating Religion and Republic* (Lanham, MD: Rowman and Littlefield Publishers, Inc., 2002).

21. See Richard John Neuhaus, "Pfefferian Inversion," *National Review* 10 (13 May 1988): 11; "Genuine Pluralism and the Pfefferian Inversion," *This World* 25 (1989): 69–98; "Contending for the Future: Overcoming the Pfefferian Inversion," *Journal of Law and Religion* 8 (1990): 115–29; and *The Naked Public Square: Religion and Democracy in America* (Grand Rapids, MI: William B. Eerdmans Publishing Co., 1984).

22. See *Burwell v. Hobby Lobby Stores*, 573 US 682 (2014) and *Masterpiece Cakeshop, Ltd. v. Colorado Civil Rights Commission*, 586 U.S. ___ (2018).

Chapter 1

Sources of Leo Pfeffer's Thought

Leo Pfeffer's career as a scholar and attorney was marked by an unwavering commitment to religious freedom and church-state separation. As the leading advocate of the separationist position before the U.S. Supreme Court during the post–World War II era, Pfeffer was a self-described absolutist with regard to First Amendment freedoms. The product of "sincerely held principle" as well as "pragmatic considerations," Pfeffer's absolutism with regard to the First Amendment was informed by his religious identity and historical context.[1]

Pfeffer's religious heritage as a Jew of East European descent, raised in a traditional Orthodox home, certainly influenced how he viewed the proper relationship of religion and the state. No less significant was his identity as a Jew in "Christian America." Pfeffer, like other Jews of his era, saw in the promises of the Constitution the opportunity to achieve "equal footing" in American society.[2] This quest, in part, drew Pfeffer to the law which not only shaped his constitutional convictions but also led to his career as an attorney for the American Jewish Congress. Pfeffer's career coincided with the U. S. Supreme Court's application of the Establishment and Free Exercise clauses to the states, further setting the stage for Pfeffer's scholarship and advocacy.

LEO PFEFFER AND PRE–WORLD WAR II AMERICAN JEWRY

Leo Pfeffer's understanding of religious freedom and church-state separation cannot be properly understood apart from his identity as an American Jew. To a large degree, the American Jewish experience has been marked by a quest for religious and civil equality. While in colonial America, Jews fared better than most of their European counterparts, they still faced restrictions with regard to holding public office or exercising the right to vote. Moreover, Sunday laws, Christian oaths, and church taxes were a part of their daily existence. Numbering about 5,000 by the time of the Revolutionary War, these predominantly Sephardic Jews became increasingly enamored with the egalitarian promises of liberal republicanism. With American Independence and the adoption of the Constitution's guarantees of religious freedom and separation of church and state, as well as Article VI's ban on religious tests for public office, American Jews began advocating not only freedom of conscience but also full equality for all religions.[3] A primary objective of Jews in the early Republic was the removal of legal or constitutional barriers to their full and equal participation in public life. "This interest," James Reichley has observed, "naturally drew them to the party of equality and particularly to Jefferson, the nation's leading proponent of religious freedom."[4]

Nevertheless, throughout the nineteenth century, obstacles continued to be placed in front of the Jewish quest for equality. Jews in turn mobilized at the local and state level to challenge various forms of discrimination.[5] A chief barrier was the Christian test oaths that often blocked Jews from holding public office. One of the chief battles to remove oaths occurred in Maryland whose constitution required a "belief in the Christian religion." Jews challenged the oath as early as 1779, but were rebuffed. Emboldened by the new Constitution and promises of religious freedom in the Bill of Rights, Jews renewed their efforts. For nearly thirty years, the Baltimore Jewish community would petition the legislature, but it would not be until 1826, and on a narrow vote, that an alternative oath for Jews was approved by Maryland lawmakers.[6] Similar efforts were mounted nationwide, and by 1840, twenty-one of twenty-six states were granted Jews political equality.[7]

The ongoing battle of Jews to counter the Protestant quest for a "Christian America" was often an uphill endeavor as various manifestations of American Christian heritage permeated legislation, court decisions, and public institutions during the nineteenth century. Nevertheless, the American Jewish population was growing rapidly with the immigration of Ashkenazic Jews. With numerical growth came greater organization and communication. Through newly formed Jewish periodicals such as the *Occident*, the *American Israelite*, and the *Jewish Messenger*, American Jews of all traditions were able to mobilize in defense of Jewish rights in the face of Sunday laws, Thanksgiving Day proclamations, religion in the public schools, and other practices that reflected the Protestant culture of the nation. U.S. Supreme Court decisions, such as *Holy Trinity* v. *United States*,[8] in which Justice David J. Brewer proclaimed that America was a "Christian nation," stirred in Jewish minds the pernicious notion of a Christian state, which relegated Jews to a mere tolerated minority. As a result, American Jews became more vigilant advocates of separation of church and state. No longer satisfied with exemptions and accommodations for their religious beliefs and practices, American Jews, during the late nineteenth century, began to renew the calls of Jefferson and Madison for a secular state, considering it to be the best guarantor of religious freedom.[9]

After World War I, American Jews faced a growing tide of anti-Semitism. Fostered by Henry Ford's *Dearborn Independent*, accusations of a Jewish conspiracy to dominate the world found a frighteningly open reception among many Americans and coincided with the revival of the Ku Klux Klan. The passage of restrictive immigration laws during the 1920s, which dramatically reduced Jewish immigration in the United States, was but one consequence of the anti-Semitism and nativism during this period. In the 1930s, anti-Semitism reemerged during the Great Depression. Jews were one of many scapegoats targeted as Americans sought to cope with the harsh realities of economic uncertainty.[10]

American Jews also became regular targets of anti-Semitism due to the participation of some Jews in radical political activity. The political idealism and egalitarianism of the socialist message found a receptive audience among many American and European Jews who were attracted specifically to its promises of a welfare state, international brotherhood, and civil reform. For others, it was a middle-class radicalism that was a response to the continued deprivation of true equality in American society.[11] During World War II, Jewish radicalism conflicted with the heightened patriotism of the war context and the reduction of toleration for those challenging political orthodoxy. Jews regularly faced the consequences of patriotic paranoia due to their comparatively significant involvement in communist and socialist political groups. Through his publications and radio broadcasts, Father Charles Coughlin ignited an anti-Semitic campaign by identifying communism as a Jewish conspiracy. Coughlin contended that America's entry into World War II was engineered by Jews, whom he believed had an inordinate amount of influence on President Franklin D. Roosevelt.[12]

The massacre of six million Jews during the Holocaust forced American Jews to reflect upon their status in American society as well. For most Jews, the Holocaust reinforced the tenuous status of Jewry in a Christian majority state. In the aftermath of the Holocaust, American Jews had to answer the question of whether, as one historian concluded, "Jewish existence continued to have any purpose. A minority of American Jews concluded that the price of identifying with the Jewish people had simply become too high."[13] For most Jews, however, the response to the Holocaust was a reevaluation of their strategy for seeking freedom and equality in American society. Increasing numbers of Jews viewed the notion of a "Christian America" as an obstacle to Jewish equality. No longer would Jews seek mere accommodations for their religious beliefs and practices. Rather, Jews saw their quest for freedom and equality as dependent upon the separation of church and state.[14]

EARLY LIFE AND INTELLECTUAL INFLUENCES

Leo Pfeffer was part of the massive immigration of East European Jews to the United States early in the twentieth century. These Jewish immigrants established Orthodox communities in the ghettos of America's Northern industrial cities. Many were uneducated and unskilled and were viewed with disdain by the acculturated and largely Reformed German Jews. But by the 1920s, they began to enjoy social mobility and greater assimilation into American life. For many, the promises of social and economic advancement often diminished strict observance of Orthodox practices.[15]

Born in Hungary, Pfeffer was brought to the United States in 1911, at the age of two, by his father, an Orthodox Jewish rabbi. His family, which included three sisters and an older brother, settled in the lower east side of New York City.[16] The importance of education was evident in the Pfeffer household as Leo was sent to the local Public School 15. Pfeffer's childhood experiences in the public school presaged his church-state activity of later years. It was there where he experienced firsthand the tensions between a nation constitutionally committed to religious liberty and a society whose public institutions retained Christian symbols and practices. For instance, Pfeffer recalled the daily Bible reading at the school assembly led by the school's principle, although it was limited to the book of Psalms due to the large number of Jewish students.[17] Bible reading in the public schools had been a continual area of church-state contention ever since Catholics protested the use of the King James Version of the Bible during the mid-nineteenth century. Moreover, the Bible-reading controversy provided a primary impetus for the establishment of the Catholic parochial school system in the United States. In the twentieth century, state legislators passed statutes requiring Bible reading in the public schools in response to what was considered a crisis in religious education. Years later, Pfeffer would eventually challenge the practice on First Amendment grounds. Citing its devotional and sectarian nature, Pfeffer found it to be a clear violation of the Establishment Clause.[18]

The introduction of a released time program at his public school during his fourth year foreshadowed his later church-state advocacy as well. Developed by Dr. William Wirt for the public schools of Gary, Indiana in 1914, released time was a program where students, during specific periods, would be released from classes in order to obtain religious instruction. Those choosing not to participate were to remain under the supervision of school authorities. This program was deemed unacceptable to Pfeffer's parents, who soon withdrew him from the public school and enrolled him in an Orthodox Jewish school. Years later, Pfeffer's first assignment as a young lawyer for the Commission on Law and Social Action (CLSA) of the American Jewish Congress would be the constitutional battle over released time. Pfeffer was asked to prepare a memorandum citing arguments both for and against released time. This he did while also making his objections on constitutional grounds clear. As a result, Pfeffer drafted an amicus curiae brief in 1948 on behalf of the Congress in opposition to the released time program in the landmark case, *McCollum v. Board of Education*.[19] Pfeffer opposed released time as a violation of the Establishment Clause by "permitting the intrusion of religion into the public school system by classes devoted to religious instruction or worship on public school premises during regular school time."[20] Pfeffer's personal experience is clearly revealed as he objected to the "division of school children according to their religious belief." For Pfeffer, "The divisiveness which inevitably results whenever sectarianism enters the public school affects all American children, but is particularly harmful to children of minority faiths."[21] Of his objections to released time, Pfeffer once stated: "This is hardly surprising in view of my childhood experience with the released-time proposal." Consequently, his work with the released time led the CLSA to name him the point person for church-state litigation.[22]

Pfeffer's secondary education was at the Orthodox Rabbi Isaac Elchonon Talmudical Academy. He then attended the City College of New York and earned a law degree at New York University in 1933. Pfeffer's attraction to law mirrored that of other American Jews of his age. Law was an area where Jews were free to participate, and in the United States, Jews were able to reach the top in the legal profession with several Jewish justices serving on the U.S. Supreme Court. The ability to bring about social and political reform drew many Jews to the law while others found in the practice of law the opportunity to "define themselves as patriotic Americans."[23]

The Jewish commitment to higher education in general reflected one of the major values of American Judaism that helped define their commitment to political liberalism. Lawrence Fuchs noted that the love of learning (Torah) motivated Jews to support political positions that placed emphasis on intellectual freedom and protection of civil liberties. Furthermore, the value of charity (*zedakeh*) spurred Jewish efforts for social justice.[24] Jewish emphasis on intellectual freedom explains Pfeffer's insistence that freedom of conscience was the cornerstone of all freedoms.[25] And as a civil libertarian, Pfeffer was unequivocal in arguing that "liberty is one boat and that, unless the hole under the seat occupied by the Communist or atheist is plugged up, the sea will ultimately engulf all the occupants—even those who sit on the extreme right side of the boat and fear the Communist or detest the atheist."[26]

Pfeffer's religious upbringing shaped his understanding of religious freedom and church-state separation as well. As the son of an Orthodox Jewish rabbi, Pfeffer was raised in a traditional Jewish home observing the practices of Orthodox Judaism and was given a religious education. For many East European Jews who had gradually moved to the middle class during this period, religious devotion became a less conspicuous element of their suburban existence. Secularization seemed to parallel the higher social, educational, and economic status that many Jews were achieving. In part, this trend can be explained as a reaction of many East European Jews to the strictures of Orthodox Judaism. Many viewed Orthodoxy as a barrier to assimilation into American life. According to James Reichley, "Many who found religious requirements of Orthodoxy too demanding opted for secularism as opposed to Conservative or Reform Judaism."[27]

Secularization was especially evident in the various Jewish philanthropic and defense agencies.[28] Historian Naomi Cohen characterized the workers of the Jewish defense agencies this way: "Rooted in the east European immigrant experience, many had imbibed a secularist indoctrination or secularist leanings. They spoke for a religious community, but, as one longtime defense worker wrote, their actions in opposition to public religion reflected their own indifference if not hostility to religion itself."[29] Such characterizations did not hold true for Leo Pfeffer. Rather, the devout Pfeffer regularly attended synagogue and observed Jewish dietary laws. Pfeffer, his wife Freda, whom he had married in 1937, and their two children, Alan and Susan, were regular members of the Young Israel Synagogue in Manhattan. A Jewish historian has described the relationship between Pfeffer and, in his view, the largely secular American Jewish Congress as "at first glance . . . incongruous," but concluded that "the union of the American Jewish Congress and Pfeffer reveals the extent to which the strict separationist faith encompassed the broadest spectrum of American Jewry."[30]

Pfeffer's concern for the integrity of religious faith is witnessed in his critique of civil religion. In 1967, Robert Bellah's published a seminal article that described an "elaborate and well-instituted" public religion in the United States that was characterized by public symbols and rituals that bound people together in a sense of shared national identity and purpose. Pfeffer viewed civil religion as both a "common denominator faith" that provides the basis for common core religious instruction and nonsectarian prayers in the public schools and a threat to true religious faith. "I am not as sanguine as Bellah," he wrote, "that the established religions do not view this civil religion as a competitor, a bad religion which if it does not drive out the good requires them to cheapen their own wares to meet the competition." Pfeffer's indictment continued: "No doubt civil religion serves a useful purpose in a nation where everybody considers religion a good thing but few take it very seriously."[31]

Pfeffer manifested a keen interest in biblical study as well. Throughout his career, Pfeffer published numerous book reviews on Old Testament scholarship. His commitment to religious liberty was no doubt informed by the influence of the Hebrew prophets and their calls for social justice. Scholars have noted the disproportionate social conscience among Jews and have argued that it is rooted in the tradition of the Hebrew prophets and the Talmud's synthesis of biblical ethics. Jewish prophets such as Amos and Isaiah condemned injustice and championed the vulnerable and marginalized, and the Jewish teachings emphasized the absolute worth of every human being.[32]

There has been significant debate concerning the proper relationship between the Hebrew prophets and contemporary American Jews' commitment to liberal political values. Some Jewish scholars argue that the prophetic messages and biblical teachings concerning freedom, justice, and equality were particularistic and were not intended to be universal values for contemporary society. Jerold Auerbach, for example, asserted that the biblical tradition and liberalism are incompatible and that any attempt to link the two requires a selective approach to the messages of the Hebrew prophets. According to Auerbach, "Jews who rejected the authority of Torah, but wanted to remain attached to Judaism, reformulated the biblical heritage to assure its compatibility with Enlightenment values and liberal politics."[33]

Contrarily, Robert Gordis has indicated that while the tension between "a particularist ethos and the faith in a universal God," is deeply rooted in Jewish thought, both have "served as the seedbed for the flowering of a highly significant theory of religious tolerance in post-biblical Judaism."[34] For Pfeffer, the example of the Hebrew prophets informed his commitment to religious liberty. Whether the utilization of the prophetic tradition is completely congruent with political liberalism or not, Pfeffer believed there was a continuity between those teachings and the realities of Jews in a "Christian America." At times, Pfeffer and his colleagues at the American Jewish Congress were criticized for their strident advocacy of separation. Pfeffer viewed their advocacy as consistent with the prophetic tradition: "The Hebrew prophets were trouble makers rather than pacifiers; their concern was with what was right and what was wrong, not what was good community relations."[35]

American Jews have been described as "children of the Enlightenment" due to their deep commitment to civil liberties. This identification with the hallmarks of the Age of Reason is not surprising since they paved the way for Jewish Emancipation in the late eighteenth century. With integration into Western society, came the sacrifice of a distinctive Jewish tradition and organic communities such as had existed in the past. At the same time, however, emancipation allowed for the many significant contributions Jews have made to Western society. Their disproportionate involvement in issues of civil rights and social justice has become a hallmark of the American Jewish tradition.[36] Jews regularly demonstrated their belief that their rights would only be secure "when the rights of people of all faiths were secure."[37]

Pfeffer emphasized the role of Enlightenment thought in the forming of the constitutional guarantees of religious freedom and separation of church and state. He viewed John Locke's social contract theory, which placed religion outside the purview of government thus making the church a "voluntary society of men," as foundational to the American experiment of church-state separation. The Enlightenment also spawned religious liberalism or deism, which influenced many of the primary players of the American founding, including Thomas Jefferson, James Madison, and Thomas Paine. In addressing the major historical influences on the framing of the First Amendment, Pfeffer argued that many of the nation's founders "accepted the social contract as self-evident, and were greatly influenced by Deism and Unitarianism." Foremost among these was Thomas Jefferson, who "never swerved from his devotion to the complete independence of religion and government."[38]

Pfeffer described Jefferson's Act for Establishing Religious Freedom, submitted to the Virginia legislature in 1779, as the "progenitor of the First Amendment's religion clauses."[39] Advocating that religion should be placed outside the realm of government and supported voluntarily, the Statute was for Pfeffer a seminal statement of religious liberty and church-state separation. Similarly, Pfeffer emphasized Jefferson's argument that religion was a private matter. This secular ideal, born out of Enlightenment liberalism, was, for Pfeffer, a central principle of the First Amendment and the best security for religious freedom.[40]

Much of Jefferson's writings on church and state suggest that he viewed religious freedom as a negative liberty. His writings reiterate the danger of the state or the church "coercing," "depriving," or "forcing" matters of belief or conscience. Pfeffer and other separationists have been accused of overemphasizing Jefferson's influence on the First Amendment, particularly his belief that the state should be secular and religious belief relegated to the private realm. Jonathan Sarna has argued that the Jeffersonian vision of a secular government was a "decidedly minority opinion" and was one only adopted by a majority of Jews after the Civil War as a defensive measure during attempts by the Protestant majority to create a "Christian America." Similarly Mark DeWolfe Howe's widely regarded book *The Garden and the Wilderness* argued that the origin of the wall of separation metaphor was not Jefferson's fear of church interference in the state, but rather Roger Williams' call for the protection of the church with a "hedge of separation" between the "garden of the church" and the "wilderness of the state." It was not, then, Jefferson's anti-clericalism, but rather Roger Williams' friendliness to religion that should provide the interpretive framework for the Religion Clauses according to Howe. In a review of Howe's book, Pfeffer responded that Williams was equally concerned about the church utilizing the coercive power of the state especially since he had been banned from the Massachusetts Bay colony by Puritan leaders. Williams and Jefferson had similar concerns according to Pfeffer: "It was not fear and distrust alone that motivated Williams and Jefferson but, no less, a conviction that the state had no business with religion."[41]

Despite Jefferson's significance to Pfeffer, the suggestion that Pfeffer's understanding of religious freedom and church-state separation was rooted purely in Jeffersonian anti-clericalism would be misguided. Pfeffer did not view the First Amendment purely as a negative prohibition against the potential encroachment of the church or the state. Rather, he viewed an equally important historical contribution to the First Amendment to have come from religious groups and figures that viewed separation as essential for the purity and vitality of religion. Dissenting groups, particularly the Baptists, were regularly cited by Pfeffer for their contributions to the development of religious freedom in America.[42] Thus, Pfeffer emphasized both the political and theological influences that converged to provide the ideological impetus behind the First Amendment.

LEO PFEFFER AND THE AMERICAN JEWISH CONGRESS

By the mid-twentieth century, the newfound aggressiveness of Jews in securing their constitutional rights was most evident at the American Jewish Congress (AJC). The Congress had been created to present Jewish interests and concerns at the Peace Conference at Versailles in 1918. Meeting in Philadelphia in December 1918, the committee of representatives from various Jewish organizations planned to dissolve after giving its final report in 1920. A movement was begun, however, to continue the organization on a permanent basis for the purpose of serving as an advocacy group for the protection of Jewish rights. Under the leadership of Louis Brandeis and Rabbi Stephen Wise, the AJC became a permanent organization dedicated to a more democratic approach to Jewish advocacy.[43]

Prior to 1945, the American Jewish Congress focused most of its energies on the protection of Jews and Jewish interests abroad. Any domestic agenda was superseded by a need to "rescue European Jews from the tightening noose of Hitler's Nazi regime."[44] Motivations for a domestic agenda, to be carried on by the AJC's newly established Commission on Law and Social Action (CLSA),[45] came as a result of studies on anti-Semitism in America and a growing realization that "the institutions of American government and the courts could aid in the preservation of constitutional rights."[46]

The ideological impetus for the Commission on Law and Social Action was provided by AJC consultant, Alexander Pekelis, in his essay "Full Equality in a Free Society: A Program for Jewish Action." Pekelis's document represented his commitment to cultural pluralism, the political theory of the Declaration of Independence, the Bill of Rights, and the teachings of the Hebrew prophets. For Pekelis, anti-Semitism and Jewish discrimination in America were private or social rather than governmental as in Europe. As a result, Pekelis sounded a clear voice for moving beyond mere education to an assertive legal agenda to end all forms of discrimination. Jewish survival, according to Pekelis, relied upon transforming "the practices and habits of American society and to change public policy through the courts."[47]

Securing equality for American Jews was only half of the equation for Pekelis. Preserving Jewish distinctiveness was essential to survival as well: "The Jewish cause in the United States thus depends on the traditional American aversion to a leveling centralized government and to the compulsory uniformity of all members of a society."[48] Thus, a commitment to preserving religious or cultural pluralism was central to the agency's purpose. This commitment to pluralism motivated the call for "collective security" or an alliance between American Jews, liberal America, and minorities facing discrimination. Pekelis's understanding of collective security would be echoed later by Pfeffer: "One thing I feel certain: intolerance is contagious, and a threat to the religious freedom of any group, including those whose beliefs are repugnant to us, is a threat to us as Jews and commands our concern."[49] This belief in collective security explains the American Jewish Congress' active involvement in the Civil Rights movement. Jews had played a leading role in the formation of the National Association for the Advancement of Colored People (NAACP) and the American Civil Liberties Union (ACLU). The extent of Jewish involvement in the civil rights movement from 1945 to 1960 led one scholar to conclude: "It is probably no exaggeration to say that the period was the 'Jewish phase' of the civil rights revolution."[50]

Pekelis and other intellectual leaders of the Jewish defense agencies were strong defenders of the public school system. For many Jews, the public schools had played a primary role in their integration into American society and were essential for the success of an enlightened liberal democracy.[51] Jewish support for public education could be traced back to the mid-nineteenth century as could their commitment to the secularity of public schools. In 1869, Rabbi Isaac Wise stated the Jewish position unequivocally: "The public schools are institutions for the education of free, intelligent and enlightened citizens. That is all. To this end we need good secular schools and nothing else."[52]

Leo Pfeffer's association with the Commission on Law and Social Action of the American Jewish Congress began in October 1945. His involvement with church-state relations came by "sheer chance," as he later recalled. Pfeffer's wife Freda, who had worked for the Women's Division of the American Jewish Congress, informed him of an opening with the recently expanding CLSA. Pfeffer was subsequently hired by the CLSA where he eventually served as counsel, director and later, special counsel during his forty-year tenure.

In many respects, Pfeffer mirrored the philosophy of the Commission laid out by Alexander Pekelis. For instance, Pfeffer's first legal assignments involved civil rights as he, too, saw the plight of other minorities, whether ethnic, religious, or political, as directly relevant to Jewish freedom. Pfeffer filed briefs of amicus curiae in several civil rights cases.[53] More significantly, he served as president of the Lawyers Constitutional Defense Committee (LCDC), an organization whose purpose was to enlist lawyers to provide legal assistance for those engaged in the effort to end racial segregation.[54] This involvement in the civil rights effort reflected Pfeffer's commitment to cultural pluralism as well. In his book, *Creeds in Competition: A Creative Force in American Culture*, Pfeffer hailed the "creative competition" that is a consequence of America's religious pluralism:

> Our society is composed of a multiplicity of elements each of which seeks to shape the institutions of American culture according to its own scale of values. Out of this never-ending competition comes America's pluralistic culture, ever dynamic, ever changing, ever reflecting the stresses and pulls of the multifarious and contradictory elements and yet somehow coming out as a substantially harmonious orchestration of these components.[55]

Like Pekelis, Pfeffer viewed religious freedom and cultural pluralism to be complementary values.

Pfeffer shared his colleagues' support for public education as well. "There are many who believe," he once asserted, "that the American public school, freed, secular, and open to all, is the supreme achievement of American democracy." And when public schools were attacked after the Court ruled unconstitutional school-sponsored religious exercises, Pfeffer responded: "The principle upon which the public school system is based is the principle upon which our entire democratic society is based, and an attack upon the principle of public education is an attack upon the principle as it relates to our entire democratic way of life."[56] Secular public schools, free from the divisiveness of religious education and activities, were best suited to play their democratic role, according to Pfeffer.

The principles of equality, pluralism, and support for public education shaped much of Pfeffer's church-state advocacy in his role with the CLSA. As Gregg Ivers has shown, Pfeffer "honed" litigation in defense of separation "to a fine art" and, in large measure, shaped the policies of the American

Jewish Congress and the National Community Relations Advisory Council (NCRAC), an umbrella organization representing American Jewish opinion on matters of public policy. It also led to Pfeffer's recognition nationwide as an expert in church-state relations and initiated a twenty-five year period in which Pfeffer was constantly before the U.S. Supreme Court as either lead counsel or filing amicus curiae briefs.[57]

While Pfeffer became the face of separationist advocacy, it is worth noting that the commitments of Pekelis, plus the litigation tactics of Pfeffer and the American Jewish Congress, were not universally supported by American Jews. Some feared the more aggressive litigation strategies might lead to backlash from the Christian majority, while others, including sociologist Will Herberg, criticized their commitment to a broad reading of the Establishment Clause. Fearing an "eviction of religion from public life," Herberg called on Jews to have "sufficient confidence in the capacity of democracy to preserve its libertarian character without any (absolute) wall of separation between religion and public life."[58]

THE POST—WORLD WAR II CHURCH-STATE MILIEU

Leo Pfeffer's prominence in the field of church and state would not have come about without certain legal developments in the second half of the twentieth century. Most important among these was a U.S. Supreme Court that showed an increasing willingness to apply the Bill of Rights' guarantees to the states. The process of "incorporation" began in 1925 with the free speech case of *Gitlow v. New York* when Justice Edward T. Sanford declared: "For present purposes we may and do assume that freedom of speech and of the press—which are protected by the First Amendment from abridgment by Congress—are among the fundamental personal rights and 'liberties' protected by the due process clause of the Fourteenth Amendment."[59] Not without controversy, the Court's practice of applying these protections to the states opened a floodgate of litigation in the federal courts. In 1940, the Free Exercise Clause of the First Amendment was incorporated in the case of *Cantwell v. Connecticut*.[60] Seven years later, the U.S. Supreme Court held the Establishment Clause to be applicable to the states as well.[61] The Court now found itself in the position of final arbiter of First Amendment controversies with an ever-increasing docket of cases.

Incorporation was in part a byproduct of the increased litigiousness of marginalized religious groups who hoped to secure equal rights and avoid discriminatory laws. Among these were the Jehovah's Witnesses whose frequent appearances before the Court forced the justices to define the limits of free speech and the free exercise of religion. Their aggressive evangelistic tactics and other controversial beliefs led to their involvement in numerous legal disputes over the limits of religious and political freedom. "America owes a great debt of gratitude to the Witnesses," Pfeffer once declared. "Much of the current law relating to religious freedom resulted from the Witnesses' persistence in asserting their constitutional rights in the teeth of persecution and doggedly appealing adverse lower court verdicts to the Supreme Court."[62] The example of the Jehovah's Witnesses provided courage for other religious minorities to seek security of their religious rights in an increasingly sympathetic Court.[63]

Another impetus for church-state controversy stemmed from the religious revival that emerged soon after World War II. The revival spanned the theological spectrum with a renewed interest in religion, manifesting itself in increases in church membership. Large sums of money were spent on new church buildings. Religious books frequently became best sellers. The Baptist evangelist Billy Graham was the key figure of evangelicalism during the period advocating "primacy of faith and the centrality of the Bible" as hallmarks of spiritual renewal. Among mainline Protestants, the religious renewal had an ecumenical flavor witnessed in organizations such as the National Council of Churches.[64]

This nationwide religious resurgence was given official sanction by President Dwight D. Eisenhower whose conspicuous forms of public religiosity exemplified much of what the nation was experiencing.[65] In fact, this "piety along the Potomac" represented a type of religious nationalism that grew out of the anxieties of the Cold War. The concern to safeguard America from any influences of "godless" and "atheistic communism" led many to push for religious education in the public schools. As a result, a renewal of religious activities entered many public school classrooms during this period, preparing the way for church-state legal contests over religion and public education.[66]

Conflicts between Protestants and Catholics renewed during the postwar years as well with many Protestants threatened by a growing and upwardly mobile Catholic population. Protestants sought to mitigate Catholic political power and cultural influence in part by embracing the separation of church and state as an antidote to what they perceived to be authoritarian tendencies of the Catholic Church. Most Catholics advocated an accommodationist view of the Establishment Clause that would allow for greater cooperation between church and state. The political and cultural battles between Protestant and Catholics hardened their views of the Establishment Clause.[67]

The most persistent church-state controversy of the Protestant-Catholic divide involved aid to parochial schools. By the 1960s, the Catholic Church faced a crisis in funding its parochial school system. Declining revenues were in part due to the increasing unavailability of clergy to staff the schools, the decline of aging facilities, and the flight of many Catholic families to the suburbs. As a result, the Catholic Church made a concerted effort to gain public funds for their schools. Special attention was given to include private schools in the Elementary and Secondary Education Act in the mid-1960s. Moreover, state legislatures, especially in northeastern cities where Catholic populations were high, passed various forms of parochiaid.[68]

The massive growth of the federal government, especially after the New Deal policies of President Franklin Roosevelt, would provide still other areas of church-state controversy. Disputes over funding, regulation, and control resulted as the federal government encroached on areas of health, labor, education, and welfare. These problems were further compounded as President Johnson's Great Society expanded social welfare programs. Public-private partnerships flourished and, as one scholar observed: "Increasingly the relations between church and state would become more subtle, more complex, more wide-ranging because the state itself was taking on more of the functions that had formerly been fulfilled by private institutions."[69]

By the 1960s, America had truly become a pluralistic nation. Will Herberg's sociological characterization of America's three faiths—Protestant, Catholic, and Jewish—was no longer an apt description of America's religious diversity.[70] The more widespread pluralism of the 1960s included the growth of Eastern religions as well as an increasing interest in astrology, spiritualism, and the occult. A theological crisis emerged within mainstream Protestantism as well. Neoorthodoxy, for many theologians, no longer provided the necessary answers for the church to be relevant in a modern technocratic society. Some adopted a radical "death of God" theology while others denounced the growing secularism of society.[71] Overall, a crisis of meaning resulted. Rapid sociological, intellectual, and religious change coupled with national crises of the Vietnam War and the Civil Rights movement created a period when "presuppositions that had held firm for centuries—even millennia—were being widely questioned." "The decade of the sixties was a time," Sydney Ahlstrom concluded, "when the old foundations of national confidence, patriotic idealism, moral traditionalism, and even of historic Judaeo-Christian theism, were awash."[72]

All of these factors sounded the death knell for the last vestiges of a Protestant cultural hegemony. And they set the stage for an explosion of church-state battles between those who sought to retain expressions of America's religious heritage and those who sought to affirm America's commitment to religious pluralism and a secular state. Religious conservatives identified the prayer and Bible reading cases of the early 1960s as the beginning of a dangerous trend toward a society devoid of religious meaning. The crisis of meaning motivated several scholars to address Robert Bellah's claim that societies inevitably understand themselves in religious terms. This "civil religion," Bellah asserted, existed "alongside of and rather clearly differentiated from the churches."[73] For some commentators, civil religion provided a unifying source for an increasingly pluralistic nation.

America's anxiety as a nation was compounded by several political crises as well. The Vietnam War, the Civil Rights movement, and Watergate all added to the nation's feeling of loss of control. A response to the seeming chaos of the 1960s was a continuing growth of religious and political conservatism that would reach its apex in 1980 with the rise of the Religious Right and the election of Ronald Reagan to the U.S. presidency. The response was especially notable within the growing conservative evangelical denominations. "In the stormy sixties with its social and theological turmoil and intense conflicts in moral systems as unexpected new patterns challenged long-accepted traditional ones," one historian explained, "conservative evangelicalism gained in appeal among those who found those new patterns disruptive and unacceptable."[74]

A vocal segment of conservative evangelicalism, especially made up of Christian fundamentalists, began a crusade to reestablish America's "Christian heritage." These evangelicals and fundamentalists, who had previously shunned political activity, entered the arena of politics with great enthusiasm and gained greater political influence as Pfeffer's career came to a close. Conservative theology would become enmeshed with conservative politics as the Religious Right mobilized around various political and social issues. Chief among their concerns was the Court's rulings that public school-sponsored prayer and Bible reading were unconstitutional. Some argued that America's moral and social ills were due to the lack of religious exercises practiced in the public schools, while others saw in Ronald Reagan an advocate of their moral, political, and social agenda. Thus, by the 1980s, the Religious Right developed a sociopolitical agenda that included opposition to the Supreme Court's decisions prohibiting religious exercise in the public schools, abortion rights, the Equal Rights Amendment, and political liberalism in general. The Religious Right took a proactive stance in favor of school prayer and other forms of religious exercises in the public schools. They also sought to lower the barriers to public subsidization of religious institutions. As a result, many of the legal battles Leo Pfeffer had previously won found new life in the 1980s.[75]

Concomitant with the conservative political and religious direction of the nation was the growing acceptance of a more accommodationist approach to the Establishment Clause. From the 1940s to the 1980s, the U.S. Supreme Court generally accepted the separationist interpretation of the Establishment Clause as well as the Pfeffer-inspired historical narrative on which it was based. It was not without its critics, though, who championed either a strict neutrality[76] or accommodationist[77] approach to the religion clauses that would have allowed greater support by the state to religion. By the 1980s scholars such as Robert Cord challenged these assumptions and claimed that an accommodationist reading of the Establishment Clause was more historically accurate. Armed with a philosophy of "original intent," Chief Justice William Rehnquist concurred with Cord's historical understanding of the First Amendment. And in his dissent in the moment of silence case, *Wallace v. Jaffree*, Rehnquist chided the Supreme Court's adherence to church-state separation.[78] Similarly, Cord argued that there was little historical evidence for precluding governmental aid to religion on a nondiscriminatory basis. "Nor does there appear to be any historical evidence," he argued, "that the First Amendment was intended to provide an absolute separation or independence of religion and the national state."[79] Thus Pfeffer, near the end of his career, had to face the most serious challenge to church-state separation since he began working for the American Jewish Congress in 1945. While many of the historical and constitutional arguments were not new, the accommodationist approach enjoyed a growing number of followers among scholars and jurists.[80] Pfeffer spent the latter years of his life continuing the defense of the separation of church and state as the guarantor of religious freedom. While his debate with the accommodationists centered primarily on the Establishment Clause, it was Pfeffer who argued that the historical record bore out both a broad and unitary reading of the religion clauses: "The fathers of the First Amendment were convinced that the free exercise of religion and the separation of church and state were two ways of saying the same thing: that separation guaranteed freedom and freedom required separation."[81]

SUMMARY

Pfeffer's understanding of the proper relationship between church and state can be traced to several sources. As the son of a rabbi, Pfeffer was versed in the Hebrew Scriptures and their teachings of social justice. His commitment to Judaism, including regular observance of the Sabbath and dietary laws, was lifelong. Pfeffer's concern for the freedom and integrity of religion no doubt stemmed from his faith.

The fact that Pfeffer frequently argued for the equality of religion, along with religious freedom and church-state separation, coincides with his identity as a religious minority in America. As a Jew, Pfeffer was keenly aware of the need to remove any legal barriers to full Jewish participation in American public life. His experiences in public education as a child presaged his later legal opposition to school-sponsored religious education and exercises.

As a young lawyer with the American Jewish Congress in the 1940s, Pfeffer was influenced by the public philosophy of Jewish leaders such as Alexander Pekelis and Horace M. Kallen. Pekelis and Kallen articulated the need of cultural pluralism for the security and equality of American Jewry. Pfeffer argued throughout his career that the religious pluralism was one of the key First Amendment values to be protected. The Holocaust attuned Pfeffer to the potential outbreak of anti-Semitism in certain segments of American society. As a result, Pfeffer was especially cognizant of the vulnerability of Jews in a Christian majority state. Pfeffer's legal advocacy was not motivated solely by a belief in the principle of religious liberty but also out of a concern for the interests of American Jews.

Social and religious developments in post–World War II America provided the context for Pfeffer's legal advocacy, and by consequence, influenced his perspective on church-state relations. Fundamentally, the U.S. Supreme Court's willingness to apply the Religion Clauses of the First Amendment to the states enabled Pfeffer to articulate his view of the First Amendment, through various roles, to the nation's highest court. This, along with the litigiousness of other religious minorities, emboldened Jewish organizations, such as Pfeffer's American Jewish Congress, to utilize the courts to an ever greater extent in securing religious and political rights.

The post-war religious revival, combined with the advent of the Cold War, spawned a renewal of displays of religiosity in public schools and other public institutions. Church-state controversies resulted as religious minorities and others opposed the public displays of America's civil religion. The rapid growth of a Catholic school system which looked increasingly to state legislatures for financial subsidies precipitated much of Pfeffer's involvement in the legal arena.

Rapid changes in American society in the 1960s compounded the conflicts in church-state relations. Ironically, a broadening of religious pluralism coincided with what many traditionalists feared was an increasing secularism in society. These developments, along with national crises such as the Vietnam War and the Civil Rights movement, led to a period of national anxiety. This led to an increase in church-state battles between those who sought to retain public expressions of America's religious heritage and those who sought to affirm America's commitment to religious pluralism and a secular state. Thus, Pfeffer's intellectual and legal contributions to American church-state relations were shaped by the religious and social context of post–World War II America.

NOTES

1. Pfeffer, "An Autobiographical Sketch," 529.

2. See Jonathan D. Sarna, *American Jews and Church-State Relations: The Search for "Equal Footing"* (New York: American Jewish Committee, Institute of Human Relations, 1989).

3. Anson Phelps Stokes, *Church and State in the United States*, 3 vols. (New York: Harper and Brothers, 1950), 1: 854–59; Cohen, *Jews in Christian America*, 11–36.

4. A. James Reichley, *Religion in American Public Life* (Washington, DC: The Brookings Institution, 1985), 230.

5. Morton Borden, *Jews, Turks, and Infidels* (Chapel Hill, NC: The University of North Carolina Press, 1984), ix–x.

6. Ibid., 36–41; Stokes, *Church and State*, 1: 865–78; Sarna, *American Jews and Church–State Relations*, 3–4.

7. Jonathan D. Sarna and David G. Dalin, *Religion and State in the American Jewish Experience* (Notre Dame, IN: University of Notre Dame Press, 1997), 4.

8. 143 U.S. 457 (1892).

9. Jonathan D. Sarna, "Church-State Dilemmas of American Jews," in Mittleman et al., eds. *Jews and the American Public Square: Debating Religion and Republic* (Lanham, MD: Rowman and Littlefield, 2002), 55.

10. Stokes, *Church and State*, 2: 390–91; Ahlstrom, *A Religious History*, 918–21.

11. Lawrence H. Fuchs, *The Political Behavior of American Jews* (Westport, CT: Greenwood Press, 1956), 169; Stephen J. Whitfield, *Voices of Jacob, Hands of Esau: Jews in American Life and Thought* (Hamden, CT: Archon Books, 1984), 109.

12. Ahlstrom, *A Religious History*, 928–29.

13. Edward S. Shapiro, *A Time for Healing: American Jewry Since World War II*. Vol. 5 of *The Jewish People in America* (Baltimore, MD: The Johns Hopkins University Press, 1992), 1.

14. Oscar Handlin, *Adventure in Freedom: Three Hundred Years of Jewish Life in America* (New York: McGraw-Hill Book Company, Inc., 1954), 214; Naomi W. Cohen, "In Defense of Equality: American Jews and the Constitution Before WWI," in *In Celebration: An American Jewish Perspective on the Bicentennial of the United States Constitution*, ed. Kerry M. Olitzky (Lanham, MD: University Press of America, 1989), 11–17; Cohen, *Jews in Christian America*, 99.

15. Ahlstrom, *A Religious History*, 972; see also Handlin, *Adventure in Freedom*, 80–142.

16. Pfeffer, "An Autobiographical Sketch," 487.

17. Ibid.

18. See Brief for Synagogue Counsel of America and National Community Relations Advisory Counsel as Amici Curiae Supporting Petitioners, *Abington v. Schempp*, 374 U.S. 203 (1963) (Nos. 142 & 149).

19. See Brief for Synagogue Council for America, et al. as Amici Curiae Supporting Appellants, *McCollum v. Board of Education*, 333 U.S. 203 (1948) (No. 90).

20. Ibid., 12.

21. Ibid., 2–4.

22. Pfeffer, "An Autobiographical Sketch," 488–89.

23. Stephen Reinhardt, "Jews, Jewish Justices and the Supreme Court," May 4, 1990, unpublished manuscript, 2; Jerold S. Auerbach, *Rabbis and Lawyers: The Journey from Torah to Constitution* (Bloomington: Indiana University Press, 1990), xix.

24. Fuchs, *The Political Behavior of American Jews*, 180.

25. Leo Pfeffer, "Freedom and Separation: America's Contribution to Civilization," *Journal of Church and State* 2 (November 1960): 101.

26. Leo Pfeffer, *Liberties of an American: The Supreme Court Speaks*, 2nd ed. (Boston: Beacon Press, 963), xii.

27. Reichley, *Religion in American Public Life*, 233.

28. Nathan Glazer, *American Judaism* (Chicago: University of Chicago Press, 1957), 87–88; see also Hasia R. Diner, *The Jews of the United States, 1654–2000* (Berkeley, CA: University of California Press, 2004), 222–25.

29. Cohen, *Jews in Christian America*, 126.

30. David Dalin, "Leo Pfeffer and the Separationist Faith," *This World* 24 (Winter 1989): 138; see also Shapiro, *A Time For Healing*, 56.

31. Leo Pfeffer, "Commentary on `Civil Religion in America' by Robert N. Bellah," in *The Religious Situation: 1968*, ed. Donald R. Cutler (Boston: Beacon Press, 1968), 361–64.

32. Robert Gordis, *The Root and the Branch: Judaism and the Free Society* (Chicago: University of Chicago Press, 1962), 14; Murray Friedman, *The Utopian Dilemma: American Judaism and Public Policy* (Washington, DC: Ethics and Public Policy Center, 1985), 4.

33. Jerold S. Auerbach, "Liberalism and the Hebrew Prophets," *Commentary* 84 (August 1987): 58–60; see also Auerbach, *Rabbis and Lawyers*.

34. Gordis, *The Root and the Branch*, 14.

35. Leo Pfeffer, "Counterrflections on Church and State," *Midstream* 8 (December 1962): 19.

36. Gordis, *The Root and the Branch*, 13–14; see Arthur Hertzberg, *The French Enlightenment and the Jews* (New York: Columbia University Press, 1968).

37. Samuel Rabinove, "How—and—Why American Jews Have Contended for Religious Freedom: The Requirements and Limits of Civility," *The Journal of Law and Religion* 8 (1990): 140.

38. Pfeffer, *Church, State, and Freedom*, 105.

39. Pfeffer, *God, Caesar, and the Constitution: The Court as Referee in Church-State Confrontation* (Boston: Beacon Press) 159.

40. Ibid., 224–25.

41. Leo Pfeffer, "Review of Mark DeWolfe Howe's *The Garden and the Wilderness: Religion and Government in American Constitutional History*," *Political Science Quarterly* 81 (December 1966): 656.

42. Pfeffer, *Church, State, and Freedom*, 99–100.

43. Pfeffer, "An Autobiographical Sketch," 488; see also Morris Frommer, "The American Jewish Congress: A History, 1914–1950" (PhD diss., Ohio State University, Columbus, OH, 1978).

44. Ivers, *To Build a Wall*, 49.

45. Hereafter CLSA.

46. Frommer, "The American Jewish Congress," 497.

47. Ibid., 524; Alexander H. Pekelis, "Full Equality in a Free Society: A Program for Jewish Action," in *Law and Social Action: Selected Essays of Alexander H.*

Pekelis, ed. Milton R. Konvitz (Ithaca, NY: Cornell University Press, 1950), 226–32; Ivers, *To Build a Wall,* 51–54.

48. Pekelis, "Full Equality," 224.

49. Pfeffer, "Religious Freedom," 137.

50. Friedman, *The Utopian Dilemma*, 24; Jonathan Sarna, *American Judaism* (New Haven, CT: Yale University Press, 2004), 308–12.

51. Ibid., 29; Henry L. Feingold, *A Time for Searching: Entering the Mainstream, 1920–1945* (Baltimore: The Johns Hopkins University Press, 1992) 90.

52. Quoted in Sarna and Dalin, *Religion and State*, 188.

53. See, for example, *National Association for the Advancement of Colored People* v. *Alabama*, 357 U.S. 449 (1958).

54. Pfeffer, "An Autobiographical Sketch," 505–06.

55. Leo Pfeffer, *Creeds in Competition: A Creative Force in American Culture* (New York: Harper and Brothers, 1958), 4.

56. Leo Pfeffer, "Church and State: The Constitutional Problem," in *The Dimensions of Freedom* (Washington, DC: Americans United for Separation of Church and State, 1969), 33.

57. Ivers, *To Build a Wall*, 71; Cohen, *Jews in Christian America*, 136–43; Pfeffer, "An Autobiographical Sketch," 492–94.

58. "Will Herberg's Challenge to Strict Separation," in Sarna and Dalin, *Religion and State,* 251; see also David Dalin, "Jewish Critics of Strict Separationism," in Mittleman et al, eds. *Jews and the American Public Square*, 291–309.

59. *Gitlow v. New York*, 268 U.S. 652 at 665. See Henry J. Abraham and Barbara A. Perry, *Freedom and the Court: Civil Rights and Liberties in the United States*, 6th ed. (New York: Oxford University Press, 1994), 38–117.

60. 310 U.S. 296 (1940).

61. *Everson v. Board of Education*, 330 U.S. 1 (1947).

62. Leo Pfeffer, *Religion, State and the Burger Court* (Buffalo, NY: Prometheus Books, 1984), 206–07; see, for example, *Cantwell v. Connecticut*, 310 U.S. 296 (1940) and *Murdock v. Pennsylvania*, 319 U.S 105 (1943) (challenging requirements prohibiting solicitation without a city license); *Minersville School District v. Gobitis*, 310 U.S. 586 (1940); *West Virginia State Board of Education v. Barnette*, 319 U.S. 624 (1943) (challenging compulsory flag salute laws in public schools); and *Prince v. Massachusetts,* 321 U.S. 158 (1944) (challenging application of child labor laws to JW evangelistic activities).

63. See Jennifer Jacobs Henderson, "The Jehovah's Witnesses and Their Plan to Expand First Amendment Freedoms," *Journal of Church and State* 46 (Autumn 2004): 811–32.

64. Robert T. Handy, *A Christian America: Protestant Hopes and Historical Realities*, 2nd ed. (New York: Oxford University Press, 1984), 186–90.

65. See William Lee Miller, *Piety along the Potomac: Notes on Politics and Morals in the Fifties* (Boston, MA: Houghton Mifflin Company, 1964).

66. Sorauf, *The Wall of Separation*, 11–12; for a compelling study assessing the relationship of big business to the Christian America agenda, see Kruse, *One Nation Under God.*

67. Steven K. Green, *The Third Disestablishment: Church, State, and American Culture, 1940–1975* (New York: Oxford University Press, 2019), 33–57.

68. Ibid., 14–15; for a history of Catholic parochial education, see Timothy Walch, *Parish School: American Catholic Parochial School Education From Colonial Times to the Present*, 2nd ed. (Washington, DC: The National Catholic Education Association, 2016).

69. Robert Wuthnow, *The Restructuring of American Religion: Society and Faith Since World War II* (Princeton, NJ: Princeton University Press, 1988), 6.

70. See Will Herberg, *Protestant-Catholic-Jew: An Essay in American Religious Sociology* (New York: Doubleday and Co., Inc., 1955).

71. See Hugh McLeod, *The Religious Crisis of the 1960s* (New York: Oxford University Press, 2007).

72. Ahlstrom, *A Religious History*, 1080.

73. Robert N. Bellah, "Civil Religion in America," in *American Civil Religion*, ed. Russell E. Richey and Donald G. Jones (New York: Harper and Row, 1974), 21.

74. Handy, *A Christian America*, 204; see also Dean M. Kelley, *Why Conservative Churches Are Growing* (New York: Harper and Row, 1977); William Martin, *With God on Our Side: The Rise of the Religious Right in America* (New York: Bantam Doubleday, 1996); and Daniel K. Williams, *God's Own Party: The Making of the Christian Right* (New York: Oxford University Press, 2012).

75. Williams, *God's Own Party*, 187–200.

76. See Philip B. Kurland, *Religion and the Law: Of Church and State and the Supreme Court* (Chicago: University of Chicago Press, 1975).

77. See, for example, O'Neill, "Nonpreferential Aid," 242–66; and John Courtney Murray, "Law or Prepossessions? "*L*aw and *C*ontemporary *P*roblems 14 (Winter 1949): 23–43.

78. *Wallace* v. *Jaffree*, 472 U.S. 38 (1985) at 72.

79. Cord, *Separation of Church and State*, 104; see James E. Wood, Jr., "Separation vis-à-vis Accommodation: A New Direction in American Church–State Relations?" in *Reflections on Church and State*, ed. James E. Wood, Jr. (Waco, TX: J.M. Dawson Institute of Church-State Studies, Baylor University, 1995), 597–608.

80. See, Michael W. McConnell, "Accommodation of Religion," *Supreme Court Review* (1985): 1–59; and Justice Antonin Scalia's dissents in *Edwards v. Aguillard*, 482 U.S. 578 (1987) and *Texas Monthly* v. *Bullock*, 489 U.S. 1 (1989).

81. Leo Pfeffer, "The Unity of the First Amendment Religion Clauses," in *The First Freedom: Religion and the Bill of Rights*, ed. James E. Wood, Jr. (Waco, TX: J.M. Dawson Institute of Church-State Studies, Baylor University, 1990), 133.

Chapter 2

The Unitary Guarantee

For Leo Pfeffer, the concepts of religious freedom and church-state separation were inextricably intertwined. He often referred to freedom and separation as "two sides of the same coin," in that "separation guaranteed freedom and freedom required separation." This "unitary guarantee," as he also described it, was central to his thought and provided the basis for his interpretation of the First Amendment.[1] Pfeffer found support for the unitary guarantee in Justice Wiley Rutledge's dissenting opinion in *Everson v. Board of Education*: "'Establishment' and 'Free Exercise' were correlative and coextensive ideas," Rutledge declared, "representing only different facets of the single great and fundamental freedom."[2] Pfeffer also cited regularly Italian scholar Francesco Ruffini, whose observations on American church-state relations led him to conclude: "'Religious liberty and separatism have become in America two terms which, ideally, historically, and practically, are inseparable.'"[3] Pfeffer thus argued that any dichotomy between the values of freedom and separation could not be justified historically or constitutionally.[4]

Pfeffer fashioned a compelling historical narrative to support the unitary guarantee. He frequently argued that religious freedom and church-state separation "were parts of the same single evolutionary process that culminated in the First Amendment."[5] Emphasizing the eighteenth-century disestablishment battles in Virginia, the writings of Thomas Jefferson and James Madison, the advocacy of dissenting Protestants, and the debates over the Constitution, Pfeffer drew from this historical narrative in shaping legal arguments in his briefs for a broad reading of the First Amendment. The basic elements of his separationist narrative were not new. It drew from leading religious historians of Pfeffer's day and echoed the historical arguments Justices Black and Rutledge utilized in *Everson v. Board of Education*.

Pfeffer's historical narrative did not go uncontested. A spate of publications appeared after the *Everson* and *McCollum v. Board of Education* decisions criticizing the Court's historical interpretation of the Establishment Clause. These criticisms were renewed in the 1980s and 1990s when a scholarly debate over the "original intent" of the framers of the Constitution led to the publication of numerous works on religious liberty and church-state relations.[6] Many of these argued that Pfeffer and the Court placed too great an emphasis on the Madisonian and Jeffersonian interpretations of the religion clauses, had overstated the influence of the Virginia disestablishment battles, and relied too readily upon the "wall of separation" metaphor. These critics argued instead that the historical evidence supported an accommodationist or narrow reading of the Establishment Clause. Nonetheless, Pfeffer's influential scholarship and legal advocacy helped solidify the Court's acceptance of the separationist understanding of the First Amendment during his career. "For the first forty years of modern Establishment Clause jurisprudence," one historian concluded, "the Court's resort to history generally reinforced separationist principles."[7]

LEO PFEFFER AND THE ARGUMENT FROM HISTORY

Much of the debate surrounding constitutional interpretation of the religion clauses centers on the historical meaning and purpose of the First Amendment. As Justice Rutledge declared in *Everson v. Board of Education*: "No provision of the Constitution is more closely tied to or given content by its generating history than the religious clause of the First Amendment."[8] Leo Pfeffer gave special attention to the historical ingredients that gave rise to the unitary guarantee in his magnum opus, *Church, State, and Freedom*. Significantly, Pfeffer began not with colonial America, but with a survey of the relationship of religion and government through Western civilization. Citing standard works on the history of religion, Pfeffer began his survey with the earliest civilizations and traced what he considered to be the long history of competition, compromise, and coercion between religion and the state.[9] "In this struggle the church has sought to dominate the state and use it as an engine for its purposes," Pfeffer observed, "and the state has sought to dominate the church and use it as an engine for its purposes."[10]

Tracing the evolution of church-state relations in the West was especially important to Pfeffer for understanding the unique American tradition of religious freedom and church-state separation. And by focusing on the consequences of church-state union, Pfeffer highlighted not only his concern with the freedom of religion, but its integrity as well. "With minor exceptions," Pfeffer observed, "the history of church-state relationships was a history of persecution, oppression, hatred, bloodshed, and war." "With equally minor exceptions," he continued, "that history was the history of the unscrupulous use of religion by secular powers to promote their purposes and policies."[11]

CHURCH-STATE PATTERNS IN COLONIAL AMERICA

Pfeffer identified how the Old World patterns of church and state were transplanted in the New World and utilized the well-documented Puritan regime Massachusetts Bay, the Anglican establishments in the Southern colonies, and the multiple establishments of the middle colonies to illustrate the persistence of church-state unions.[12] By the time of the American Revolution, nine of the thirteen colonies still had established churches. In many of these, persecution was visited upon nonconformist Protestants, Catholics, Jews, and nonbelievers through compulsory taxation and restrictions on their civil liberties. Such evidence led Pfeffer to conclude that in colonial America, "compulsory support of religion was the rule rather than the exception."[13]

Nonetheless, an ideological transformation was taking place in Revolutionary America. The trend toward disestablishment and religious liberty found its birth in the last quarter of the eighteenth century and was the result of both practical and ideological factors.[14] Religious pluralism, for instance, was a key pragmatic factor according to Pfeffer. With no religion enjoying a clear majority in the colonies, "there was no alternative but to learn to live together." A variety and multiplicity of sects consequently mitigated against religious uniformity, making establishments either impossible or difficult to maintain.[15] Religious pluralism both in England and the New World contributed to the passage of the English Act of Toleration of 1689. Providing freedom of worship for Protestant dissenters, the Act was a major step in the evolutionary development of freedom and separation.[16] As the British colonies flourished in the eighteenth century, so did their religious pluralism. Rather than seeing this as a threat, key figures such as James Madison and Thomas Jefferson extolled the benefits of diversity. Politically, Madison viewed the multiplicity of interests as a check against tyranny of the majority, and Jefferson argued that diversity of opinion was beneficial to religion.[17]

Historians have long noted the limited number of colonial Americans having formal membership in a church. The minimal institutional presence of religion would further undermine established churches.[18] Pfeffer argued that less than five percent of the population were church members. This was not evidence to him, of course, of a secular culture. "It is probably true that religion was widespread," Pfeffer concluded, "but was mostly a personal, non-institutional matter."[19] More recent historical works have challenged these figures, suggesting that the colonial religious context was more complex and that church attendance was more extensive than these statistics reveal.[20] At any rate, Pfeffer didn't believe that low-church membership reflected an antipathy toward religion, but rather a growing religious individualism that fostered tolerance and the respect for other's religious beliefs.[21]

Pfeffer highlighted the role economic considerations played in the development of religious freedom in America as well. Many of the colonies were initiated as economic ventures and their success was of vital interest to the political rulers of the mother country. Consequently, tolerance was seen as an important tool to attract new colonists and ensure economic viability. Pfeffer noted the active role many merchants played in securing colonial charters, which often included protections for liberty of conscience.[22] The British Plantation Act of 1740, for instance, eased the way for settlement not only for dissenting Protestants but also Jews.[23] Commerce, Pfeffer noted, "tended to distract the colonies from their absorbing preoccupations and their exclusiveness in the matter of religion."[24] Similarly, Pfeffer drew parallels between the Revolutionary cries of "no taxation without representation," with pleas for exemption from religious taxation. The support of Protestant dissenters for the Revolutionary cause was due to the fact they were embroiled in a battle for both political and religious freedom. Religious taxes loomed large in the quest for disestablishment, leading Pfeffer to conclude that the "history of religious liberty in this country is in large measure a history of the struggle against compulsory taxation for religious purposes."[25]

Pfeffer argued that the Revolutionary War had a liberalizing and unifying effect on Americans as well. Religious differences were diminished as leaders sought support from all constituents, including Catholics and Protestant dissenters. From an ideological standpoint, Pfeffer argued that the expansion of religious liberty during the Revolutionary War was also the product of a people attempting to reconcile their own practices with the lofty ideals of the Declaration of Independence. According to Pfeffer, "It was difficult to justify inequality in religious treatment by a nation which severed its political bonds with the king of England because he violated the self-evident truth that all men are created equal."[26]

Pfeffer insisted that the revolutionary changes in church-state relations were not merely pragmatic considerations of religious pluralism, low-church membership, the desire of economic prosperity, or the Revolutionary War. Rather, he argued that it was also the culmination of a variety of intellectual influences represented in both the theological influences of pietism and the philosophical contributions of Enlightenment rationalism. Pfeffer's insistence on the ideological forces that helped shape the unitary guarantee was not intended to diminish the practical considerations weighing on the minds of the early American statesmen. For Pfeffer, the ideological and practical were interrelated.

Ideologically, those who embraced the religious individualism of the Great Awakening—Pfeffer used the word Pietists or Evangelicals—shared a fundamental commitment with Enlightenment rationalists: Government should have no power over religion. Expressed in another way, Pfeffer held that the First Amendment provided a unitary freedom guaranteeing "voluntariness in matters of belief" and a government "without inherent powers but limited to those specifically conferred upon it."[27] Just as freedom and separation were interrelated, so were voluntarism and limited government. Limited government required voluntarism in religious matters, and voluntarism depended on a limited government. Protestant historians and Pfeffer's contemporaries, Winthrop S. Hudson and Franklin H. Littell, emphasized the interrelationship of voluntarism and limited government in their widely regarded books.[28] Hudson described the voluntary principle as the "great tradition of the American churches," while Littell suggested that voluntaryism and pluralism reshaped "the nature of the political covenant." These rearticulations of the unitary guarantee supported Pfeffer's contention that for the Pietists, the "source of all power was Christ who saw fit not to grant authority over religion to temporal government."[29]

Pfeffer carefully documented the religious or pietistic roots of the religion clauses. "It is therefore appropriate to emphasize," he once declared, "that the principle of the separation of church and state was advocated by devoutly Christian leaders and thinkers long before it was espoused by the nonreligious and long before it was elevated to a constitutional principle in the First Amendment."[30] Roger Williams was an especially important figure to Pfeffer.[31] Williams, whose influence has been traced to John Locke, Thomas Jefferson, and James Madison among others, based his early advocacy of church-state separation on a strong theological separatism that sought to protect the "garden of the church" from the "wilderness of the state."[32] In mid-seventeeth-century Rhode Island, Williams embarked upon a revolutionary experiment in full religious liberty where "no person . . . shall hereafter be any wise be molested or called in question for any difference in opinion in matters of religion." In his pamphlet, *The Bloudy Tenent of Persecution for cause of Conscience, discussed in a Conference between Truth and Peace*, Williams outlined twelve principles in defense of religious freedom and the separation of church and state. Described by Pfeffer as "an epochal milestone in the history of religious freedom and the separation of church and state" the *Bloudy Tenent* opposed "enforced uniformity of religion" because it "confounds the Civil and Religious."[33]

In his letter to the Town Providence in 1654, William's utilized a "ship of state" analogy to argue for limited government and freedom of conscience.

Challenging the claim that his emphasis on freedom of conscience would lead to anarchy, Williams drew a distinction between the sacred and the secular. While the ship or commonwealth would grant liberty of conscience to the "papists, protestants, Jews, or Turks," the ship's captain or civil magistrate could exercise compulsion in civil but not religious matters. Moreover, religious conscience would not be a valid excuse where the safety and security of the state are concerned.[34] Williams's "doctrine of the two tables" articulated in another useful way the limitations of government with regard to religion. Williams believed that government could "enforce the injunctions of the second table of the Decalogue, which concerned man's dealings with his fellow men," but those of the first table, which concerned one's relationship with God, "was not in the proper sphere of the state."[35] Williams provided influential theological rationales for the unitary guarantee, though Pfeffer once dryly noted: "Seventeenth century America was not ready for Roger Williams. In view of the still current attack on the principle of separation of church and state . . . we are perhaps even now not ready for those ideas."[36]

The Great Awakening of the early eighteenth century fostered greater individualism and voluntarism in religion in colonial America as well as a growing skepticism toward religious establishments. Indeed, freedom and separation found broad support among those that embraced the revivalism of the Great Awakening, many of whom were religious dissenters. Their growth and eventual political mobilization made them a formidable force in the movement toward disestablishment. As Pfeffer concluded: "The result was that the ardent revivalist groups which formed the movement became staunch partisans of the separation of church and state."[37]

Among these revivalist groups were the Baptists. Baptists emphasized voluntarism in religious faith manifested in the practice of believer's baptism. Such a theological position had significant consequences for church-state relations. Baptists' advocacy of soul liberty, for example, stressed the necessity and responsibility of each person to deal directly with God, free from any interference from creeds, clergy, or civil government. Their contribution to the American tradition of religious freedom and church-state separation was frequently highlighted by Pfeffer. "All in all," he once declared, "the Baptists were by far, but by no means the only conventional major religious group that could claim credit for the exclusion of religion and man's relationship to God from the jurisdiction of civil government."[38]

Pfeffer noted Isaac Backus's efforts as one of the most "active and effective" Baptist advocates for religious freedom.[39] Backus was a pastor who, as an agent for the Warren Association, represented Baptists before the Massachusetts legislature in the late eighteenth century. Most of his energies were given to the advocacy of religious freedom and separation of church and state and were most often directed against the Congregational establishment.

Pfeffer believed that Backus's protestations articulated the theological basis for the separation of church and state. In opposing a religious tax in Massachusetts, Backus argued that freedom relied upon separation by insisting that religion was outside the jurisdiction of government: "Nothing can be true religion but a voluntary obedience unto God's revealed will, of which each rational soul has an actual right to judge for itself . . . . And civil rulers are so far removed from having any right to empower any person or persons to judge for others in such affairs, and to enforce their judgments."[40] Backus opposed religious tests for these same reasons. "Nothing is more evident, both in reason, and in the holy scriptures," he once argued, "than that religion is ever a matter between God and individuals; and therefore no men or man can impose any religious test, without invading the essential prerogatives of our Lord Jesus Christ."[41]

John Leland, a contemporary of Backus, was a colorful Baptist evangelist from Virginia whose commitment to Jeffersonian republicanism was matched by his ardent advocacy of religious freedom and his strident opposition to religious establishment. Pfeffer included Leland as a significant figure in the evolutionary development of the American tradition of church-state separation not only for his advocacy of religious freedom but also because he was an influential figure in Virginia politics. Leland's rationale for advocating freedom and separation was unambiguous. He declared in his most famous tract, *The Rights of Conscience Inalienable*, that "government has no more to do with the religious opinions of men than it has with the principles of mathematics." Leland insisted that attempts by the state to enforce religious uniformity had achieved nothing more than hypocrisy, clerical abuses, and persecution.[42]

Pfeffer perceived Leland to be an important transitional figure between the pietistic theological impulses for separation and the political philosophy of Enlightenment rationalists. Leland blended religious individualism with Jeffersonian political liberalism in his call for the rights of conscience.[43] Consequently, Leland was an absolutist with regard to separation of church and state.[44] Like Williams, Leland was far ahead of his time in the application of his views. He opposed religious oaths, government-sanctioned Sabbath observance, and government-paid chaplains, which he considered, "unconstitutional, inconsistent with religious liberty, and unnecessary in itself."[45] Leland gained a reputation as a radical. While this reputation has led some scholars to question his influence,[46] others have argued that his views were not so far outside the mainstream, especially for Virginia Baptists.[47]

While Pfeffer gives special attention to the Baptists, due to their consistent and influential advocacy of religious freedom and church-state separation, they were by no means the only evangelical or pietistic ideological influences on the evolution of the American tradition of religious freedom and church-state separation. William Penn and his fellow Quakers were frequently noted by Pfeffer for their contributions to religious liberty. Like Rhode Island, Pfeffer praised Penn's "holy experiment" in Pennsylvania where widespread religious toleration was practiced. Pfeffer found support for the coextensive nature of separation and freedom in Penn's writing's as well. Penn's "The Body of Laws" included these protections of religious conscience:

> That no person . . . who professes, him or herself Obliged in conscience to Live peaceably and quietly under the civil government, shall in any case be molested or prejudiced for his, or her Conscientious persuasion or practice. Nor shall hee or shee at any time be compelled to frequent or Maintain anie religious worship, place or Ministry whatever, Contrary to his, or her mind, but shall freely and fully enjoy his, or her Christian Liberty in that respect, without any Interruptions or reflection.[48]

Pfeffer noted that Presbyterians made "an effective contribution to the evolution of separation and freedom" as well. The Presbytery of Hanover were some of the most vocal opponents to religious taxes in Virginia arguing that "religion is altogether personal and the right of exercising it unalienable." Pfeffer suggested that Presbyterian president of Princeton University, John Witherspoon, likely influenced James Madison's views on voluntary support of religion. Virginia Presbyterian leader, Samuel Davies, was identified as Pfeffer as an "ardent advocate of the separation of church and state."[49]

Ideological influences in the evolution of religious freedom and church-state separation came from less orthodox sources as well. Enlightenment rationalism spawned a religious liberalism or deism known for its suspicion of institutional religion. Reacting in part to the religious wars and persecution that had been a regular part of the fabric of Western history, deists opted for a God of transcendence whose interaction with the world was minimal and consistent with human reason and experience. Deism significantly influenced many prominent leaders of colonial and early America including Thomas Jefferson, Thomas Paine, John Adams, George Washington, Benjamin Franklin, and James Madison. Pfeffer argued that Enlightenment deism's influence was widespread in light of the fact that "none of the first seven Presidents was at the time off his election a member of any church." He also described the "two basic documents of American freedom," the Declaration of Independence and the Bill of Rights, as breathing "the spirit of deistic humanism."[50]

The Enlightenment also spawned a liberal political philosophy classically expressed in the late seventeenth century by John Locke in his *Second Treatise on Government* (1690).[51] In the Lockean scheme, political society was entered into by autonomous individuals by an agreement or social contract. Government was limited in its powers and individuals possessed natural rights that were outside the purview of political society. This social contract theory was the basis for Locke's *Letter Concerning Toleration* (1689) where he addressed specifically the relationship of church and state. In this work, Locke sought to address the political problem of religion. Since religion had been a source of civil conflict and warfare throughout history, Locke concluded that religious toleration rather than religious uniformity would better bring about peace and prosperity. Locke's political solution echoed Roger Williams's theological one by essentially advocating for a separation of church and state. Convinced that "saving religion consists of the inward persuasion of the mind," Locke defined the church as a "voluntary society of men" that would have no coercive power and would primarily be concerned with "care of the souls." The state would be limited to "civil interests."[52] Pfeffer noted that Locke did not pursue his ideas to their "logical conclusion." Locke did not extend toleration to Catholics and atheists, arguing that neither could be trusted to uphold the social contract. Nevertheless, a century later, his social contract theory was very influential on American founders, such as Jefferson and Madison, and provided the theoretical basis for American constitutional democracy. Moreover, his views on church and state were consonant with the theological convictions of the evangelicals or pietists who placed religion or conscience outside governmental jurisdiction. Thus, Locke contributed as well to the convergence of the pietistic and rationalistic justifications for religious freedom and church-state separation. According to Pfeffer:

> The concept that religion was outside the jurisdiction of civil government was acceptable to and accepted both by the religionist and the rationalist. To the religionist, God or Christ did not desire the magistrate to have such jurisdiction ("render unto Caesar that which is Caesar's"; "my kingdom is not of this world," etc.); to the rationalist, the power to act in religion was not one of the powers conferred on government as part of the social contract.[53]

Pfeffer frequently cited Thomas Paine as a demonstration of the deist position as well. In his widely circulated pamphlet, *Common Sense*, Paine declared: "As to religion, I hold it to be the indispensable duty of government to protect all conscientious professors thereof, and I know of no other business which government hath to do therewith."[54] Pfeffer believed Paine's quote expressed well the dual concepts of freedom and separation.[55] Yet the most significant historical figure for Pfeffer in the evolution of freedom and separation in America was Thomas Jefferson. Pfeffer obviously admired Jefferson whom he claimed stood above the many famous individuals fighting for religious liberty in colonial America. For Pfeffer, Jefferson's commitment to the separation of church and state was unwavering and his influence was noticed far beyond his introduction of the phrase "wall of separation between church and state" in his famous letter to the Danbury Baptists.[56]

Jefferson provided not only ideological but also practical arguments for the relationship of religious freedom and church-state separation. In his *Notes on Virginia*, which Pfeffer considered one of the most eloquent defenses of religious liberty, Jefferson challenged the efficacy of religious coercion and uniformity. Reflecting on the religious pluralism of colonial Virginia, Jefferson questioned whether religious uniformity was attainable and whether persecution created anything but "fools" and "hypocrites." Instead, he declared the limited nature of government: "But our rulers can have no authority over such natural rights, only as we have submitted to them."[57]

According to Pfeffer, Jefferson's *Bill for Establishing Religious Freedom*, which had been introduced to the Virginia legislature by Jefferson in 1779, encapsulated what he considered to be an eloquent articulation of the unitary guarantee. In the language of the social contract, Jefferson argued that "our civil rights have no dependence on our religious opinion" and "the opinions of men are not the object of civil government."[58] Government's incapacity to concern itself with religion included for Jefferson the provision of tax funds for religious causes. Pfeffer utilized language from Jefferson's *Bill for Establishing Religious Freedom* frequently, especially in his battles over public aid to religious schools. Jefferson's famous declaration "It is sinful and tyrannical to compel a man to furnish contributions for the propagation of opinions which he disbelieves and abhors; and it is also wrong to force him to support this or that teacher of his own religious persuasion" was often the starting point for Pfeffer's no-aid advocacy.[59]

Jefferson's *Bill for Establishing Religious Freedom* was introduced as part of a larger battle for religious freedom in Virginia. For many scholars, Virginia provided the context for the better understanding the debates surrounding the passage of the First Amendment of the Constitution just a few years later. James Madison and other key figures in the framing of the U.S. Constitution and Bill of Rights were deeply involved in the religious liberty developments in Virginia as well.[60] Pfeffer described the developments in colonial Virginia as revolutionary considering the well-entrenched Anglican establishment and the ongoing persecution of dissenting sects. Dissenting ministers were prohibited from performing marriages or engaging in public worship, plus their parishioners faced fines and physical punishment for failure to pay the "tithe" that supported the Anglican Church. Religious and political turmoil engulfed the colony in the 1760s and 1770s as dissenters protested discriminatory laws. The Anglican establishment diminished during the Revolutionary era as did a number of the legal disabilities faced by dissenters. Nonetheless, the idea that the state should support the church or even Christianity in general set the context for the climax of the struggle in Virginia over disestablishment. Introduced in 1784, a "Bill Establishing a Provision for Teachers of the Christian Religion" established a universal taxation "for the support of religion, permitting each taxpayer to designate the minister to whom he wished his contribution allocated."[61] The ensuing debate over the General Assessment bill was significant to Pfeffer because it revealed a growing consensus that separation of church and state prohibited more than a single church from enjoying a monopoly of state recognition and support. It also provided the context for the one of James Madison's most significant contributions to the American tradition of church-state separation. In opposition to the General Assessment Bill, Madison introduced his famous *Memorial and Remonstrance against Religious Assessments*. Pfeffer believed the *Memorial and Remonstrance* to be "one of the great documents in the history of human liberty"[62] because it "presents a fifteen-point socio-political foundation for the basically integral unity of religious freedom and church-state separation."[63] Written just seven years before the adoption of the First Amendment and composed by the "architect of the United States constitution," Pfeffer believed the *Memorial and Remonstrance* to be the most reliable source for determining the meaning of the religion clauses of the First Amendment.

In summarizing the *Memorial and Remonstrance*, Pfeffer identified two basic classes of arguments. First, there were arguments emphasizing voluntarism with regard to religion. Second, there were arguments based on the belief that religion was outside the jurisdiction of the government. "Since religion is exempt from the authority of the Society at large," Madison declared, "still less can it be subject to that of the Legislative Body whose jurisdiction is both derivative and limited." According to Pfeffer, these two sets of arguments would form "the two aspects of what five years later was to become the religion clauses of the First Amendment."[64] Pfeffer believed Madison advanced the argument for a wall of separation between church and state was necessary for true religious freedom. Crucial to Pfeffer's argument was Madison's famous assertion: "The same authority which can establish Christianity, in exclusion of all other religions, may establish with the same ease, any particular sect of Christian, in exclusion of all other sects, and the same authority which can force a citizen to contribute three pence only of his property for the support of any one establishment, may force him to conform to any other establishment in all cases whatsoever."[65] Pfeffer did not believe Madison's argument about religious taxes could be reconciled with a narrow or accommodationist interpretation of the religion clauses. Instead, the *Memorial and Remonstrance* exemplified the unitary guarantee and justified a broad interpretation of the First Amendment.

With the defeat of the General Assessment Bill and the passage of Jefferson's Bill for Establishing Religious Freedom in 1786, the Virginia battle for religious freedom and church-state separation was essentially complete. Pfeffer believed the significance of the developments in Virginia on the eventual framing and passage of the First Amendment were manifest:

> Jefferson's statute, and the struggle against the Assessment Bill that preceded it, were incidents that showed the growing American tradition of voluntary support of religion that culminated in the adoption of the First Amendment. The tradition can be traced back to Milton and Locke in England. Roger Williams, Benjamin Franklin, and George Mason were some of the better-known molders of public opinion in America who expressed the same tradition. It was because the Assessment Bill violated the principle of voluntariness rather than because Christianity was selected as the exclusive beneficiary of the state's bounty that Jefferson and Madison opposed it so strenuously.[66]

Disestablishment in Virginia proceeded at a faster pace than most states. Massachusetts, for example, did not fully disestablish the Congregationalist Church until 1833.[67] Nonetheless, Pfeffer's emphasis on the Virginia experience was crucial to understanding the "ferment taking place throughout the nation."[68]

THE FRAMING AND RATIFICATION OF THE FIRST AMENDMENT

The original Constitution's silence on religion, except for the No Religious Test Clause of Article VI, was for Pfeffer further evidence for the widespread acceptance of the unitary guarantee at the nation's founding. Both the constitution's agnosticism and its prohibitions on religious tests to hold public office were foundational for understanding religious freedom: "This concept—that religion is beyond the jurisdiction of the government of men—" Pfeffer once argued, "is the alpha and omega of our Constitution"[69]

Pfeffer considered it significant that the Constitution's silence on religion appeared less controversial to early Americans than its lack of a bill of rights. This was further evidence for Pfeffer to claim that the idea of a secular state was widely accepted at the time: "The opening words of the bill, 'Congress shall make no law,' constituted a seal of approval rather than a repudiation of the absence of reference to the Deity in the Constitution."[70] Nevertheless, virtually every state's ratifying convention did register dissatisfaction that no explicit protection of religious liberty appeared in the proposed Constitution. The call for a bill of rights included Thomas Jefferson, who wrote Madison from Paris encouraging a bill of rights to be submitted to the states. Madison's initial recalcitrance and other leaders' opposition to a bill of rights were not based on the belief that government should be able to work cooperatively with religion. Rather, he believed a bill of rights to be superfluous since religion was to be "outside the cognizance" of government.[71] To secure ratification of the Constitution, Madison was ultimately persuaded to support of bill of rights.

Debate over the Framer's intended meaning behind the First Amendment's religion clauses was vigorous during Pfeffer's career. Partisans for both a narrow and broad reading mined the depths of the historical record to support their interpretation. The debate often hinged on the Congressional debates that led to the final language of the religion clauses: "Congress shall make no law respecting an establishment of religion or prohibiting the free exercise thereof." What often confused the debate was Madison's use of "national religion" in his original proposal, suggesting to some that he was proposing a narrow reading of non-establishment. Nevertheless, Madison's proposal was modified by the House to read "Congress shall make no law establishing religion, or to prevent the free exercise thereof, or to infringe the rights of conscience." The Senate responded with its own language: "Congress shall make no law establishing articles of faith, or a mode of worship, or prohibiting the free exercise of religion." Madison would ultimately chair the conference committee that crafted the final version. While some read the historical record and final language as merely a ban on a single national church, Pfeffer contended that the final version reflected a broader prohibition than earlier proposals. "The rejection of these versions," Pfeffer urged, "each of which unambiguously spells out the narrow interpretation of the First Amendment, would seem to indicate that Congress did not intend such narrow interpretation."[72] Furthermore, Pfeffer identified historical evidence that suggested the word "establishment," at the time of the framing, did not mean the exclusive establishment of one church. The meaning of "establishment of religion," he once argued, had "a much broader meaning in 1791 than it has today in common parlance."[73] Pfeffer ultimately rooted his interpretation in the notion that the religion clauses divested government from power over religion thus making any interpretation that allowed government support for religion to be contrary to the purpose of the First Amendment. In fact, Pfeffer claimed that "before the First Amendment was adopted, it was generally accepted that Congress had no jurisdiction or power to deal with religion on a preferential or nonpreferential basis."[74] Consistent with his unitary understanding of the religion clauses, Pfeffer argued as well that investing the government with the power to aid religion even on a nonpreferential basis was irreconcilable with the purposes of the Free Exercise Clause. Noting that opposition to the Virginia General Assessment Bill was as much about freedom of religion as no-establishment, Pfeffer concluded that Jefferson and Madison "did earnestly believe that the 'free exercise of religion' would be restrained 'by establishing funds for the support of ministers' or 'the endowment of churches'."[75]

POST-RATIFICATION DEVELOPMENTS

While Massachusetts did not end its Congregationalist establishment until 1833, Pfeffer found it significant that state constitutions adopted separation and freedom guarantees voluntarily. By the end of the nineteenth century, many states adopted religious liberty and no-aid provisions that were more explicit than what was articulated in the Establishment Clause of the First Amendment. Much like the evolution of the First Amendment, state provisions followed a discernable pattern according to Pfeffer. Gradually "vestiges of colonial intolerance" aimed primarily at Jews and Catholics were repealed while "a gradual extension of the areas of religious liberty, first to include all Protestant sects, then all Christians, then all believers in God, and finally elimination of all religious tests" took place. States broadened their separationist provisions during this period culminating in the "abolition of all tax support."[76]

Pfeffer noted that the U. S. Congress had never passed an appropriations bill for religious institutions.[77] Moreover, President Ulysses S. Grant's called for a constitutional amendment prohibiting religious instruction in the public schools and tax support for religious schools in his 1876 annual message. The subsequent "Blaine Amendment" banned public funds for religious schools.[78] While it did not receive the necessary two-thirds vote in the Senate, thirty-seven states would ultimately adopt similar provisions in their own constitutions. These state constitutional provisions have been hotly debated due to the role of anti-Catholicism in their origins,[79] but Pfeffer found them instead to be further evidence for a growing consensus that no-establishment meant no-aid.

Pfeffer found overwhelming support for the broad reading of the religion clauses in the federal courts as well. Prior to the *McCollum v. Board of Education* case in 1948,[80] the only major jurist to voice opposition to the broad interpretation of the First Amendment was that of early nineteenth-century justice Joseph Story. Story, whose influential *Commentaries on the Constitution of the United States* articulated a nonpreferentialist interpretation of the Establishment Clause, was often cited by Pfeffer's accommodationist opponents. "The real object of the amendment was not to countenance, much less to advance, Mahometanism, or Judaism, or infidelity, by Prostrating Christianity;" Story asserted, "but to exclude all rivalry among Christian sects." Pfeffer believed Story's narrow reading to be an anomaly among nineteenth-century jurists and noted Chief Justice Morrison Waite's opinion in *Reynolds v. United States* where he declared that Jefferson's "wall of separation" metaphor was "accepted almost as an authoritative declaration of the scope and effect of the amendment thus secured."[81]

THE UNITARY GUARANTEE DEFINED

No U.S. Supreme Court decision was more important to Leo Pfeffer's church-state advocacy than *Everson v. Board of Education.* Justice Hugo Black's majority opinion in the 1940 New Jersey bus case not only marked the incorporation of the Establishment Clause but also affirmed its broad or separationist interpretation. According to Black:

> The "establishment of religion" clause of the First Amendment means at least this: Neither a state nor the Federal Government can set up a church. Neither can pass laws which aid one religion, aid all religions, or prefer one religion over another. Neither can force nor influence a person to go to or to remain away from church against his will or force him to profess a belief or disbelief in religion. No person can be punished for entertaining or professing religious beliefs or disbeliefs, for church attendance or non-attendance. No tax in any amount, large or small, can be levied to support any religious activities or institutions, whatever they may be called, or whatever form they may adopt to teach or practice religion. Neither a state nor the Federal Government can, openly or secretly, participate in the affairs of any religious organizations or groups and *vice versa.* In the words of Jefferson, the clause against establishment of religion by law was intended to erect "a wall of separation between church and state."[82]

This frequently cited paragraph in First Amendment cases became for Pfeffer a starting point in virtually every brief he wrote concerning the Establishment Clause. Simply, Black's separationist language was consonant with what Pfeffer considered to be the unitary guarantee. Black's definition reflected the interrelationship of freedom and separation by not only banning aid to religion but also proscribing punishment for belief or non-belief in religion, attendance or non-attendance at worship, and coercion with regard to religious matters.[83] Black's opinion is noteworthy as well for the attention he gave to the historical record. In doing so, he emphasized the disestablishment battle in Virginia and the contributions of Madison and Jefferson: "This Court has previously recognized that the provisions of the First Amendment, in the drafting and adoption of which Madison and Jefferson played such leading roles, had the same objective and were intended to provide the same protection against governmental intrusion on religious liberty as the Virginia Statute."[84]

At the heart of Black's majority opinion was the "no-aid" principle, yet he and four other justices voted to uphold the New Jersey program of reimbursing the transportation costs of parents sending their children to parochial schools. Black justified this exception to his "high and impregnable wall," by arguing that the New Jersey aid program "does no more than provide a general program to help get their children, regardless of their religion, safely and expeditiously to and from accredited schools." This irony was not lost on Justice Wiley Rutledge who, in his dissenting opinion, criticized the majority decision while affirming its separationist philosophy. Like Black, Rutledge gave significant attention to the history of American church-state relations to argue that the Framers intended to ban "not simply an established church, but any law respecting an establishment of religion." The "correlative and coextensive" nature of the religion clauses was evident in the language of the First Amendment: "'Religion' appears only once in the Amendment. But the word governs two prohibitions and governs them alike. It does not have two meanings, one narrow to forbid 'an establishment' and another, much broader, for securing 'the free exercise thereof.'"[85] Rutledge concluded that the religious clauses created "a complete and permanent separation of the spheres of religious activity and civil authority, by comprehensively forbidding every form of public aid or support for religion."[86]

Pfeffer believed it was significant that the majority and dissenting justices adopted the broad interpretation of the religion clauses, even though they were narrowly divided on the outcome of the case. He also noted their use of history supported his conviction that the unitary guarantee was the product of a historical evolution:

> The unity of the struggle is manifested in every great document in the history of American religious freedom—Roger Williams' *Bloody Tenet of Persecution*, Madison's *Memorial and Remonstrance*, and Jefferson's *Statute for Establishing Religious Freedom* are the most significant. Indeed, the text of the First Amendment prohibits laws respecting an establishment of religion before it prohibits laws prohibiting the free exercise thereof, expressing the conviction of the Constitutional Fathers that the free exercise of religion could not be guaranteed unless non-establishment were also guaranteed.[87]

Pfeffer's first foray into the church-state field as a young lawyer for the Commission on Law and Social Action of the American Jewish Congress was to help draft a brief challenging the constitutionality of the released-time program in *McCollum v. Board of Education*. Introduced as a way to allow students to receive religious education during the school day,[88] the Illinois plan, at issue in *McCollum*, brought clergy into public school classrooms to provide religious instruction. Students choosing not to participate were sent to study hall. As will be discussed in detail in the next chapter, Pfeffer used the language of the *Everson* decision to argue that the released-time program was unconstitutional. The AJC brief challenged the released-time program on both no establishment and free exercise grounds. The brief argued that the released-time program unconstitutionally aided religion by utilizing the tax supported schools for religious instruction and violated students' free exercise rights by isolating nonparticipants.[89]

Reiterating the principles laid down in *Everson*, the Court found that the released-time program constituted a "utilization of the tax-established and tax-supported public school system" to aid religious groups in the propagation of their message. Such involvement, Hugo Black declared for the majority, "falls squarely under the ban of the First Amendment (made applicable to the States by the Fourteenth) as we interpreted it in *Everson*."[90] Black's call for a "high and impregnable" wall of separation was echoed by Justice Felix Frankfurter in his concurring opinion. Frankfurter's commitment to a high wall of separation, as the best protector of religious freedom, was clear as he considered the "basic Constitutional principle" of separation "absolute." According to Frankfurter, "Separation means separation, not something less."[91] The significance of *McCollum*, for Pfeffer, then, was not only that it reiterated the coequal, coextensive nature of the freedom and separation concepts but also that it upheld Black's broad definition as the Court's understanding of the First Amendment.[92] Pfeffer's brief in *McCollum* was significant as well because it provided the framework for his arguments in future Establishment Clause cases.

THE ACCOMMODATIONIST CHALLENGE

Students of American religious history will find Pfeffer's historical narrative of the rise of religious liberty and the separation of church and state familiar. In *Church, State, and Freedom*, Pfeffer drew from the standard religious history texts of the day, including Sanford H. Cobb's *The Rise of Religious Liberty in America*, William Warren Sweet's *Religion in Colonial America*, and Anson Phelps Stokes's three-volume, *Church and State in the United States*—a work Pfeffer would later publish as a one-volume abridgement.[93] As a result, Pfeffer's general historical narrative of the rise of religious liberty in the West and, in colonial America, was largely uncontested. Nonetheless, stark divisions arose as to what the historical record revealed regarding the nation's founders and constitutional framer's intentions with regard to the religion clauses of the First Amendment. Some of this division centered on differing interpretations of Thomas Jefferson and James Madison's intent and role in the framing of the First Amendment, the developments in the early state constitutions, and the Ratification Conventions, as well as the actions of the First Congress. Others argued that Pfeffer and the *Everson* opinions were selective in their use of history to shape a narrative that conformed to their broad and separationist reading of the First Amendment's religion clauses. Pfeffer increasingly became a target of criticism after distinguishing himself through his litigation and scholarly works as the leading advocate of strict separation of church and state. "Indeed, in a reading of many of the Court's separationist opinions," concluded one scholar, "it is difficult at times to know when the Court's language ends and Pfeffer's begins."[94]

The most influential criticism of the historical account in *Everson* and *McCollum* was James O'Neill's *Religion and Education under the Constitution* published in 1949. Described by one scholar as the "leading manifesto for the nonpreferentialist position"[95] O'Neill argued that "there is no such great principle (of complete separation of Church and State) and there never has been."[96] O'Neill offered a revisionist account of the historical record concluding instead that at the time of the framing of the Constitution, "establishment of religion" was a "formal, legal union of a single church or religion with government." O'Neill rejected the no-aid interpretation of the Establishment Clause that prohibited "non-preferential assistance by government to religion." Such an interpretation was "a modern invention which has no basis in language, tradition, law, or history."[97] O'Neill was joined by legal scholar Edward Corwin who accused Justice Rutledge of selling "his brethren a bill of goods when her persuaded them that the 'establishment of religion' clause of the First Amendment was intended to rule out all government 'aid to *all* religions'."[98] Corwin argued that a proper reading of history, including Jefferson's and Madison's contributions, would lead one to the following conclusion: "The historical record show beyond peradventure that the core idea of 'an establishment of religion' comprises the idea of <preference>."[99]

One scholar has called the early debates between Pfeffer and his accommodationist critics a "confrontation with Catholicism."[100] Indeed, many of the accommodationist scholars came from the Catholic community, and they parted ways not just in their historical understanding of the Establishment Clause but also in its application—particularly in the arena of religion and education. As chapter 3 will discuss in more detail, some scholars have argued that the strict separationist interpretation was the product of nineteenth-century nativism and anti-Catholicism that resurfaced with a renewed intensity during the Protestant-Catholic church state struggles of the mid-twentieth century.[101] Such broad assertion have been challenged, but the fact that Pfeffer found himself at odds so frequently with the Catholic Church forced he and other separationists to fend off claims that their First Amendment views were the product of animus toward Catholics.[102]

Despite this lively debate involving leading scholars of the day, the separationist historical narrative enjoyed broad consensus for the next several decades. By the 1980s, however, new voices would be raised challenging the separationist historical interpretation. Among these was political scientist Robert Cord whose *Separation of Church and State: Historical Fact or Current Fiction* became an influential work for accommodationist scholars and jurists alike. Cord began his critique by challenging Pfeffer's interpretation of Madison's and Jefferson's church-state views. Neither Madison nor Jefferson, Cord contended, envisioned a First Amendment banning all aid to religion. Cord was careful to note that Madison as a constitutional framer proposed a draft of the First Amendment that read "The Civil rights of none shall be abridged on account of religious belief or worship, nor shall any *national* religion be established." This language, for Cord, was clear indication that Madison only intended to ban a national religion.[103] Madison's draft, along with the resolutions at the state ratifying conventions and the text of the final version, clearly demonstrated to Cord that the primary concern of the framers was to prevent "the Federal Government from establishing a national religion or raising one religion above the others."[104] Cord relied heavily on political scientist Michael Malbin who also placed great emphasis on the wording of the final version of the First Amendment. For Malbin, the use of the word "an" before "establishment of religion" rather than "the" indicated that "they [the Framers] wanted to prohibit only those official activities that tended to promote the interests of one or another particular sect."[105] Cord dismissed Jefferson's influence on the First Amendment due to the fact that he was residing in Paris during its framing and ratification.

As a member of the First Congress, Madison sat on a committee that approved a Congressional chaplain. Cord, echoing O'Neill and other early critics of Pfeffer's separationist historical narrative, argued as well that Madison apparently found no constitutional problem with presidential Thanksgiving Day proclamations since he issued four during his presidency. These examples proved for Cord that Madison did not intend to erect a high wall of separation between church and state as Pfeffer argued.[106] Jefferson's actions indicated that he, like Madison, was certainly no absolutist with regard to governmental aid to religion. According to Cord, Jefferson supported an Indian treaty that provided funds for, among other things, building of a church and payment of a Catholic priest to perform his duties among Native Americans. He also signed federal land grant trust laws that, in part, provided funds for religious societies "to preach the gospel to the Indians."[107]

Cord went so far as to say that even Madison's famous *Memorial and Remonstrance Against Religious Assessments*, what Pfeffer considered one of the strongest pieces of evidence for the broad interpretation of the Establishment Clause, has been overemphasized and was fundamentally challenging "exclusive establishments" as opposed to nondiscriminatory aid to religion.[108] This too had been an argument raised by O'Neill who asserted that "not one of the fifteen concerns general financial support for religion."[109]

Cord's book is important not only because of its challenge to the strict separationist position but also because of its influence on jurists such as Chief Justice William Rehnquist. Rehnquist's dissenting opinion in the 1985 *Wallace v. Jaffree*[110] case was a lengthy critique of the separationist position and an advocacy of the nonpreferentialist position. Based largely on Cord's research, Rehnquist concluded that "the 'wall of separation of church and state' is a metaphor based on bad history, a metaphor which has proved useless as a guide to judging. It should be frankly and explicitly abandoned."[111]

Donald Dreisbach's *Real Threat and Mere Shadow: Religious Liberty and the First Amendment* likewise identified Pfeffer as the "leading strict separationist advocate" whose writings illustrated "the reliance of strict separationists on history."[112] Dreisbach's is a sustained analysis of the *Everson* and Pfefferian historical argument that draws equally candid, if not uncharitable, conclusions: "At the very least, Pfeffer and the Everson Court were guilty of poor scholarship and, at worst, they deliberately engaged in an intellectually dishonest manipulation of the historical record."[113] Like Cord, Dreisbach concluded that both Madison's *Memorial and Remonstrance* and Jefferson's *A Bill for Establishing Religious Freedom* "were not treatises or briefs for an absolute separation of state government and religion."[114]

Similarly, critics of the Court and Leo Pfeffer have argued that too much emphasis has been placed upon the disestablishment battles in Virginia in determining the meaning of the religion clauses. Some have asserted that Madison and Jefferson, while opposed to religious establishments, recognized that the system of federalism would have left such issues to the states individually. This contention is illustrated by the fact that Connecticut and Massachusetts did not disestablish the Congregationalist Church until well into the nineteenth century. Some scholars and jurists have gone so far as to say that the Establishment Clause was created to protect the state establishments—that church-state relationships would be determined at the state level.[115] This federalism contention was not given much attention by Pfeffer. Clearly, he would have agreed that that the First Amendment limited federal power over religion, yet it does not follow that the Framer's merely equated the Establishment Clause with federalism. Pfeffer argued that while some states maintained establishments, others adopted constitutional provisions similar to that of the First Amendment. Nonetheless, the varying approaches to disestablishment in the states have likewise led some scholars to question whether the Jeffersonian wall or the notion of a secular state was beyond the conception of most Americans during the colonial and early national periods.[116]

Particularly troublesome for critics of the strict separationist position was the *Everson* Court's and Pfeffer's reliance on Thomas Jefferson's "wall of separation" metaphor as an apt reflection of the meaning of the Establishment Clause. Cord, for example, asserted that Jefferson's 1802 letter to the Danbury Baptists, in which he used the phrase the wall of "separation of church and state," was not a statement of an absolutist with regard to the separation of church and state. Instead, he concluded that in looking at Jefferson's total record, the phrase "'separation of church and state' could only have meant that the 'wall of separation' was erected 'between church and state' in regard to possible federal action such as a law establishing a national religion or prohibiting the free exercise of worship."[117] Historian James Hutson has argued that many observers have asked "how a dictum delivered thirteen years after the composition of the First Amendment by a person who was in France at the time it was written can provide an authoritative interpretation of the language at issue."[118] While others have contended that the letter was more about federalism and the limits of the presidency, if not also a swipe at the Federalist establishment in Connecticut.[119]

Beyond critiquing Pfeffer's interpretation of Madison and Jefferson, critics have looked to executive and legislative actions to further support an accommodationist reading of the religion clauses. Cord and others identified Congressional chaplains, Thanksgiving Day proclamations, and Congressional appropriations that, under the guise of "civilizing" Native Americans, supported religious groups, missions, and churches. The Northwest Ordinance, which in part called for the provision of funds for church schools to promote religion and morality in the Western territories, was further evidence that the First Congress did not conceive of the First Amendment as broadly as Pfeffer claimed. Rather, "the new Federal Government should not be negative or neutral," one historian declared, "but rather it should be a positive force in promoting the liberty of its citizens, so long as it did not favor one particular religious sect beyond all others."[120]

Accommodationist scholars have also argued that the Court largely ignored the debates in the Ratification Conventions and gave scant attention to the debates in the First Congress over the proposed amendments. In looking at these records, Gerard Bradley concluded that the consensus view of no establishment was "no sect preference."[121] Thus, too much emphasis has been placed upon the Virginia battles, Jefferson, and Madison, rather than what the religion clauses would likely have meant to the average person.[122] In sum, the historical evidence led scholars like Robert Cord to conclude that Pfeffer's interpretation of the First Amendment was "overbroad, explicit, and rigid" and "out of harmony with American historical reality."[123]

Leo Pfeffer spilled a significant amount of ink defending his separationist account of the historical record. He and James O'Neill squared off in a debate over the historical interpretation of the Establishment Clause that was published in the *Buffalo Law Review* in 1953.[124] Their extended essays addressed many of the key points of contention that would be revisited during the debates over original intent in the 1980s. In a 1951 University *of Chicago Law Review* article entitled "Church and State: Something Less Than Separation,"[125] Pfeffer again took the opportunity to respond to many of O'Neill's nonpreferentialist critiques. This article would eventually appear as a chapter in *Church, State, and Freedom.*

In responding to O'Neill and other critics, Pfeffer granted that there were numerous proposals of the First Amendment before the Constitutional Convention that reflected a narrower or perhaps nonpreferentialist understanding of the phrase "establishment of religion." Yet he asked that if the framer's intended nonpreferentialism, why were the explicitly nonpreferentialist proposals not adopted? The adopted phrase, "*respecting* an establishment of religion" was evidence to Pfeffer that the First Amendment had a broader meaning than accommodationists were willing to accept.[126] Furthermore, Pfeffer found that numerous proposals more explicitly nonpreferential were not passed in favor of the more general wording of the final draft.[127] Other scholars have found this a particularly strong argument for the separationist position. Of the final language, leading religion clause scholar Douglas Laycock concluded that "most important, it forbids any law respecting an establishment of 'religion.' It does not say '*a* religion,' 'a national religion,' 'one sect or society,' or 'any particular denomination of religion.' It is religion generically that may not be established."[128]

Pfeffer admitted that the strongest historical argument for the nonpreferentialists were the instances of governmental support for religion, such as chaplaincies, Thanksgiving proclamations, tax exemption for religious institutions, and support for missions to Native Americans. Nevertheless, he argued that several of these practices would violate even a nonpreferentialist reading of the First Amendment. In other words, these were violations of both a broad and a narrow interpretation of the First Amendment, since they benefited Christianity over other religions.[129] Other practices Pfeffer dismissed as "vestiges of establishment" and emphasized instead "how few and comparatively minor these vestiges actually were."[130] While Madison succumbed to the "pressure of politics" to issue a thanksgiving proclamation, Jefferson refused to do so. In contrast to these manifestations of church-state interaction, Pfeffer reiterated the Constitution's silence on religion, as well as the fact that Congress had never passed an appropriations bill specifically for religious institutions.[131]

Madison's "Detached Memoranda," written during his retirement, was of special importance to Pfeffer in identifying Madison's understanding of the First Amendment. Free from the political pressures inherent in holding public office, Madison was able to reflect openly in this piece on the relationship of church and state. For instance, Madison wrote that Congressional chaplains were a violation of establishment, despite his support while in Congress. Moreover, Madison believed that military chaplains should be voluntarily supported by the churches. Religious proclamations by the government were likewise inappropriate. Not only were they beyond the jurisdiction of government, but they favored the predominant sects and threatened to make religion subservient to political interests.[132] These reflections of Madison, revealed in the "Detached Memoranda," were for Pfeffer, one of the best sources "for determining the meaning of the religion clauses."[133]

Others have contended that the "Detached Memoranda" should be given less weight than Madison's actions as president when, among other things, he had issued Thanksgiving proclamations. Pfeffer responded that the fact that there were some gaps between principle and practice did not justify abandonment of the principle itself. Several of these practices were inconsistent with the First Amendment while others, like the "reference to God on coins . . . are insignificant to the point of being trivial." Such examples were acts of "ceremonial obeisance" according to Pfeffer and hardly provided the basis for a narrow reading of the Establishment Clause.[134] The gap between principle and practice could be found in other constitutional provisions, Pfeffer argued, yet the principle of freedom of expression "is not vitiated by the widespread limitation on the freedom in actual practice."[135] For Pfeffer, these inconsistencies hardly justified jettisoning the broad interpretation of the First Amendment nor did they justify the "government expenditure of tax raised funds for religious institutions."[136]

Pfeffer challenged the criticisms of Jefferson's letter to the Danbury Baptists, arguing instead that "we have Jefferson's own testimony that the letter was prepared with extreme care and deliberation, and that in fact he merely seized upon the Danbury Baptists' address as a long-awaited opportunity to express the thought contained in the letter."[137] Noting that Jefferson had discussed the letter with his attorney general before sending it, Pfeffer concluded that "it is difficult to characterize the letter as lacking in deliberation and care."[138]

Finally, the land grants given to religious societies for the work among Native Americans provided the basis for a substantial portion of Cord's argument, and it was an area which Pfeffer did not address at great length. However, one might question the efficacy of building a theory of the First Amendment on the basis of appropriations which had as one of their consequences the payment of religious societies to provide education for Native Americans. After all, the relationship of the U.S. government to Native Americans has been one of great ambiguities in which constitutional principles have often been ignored.[139] Native American tribes were often viewed as foreign nations by presidential administrations leaving the First Amendment inapplicable. Moreover, the payment of a particular mission society to educate the Native Americans seems difficult to reconcile with the narrow interpretation of the First Amendment. Like Congressional chaplains, the missionaries typically represented a particular religious faith. In general, Pfeffer described the historical evidence that Cord and other nonpreferentialists had marshaled against the broad interpretation of the First Amendment as "relatively petty compromises of the principle of strict separation of church and state."[140]

Pfeffer believed the strongest evidence against the nonpreferentialist theory was the well-known battle in colonial Virginia over religious freedom. Scholars have argued convincingly that the developments in Virginia involved many of the key players and debates that would be involved in the framing of the Constitution.[141] The Virginia developments not only produced Thomas Jefferson's "Bill for Establishing Religious Freedom" but also James Madison's "Memorial and Remonstrance Against Religious Assessments." For Pfeffer, the General Assessment bill was a clear example of a nonpreferential aid to religion. Contrary to Cord's claim that Madison opposed the bill on nonpreferentialist grounds, Pfeffer held that "the position taken by Madison and Jefferson and their supporters during this period was that religion was exempt from and entirely outside of state authority. Their objection to the fact that the Assessment Bill provided for the support of the 'Christian Religion' stemmed at least as much from that reason as from opposition to preferential treatment."[142] The nature of the General Assessment debate led one leading law and religion scholar to conclude that "the great debate about disestablishment in Virginia culminated in a decisive vote against nonpreferential aid."[143] Further support for Pfeffer's position can be found in the highly regarded work of historian Thomas Curry. Curry's detailed study of church-state relations from the colonial period through the passage of the First Amendment led him to conclude that the discrepancy between the early American commitment to secular government and the reality of government interference in religion came out of the cultural and social context of the time. According to Curry, "Customs like days of prayer and thanksgiving appeared not so much matters of religion as part of the common coin of civilized religion."[144]

Cord and fellow critics of Pfeffer provide less analysis on the ideological origins of the First Amendment, especially Pfeffer's claims about the convergence of the concepts of limited government and voluntariness in religion. For Cord, the actions of the First Congress and early presidents are of utmost importance. There is virtually no discussion of political theory or theological developments in his study. In contrast, Pfeffer gave careful attention to the ideological influences of the period. "Jefferson's Act and the struggle against the Assessment Bill which preceded it represented incidents manifesting a growing American tradition of voluntary support of religion," Pfeffer explained. "It was because the Assessment Bill violated the principle of voluntariness rather than because Christianity was selected as the exclusive beneficiary of the State's bounty that Jefferson and Madison opposed it so strenuously."[145] Misinterpreting or at least minimizing the concepts of limited government and voluntarism in religion constitutes the fatal flaw of the nonpreferentialists according to constitutional scholar Leonard Levy. "The nonpreferential interpretation seems persuasive," Levy asserted, "if one can ignore or forget the fact that the First Amendment, no matter how parsed or logically analyzed, was framed to deny power, not vest it."[146]

Many scholars and jurists found Pfeffer's separationist historical narrative persuasive. Nevertheless, he often painted with broad strokes when drawing conclusions from history and did not always provide a particularly nuanced account of the historical record. One can rightly question some of his more sweeping claims. These included the contention that by 1787, a "widespread if not universal consensus that full religious freedom was attainable only in a secular state"[147] or that Jefferson "never swerved from his devotion to the complete independence of religion and government."[148] As an attorney, Pfeffer was given to broad claims since he used history to build a legal case for his position. As a result, Pfeffer was as seemingly complicit as some of his interlocutors for identifying a clear intent of the Framers of the Constitution.

A number of scholars have argued that applying modern notions of original intent to the constitutional Framers is misguided.[149] A strict adherence to original intent, they argue, ignores the multifarious ideological influences on those determining the language of the First Amendment. These often included competing notions as to the nature of individual rights, community interests, and the role of government.[150] Others have noted that religious establishment likely had multiple meanings. Leading First Amendment scholar John Witte has identified six principles, including liberty of conscience, free exercise of religion, religious pluralism, religious equality, separation of church and state, and disestablishment that were advocated by the nation's founders to "prevent repressive religious establishments."[151] Moreover, the fact that the Framers were politicians seeking to gain consensus on how to govern a new nation adds complexity to the quest for original intent as well. Certainly ideology was frequently sacrificed for political ends. Despite the limitations of original intent, the "lure of history" was nonetheless quite powerful for justices, particularly when it came to Establishment Clause cases.[152]

While identifying historical evidence for the broad interpretation of the First Amendment was extremely important to Pfeffer, he believed the principles underlying the Constitution were of more fundamental significance. Thus, the fact that there were deviations from the broad interpretation of the

First Amendment did not require its abandonment. "We must look to the intent of the fathers for the broad objective, the philosophy underlying the particular liberty secured by the Bill of Rights," he once wrote, "rather than the specific details of its application." Furthermore, Pfeffer recognized the shortfalls in too strict an adherence to original intent. "But the precise intent of the framers and adopters of the First Amendment, while interesting, is not decisive. Probably there was no single intent. The generation which adopted the Amendment expressed as a basic principle of American democracy the broad concept of separation of church and state. The evolution of that concept did not end in 1791."[153]

RELIGIOUS TESTS: THE ISSUE OF EQUALITY

Less attention has been given to the ban on religious tests in Article VI of the Constitution than the First Amendment's religion clauses. Pfeffer considered it significant that Article VI was the only article that mentioned of religion in the Constitution, especially considering it placed a restriction on government. The ban on religious tests affirmed the notion that religion was outside the jurisdiction of government and that freedom of conscience was inviolable. Pfeffer found it noteworthy that Article VI echoed Jefferson's opposition to religious tests in his Bill for Establishing Religious Freedom:

> That our civil rights have no dependence on our religious opinions, any more than on our opinions in physics or geometry; that therefore the proscribing of any citizen as unworthy of public confidence by laying upon him an incapacity of being called to offices of trust and emolument, unless he profess or renounce this or that religious opinion, is depriving him injuriously of those privileges and advantages to which in common with his fellow citizens he has a natural right.[154]

Religious tests had been the target of religious dissenters, including Baptists who opposed them as violations of religious conscience. Isaac Backus, for example, declared that "the imposing of religious tests hath been the greatest tyranny in the world."[155] Article VI, Pfeffer contended, presaged the First Amendment and contributed as well to the rationale for disestablishment. More importantly, he believed the ban on religious tests compelled a broader reading of the First Amendment than merely a ban on a single national church.[156]

Despite such opposition, religious tests were commonplace in colonial America and some remained in the text of a few state constitutions. Originally, their purpose had been to ban Catholics, Jews, and atheists from public office, as one opponent of Article VI declared with alarm during

Constitutional ratification: "We may have a Papist, a Mohomatan, a Deist, yea an Atheist at the helm of government."[157] Nevertheless, Article VI was passed with little debate during the Constitutional convention. More opposition was expressed during the ratification conventions, but the spirit of religious equality carried the day.

As with disestablishment, most states gradually ended religious tests and oaths of office. However, several states retained provisions requiring public officeholders to make an oath expressing belief in God. As late as 1960, Maryland's constitution still included Article 37 which stated in part: "no religious test ought ever to be required as a qualification for any office or profit or trust in this State, other than a declaration of belief in the existence of God."[158] Roy Torcaso, who was barred from serving as a notary public because of his refusal to declare a belief in God, challenged the constitutionality of the requirement. Pfeffer and the American Jewish Congress took the case, setting the stage for what would become Pfeffer's first oral arguments before the U.S. Supreme Court. Pfeffer considered Article 37 a clear violation of religious freedom and viewed the case as an opportunity for the U.S. Supreme Court to rearticulate the broad interpretation of the First Amendment stated in the *Everson* and *McCollum* decisions. He sought to buttress his religion clause arguments by contending that the Maryland test oath violated the Equal Protection Clause of the Fourteenth Amendment and the religious test ban of Article VI of the Constitution as well.[159]

As lead counsel, Pfeffer argued in his brief that the "eligibility for a State office conditioned upon a belief in the existence of God constitutes a law respecting an establishment of religion in violation of the First Amendment."[160] Utilizing the language of *Everson* and *McCollum*, Pfeffer argued that the constitutional violation was first based on the fact that the oath requirement preferred some religions over others, "specifically theistic religions over those which are non-theistic." "Such a law is no less barred by the First Amendment," Pfeffer asserted, "than one requiring a belief in Christianity, or in Trinitarian Christianity, or in Protestant Christianity."[161]

Pfeffer's next line of attack was based on the requirement of government neutrality between belief and nonbelief, as Justice Black affirmed in *Everson*. The Maryland test oath clearly violated the First Amendment, Pfeffer asserted, because it preferred belief over nonbelief. For Pfeffer, this would be the case "even if religion were narrowly defined to exclude non-theistic belief." "A law according special privilege to theism," he continued, "would violate the mandate of neutrality."[162] Pfeffer's brief also traced the history of religious tests in America as well as the framing of Article VI. In doing so, Pfeffer sought to highlight the commensurate nature of the no religious test clause with the religion clauses. Religious tests violated the no aid principle of the Establishment Clause, because religious tests led to government endorsement or support of religion.[163] The Maryland oath requirement violated Roy Torcaso's free exercise of religion as well. "The Bill of Rights that protects the Catholic and Jew from discrimination in the holding of public office or practice of law by reason of their beliefs in the field of religion," Pfeffer asserted, "protects the non-theist."[164]

Pfeffer challenged religious tests as violations of the Equal Protection Clause of the Fourteenth Amendment as well. His utilization of the Equal Protection Clause reinforced his argument for the equality of all religions and no-religion. "The net result is that discrimination on the basis of religious belief or non-belief in the granting or withholding of public office," Pfeffer asserted in his brief, "is by its very nature a deprivation of due process of law and a denial of the equal protection of the laws."[165] As discussed in Chapter 1, the quest for equality was a prime motivating factor in the strong advocacy of the separation of church and state by Pfeffer and the Jewish defense agencies.[166] Thus, Pfeffer's drew from several constitutional provisions to emphasize that the First Amendment was not merely to provide liberty of conscience and religious exercise, but to place all religions and no religion on "equal footing."[167] And "equal footing," Pfeffer argued, was best secured when there was a commitment to the separation of church and state.

In a brief and unanimous decision, the U.S. Supreme Court found Pfeffer's arguments convincing. Declaring that the Maryland religious test violated Torcaso's freedom of belief and religion, the Court, utilizing the definitions found in *Everson* and *McCollum* and reiterated by Leo Pfeffer, reaffirmed the broad interpretation of the First Amendment:

> We repeat and again reaffirm that neither a State nor the Federal Government can constitutionally force a person "to profess a belief or disbelief in any religion." Neither can constitutionally pass laws or impose requirements which aid all religions as against nonbelievers, and neither can aid those religions based on a belief in the existence of God as against those religions founded on different beliefs.[168]

Torcaso is significant not just because of its affirmation of the broad reading of the religion clauses but also because it establishes the legal basis that the First Amendment protects both religion and irreligion.[169] "The Court also affirmed what has been, or should have been, apparent all along," one constitutional scholar observed, "that the Constitution of the United States, in guaranteeing freedom of religion, by implication also guarantees freedom of *irreligion*."[170]

SUMMARY

At the heart of Leo Pfeffer's understanding of the First Amendment was his belief that religious freedom and church-state separation were interdependent elements of a single concept. Freedom and separation were "two sides of the same coin" and together created a "unitary guarantee." According to Pfeffer, this "unitary guarantee" was embodied in the religion clauses of the First Amendment.

Historically, Pfeffer believed the unitary guarantee in the First Amendment was the culmination of an evolutionary process. The theological convictions of Protestant sects and the political theory of the Enlightenment combined to articulate the philosophical premise of the unitary guarantee: religion was outside the sphere of government. Alongside these ideological influences were the practical considerations of colonial America. Religious pluralism, economic survival, and limited participation in institutional church life enhanced religious toleration and mitigated against religious establishment.

According to Pfeffer, both the framing and the ratification of the First Amendment reflected the widespread acceptance of the unitary guarantee by the Framer's. The Constitution's silence on religion, the debate surrounding the First Amendment and Bill of Rights, as well as the language of the First Amendment all reflect that religion and government were to be independent. For Pfeffer, the unitary guarantee commanded a broad prohibition of interaction between church and state, not just the ban of a single national church.

Pfeffer found in the early U.S. Supreme Court's Establishment Clause decision, *Everson v. Board of Education*, a classic articulation of the unitary guarantee. Justice Hugo Black's call for a high wall of separation between church and state became for Pfeffer the starting point for much of his future church-state litigation. Equally important to the viability of religious freedom and church-state separation was the religious test ban of Article VI of the Constitution. Affirming that religion was outside of the jurisdiction of government, Article VI guaranteed the equality of all religions and no religion.

In making his historical and constitutional case for the broad or separationist reading of the religion clauses, Pfeffer often drew sweeping conclusions that did not always reflect the diversity of perspectives or provide a particularly nuanced understanding of the relationship of church and state. Pfeffer's narrative did enjoy acceptance by the Court during his career, but it was not without criticism. Historical debate flourished at both the beginning and end of his career over the historical record and whether the "wall of separation" metaphor was an apt description of the function of the Establishment Clause. Nonetheless, Pfeffer shaped a persuasive historical narrative that he drew from regularly in his legal advocacy. For Pfeffer, the unitary guarantee required a broad reading of the First Amendment's religion clauses. Armed with separationist perspective, Pfeffer's would challenge most forms of religious exercises in the public schools as well as public aid to religious institutions.

NOTES

1. Leo Pfeffer, "Freedom of Religion and Separation of Church and State," Statement submitted to Subcommittee on Constitutional Rights, U.S. Senate Committee on the Judiciary, Washington, DC, 3 October 1955, p. 5; "The Meaning of the First Amendment," *Liberty* 44 (2nd Quarter, 1949): 8; *Church, State, and Freedom*, 727.

2. *Everson* v. *Board of Education*, 330 U.S. 1 at 40.

3. Francesco Ruffini, *Religious Liberty* (London: Williams and Norgate, 1912), 16; quoted in Pfeffer, *Church, State, and Freedom*, 138.

4. Ibid., 137.

5. Ibid., 137.

6. See, for example, Gerard V. Bradley, *Church-State Relationships in America* (Westport, CT: Greenwood Press, 1987); Thomas J. Curry, *The First Freedoms: Church and State in America to the Passage of the First Amendment* (New York: Oxford University Press, 1985); Derek Davis, *Original Intent: Chief Justice Rehnquist and the Course of American Church/State Relations* (Buffalo, NY: Prometheus Books, 1991); Leonard W. Levy, *The Establishment Clause: Religion and the First Amendment*, 2nd ed. (Chapel Hill: University of North Carolina Press, 1994); Michael J. Malbin, *Religion and Politics: The Intentions of the Authors of the First Amendment* (Washington, DC: American Enterprise Institute for Public Policy Research, 1978); and Douglas Laycock, "Original Intent and the Constitution Today," in *The First Freedom: Religion and the Bill of Rights*, ed. James E. Wood, Jr. (Waco, TX: J.M. Dawson Institute of Church-State Studies, Baylor University, 1990), 87–112.

7. Steven Green has concluded that "for the first forty years of modern Establishment Clause jurisprudence, the Court's resort to history generally reinforced separationist principles." See Steven K. Green, "'Bad History': The Lure of History in Establishment Clause Adjudication," *Notre Dame Law Review* 81 (2016): 1723.

8. 330 U.S. 1 at 33.

9. These included Henry Nelson Wieman, and Walter M. Horton, *The Growth of Religion* (Chicago: Willett, Clark, and Co., 1938), Williston Walker, *A History of the Christian Church* (New York: Charles Scribner's Sons, 1940), and M. Searle Bates, *Religious Liberty: An Inquiry* (New York: International Missionary Council, 1945).

10. Pfeffer, *Church, State, and Freedom*, 724.

11. Ibid., 30.

12. Here Pfeffer cited some of the major works of his era on religious liberty. See, for example, Sanford H. Cobb, *The Rise of Religious Liberty in America: A History* (New York: Macmillan Co., 1902) and Evarts B. Green, *Religion and the State* (New York: New York University Press, 1941).

13. Pfeffer, *Church, State, and Freedom*, 91.

14. Leo Pfeffer, "No Law Respecting an Establishment of Religion," *Buffalo Law Review* 2 (Spring 1953): 3; "The Case for Separation," in *Religion in America*, ed. John Cogley (New York: Meridian Books, 1958), 52; *Church, State, and Freedom*, 92.

15. Ibid., 95.

16. Ibid., 93.

17. James E. Wood, Jr. "The United States as a Pluralistic Society," in *Reflections on Church and State*, ed. James E. Wood, Jr. (Waco, TX: J.M. Dawson Institute of Church-State Studies, Baylor University, 1995), 119–20.

18. Pfeffer, *Church, State, and Freedom*, 95; Pfeffer cited William Warren Sweet, whose works on American religious history were the standard for many decades. According to Sweet, "There came to be more unchurched people in America, in proportion to the population, than was to be found in any country in Christendom"; William W. Sweet, *The Story of Religion in America* (New York: Harper and Row, 1950; reprinted Grand Rapids, MI: Baker Book House, 1973), 5.

19. Pfeffer, *Church, State, and Freedom*, 95–96.

20. Patricia U. Bonomi, *Under the Cope of Heaven: Religion, Society and Politics in Colonial America* (New York: Oxford University Press, 2003), 147.

21. Pfeffer, *Church, State, and Freedom*, 95–96.

22. Ibid., 96.

23. Stokes, *Church and State*, I: 254–55.

24. Pfeffer, *Church, State, and Freedom*, 96.

25. This was a regular argument used by Pfeffer in his legal challenges to aid to parochial schools. That no aid was to travel from the public treasury to religious institutions was a direct implication of the First Amendment; see Leo Pfeffer, "The Price We Pay for Federal Aid," *Midstream* 11 (March 1965): 39.

26. Pfeffer, *Church, State, and Freedom*, 97; see especially John Ragosta, *Wellspring of Liberty: How Virginia's Religious Dissenters Helped Win the American Revolution and Secured Religious Liberty* (New York: Oxford University Press, 2010).

27. Pfeffer, "Freedom of Religion," p. 5.

28. Winthrop S. Hudson, *The Great Tradition of the American Churches* (New York: Harper and Row, 1953); Franklin H. Littell, *From State Church to Pluralism: A Protestant Interpretation of Religion in American History* (New York: Macmillan Co., 1971), 5.

29. Pfeffer, "No Law," 4.

30. Pfeffer, "Freedom of Religion," p. 6.

31. See David Little, "Roger Williams and the Separation of Church and State," in *Religion and the State: Essays in Honor of Leo Pfeffer*, ed. James E. Wood, Jr. (Waco, Tex.: Baylor University Press, 1985), 3–24.

32. Edmund S. Morgan argued that above all, Williams's theological separatism lay at the heart of his church-state views; see Edmund Morgan, *Roger Williams: The Church and the State* (New York: Harcourt, Brace and World, 1967); see also John M. Barry, *Roger Williams and the Creation of the American Soul: Church, State, and the Birth of Liberty* (New York: Viking Press, 2012).

33. Pfeffer, *Church, State, and Freedom*, 86–87.

34. Leo Pfeffer, "The Establishment Clause: An Absolutist's Defense," *Notre Dame Journal of Law, Ethics and Public Policy* 4 (1990): 705.

35. Pfeffer, *Church, State, and Freedom*, 84–85.

36. Ibid., 88.

37. Ibid., 103.

38. Leo Pfeffer, "The Deity in American Constitutional History," *Journal of Church and State* 23 (Spring 1981): 216.

39. Pfeffer, *Church, State, and Freedom*, 99.

40. Quoted in *Baptists and the American Republic*, ed. Joseph Martin Dawson (Nashville, Tenn.: Broadman Press, 1956), 75.

41. Statement made in support of Federal Constitution's religious test ban; quoted in Pfeffer, *Church, State, and Freedom*, 101.

42. John Leland, "The Rights of Conscience Inalienable," in *The Writings of John Leland*, ed. L. F. Greene (New York: Arno Press, 1969), 181–84.

43. Andrew Manis has argued that Leland held a "hybrid position" composed of evangelical and Jeffersonian ideas often putting evangelical twists on Jeffersonian notions in his arguments for separation. Andrew M. Manis, "Regionalism and a Baptist Perspective on Church and State," *American Baptist Quarterly* 3 (September 1983): 213–20; see also Edwin S. Gaustad, "The Backus-Leland Tradition," *Foundations* 2 (1959): 131–52; L. Herbert Butterfield, *Elder John Leland, Jeffersonian Itinerant*. Vol. 62 American Antiquarian Society; reprinted (New York: Arno Press, 1980); and J. Bradley Creed, "John Leland; American Prophet of Religious Individualism" (Ph.D. Diss. Southwestern Baptist Theological Seminary, 1981).

44. Leland, "The Rights of Conscience," 180.

45. Ibid.; John Leland, "The Virginia Chronicle," in The *Writings of John Leland, ed. L.F. Greene* (New York: Arno Press, 1969), 119.

46. William G. McGloughlin, "Issac Backus and the Separation of Church and State in America," *American Historical Review* 73 (June 1968): 1412, n. 55.

47. Manis, "Regionalism and a Baptist Perspective," 214.

48. Charter to William Penn, and Laws of the Province of Pennsylvania, Passed between the Years 1682 and 1700; quoted in Anson Phelps Stokes and Leo Pfeffer, *Church and State in the United States*, rev. one-vol. ed. (New York: Harper and Row, 1964), 19.

49. Pfeffer, *Church, State, and Freedom*, 101.

50. Leo Pfeffer, *God, Caesar and the Constitution: The Court as Referee of Church–State Confrontation* (Boston: Beacon Press, 1975), 8.

51. See John Locke, *Two Treatises on Government*, ed. Peter Laslett (Cambridge: Cambridge University Press, 1960 [1690]) and John Locke, *Letter Concerning Toleration*, ed. James H. Tully (Cambridge, Mass.: Hackett, 1983 [1689]).

52. Pfeffer, "The Deity," 216–17; Pfeffer, "Freedom and Separation," 107–09; "No Law," 4–5; *Church, State, and Freedom*, 101–04.

53. Ibid., 103.

54. Moncure D. Conway, ed., *The Writings of Thomas Paine* (New York: AMS Press, 1967), 1: 108–09.

55. Pfeffer, *God, Caesar, and the Constitution*, 348; *Church, State, and Freedom*, 104; "No Law," 7; "The Establishment Clause," 72; "The Unity of the First Amendment Clauses," 135.

56. Pfeffer, *Church, State, and Freedom*, 105.

57. Ibid., 106.

58. Ibid., 113–14.

59. Ibid.

60. See, for example, Marvin K. Singleton, "Colonial Virginia as First Amendment Matrix: Henry, Madison, and the Establishment Clause," *Journal of Church and State* 8 (Autumn 1966): 344–64; Curry, *The First Freedoms*, 134; William Lee Miller, *The First Liberty: Religion and the American Republic* (New York: Paragon House Publishers, 1985), 7; Stokes, *Church and State*, 1: 366–96.

61. Curry, *The First Freedom*, 136.

62. Ibid., 113.

63. Leo Pfeffer, "Madison's 'Detached Memoranda': Then and Now," in *The Virginia State for Religious Freedom: Its Evolution and Consequences in American History*, eds. Merrill D. Peterson and Robert C. Vaughan (New York: Cambridge University Press, 1988), 285.

64. Pfeffer, "Freedom of Religion," 11.

65. James Madison's "Memorial and Remonstrance against Religious Assessments"; quoted in Pfeffer, *Church, State, and Freedom*, 113.

66. Ibid., 173.

67. See, for example, Carl H. Esbeck and Jonathan J. Den Hartog, eds. *Disestablishment and Religious Dissent: Church–State Relations in the New American States, 1774–1833* (Columbia: University of Missouri Press, 2019).

68. Curry, *The First Freedom*, 134.

69. Pfeffer, "Freedom and Separation," 109.

70. Pfeffer, "The Deity," 218.

71. Pfeffer, "No Law," 5–10; *Church, State, and Freedom*, 125–27.

72. Ibid., 159, see also, Brief for Appellant at 61, *Zorach v. Clauson*, 343 U.S. 306 (1952) (No. 431); "Church and State: Something Less than Separation," *The University of Chicago Law Review* 19 (Autumn 1951): 11–14.

73. Pfeffer, "Freedom of Religion," 17.

74. Pfeffer, "No Law," 11; *Church, State, and Freedom*, 174.

75. Ibid., 160.

76. Ibid., 143.

77. Pfeffer, "Church and State: Something Less," 24; "Freedom of Religion," 21.

78. Pfeffer, *Church, State, and Freedom*, 146–47.

79. See, for example, Philip Hamburger, *Separation of Church and State* (Cambridge, MA: Harvard University Press, 2002).

80. 333 U.S. 203 (1948).

81. Pfeffer, *Church, State, and Freedom*, 146.

82. *Everson v. Board of Education* 330 U.S. 1 at 15–16.

83. Ibid.; Pfeffer, "The Unity of the First Amendment Religion Clauses," 136–37.

84. 330 U.S. 1 at 13.

85. Ibid. at 31–32.

86. Ibid.; Pfeffer, "The Unity of the First Amendment Religion Clauses," 136.

87. Leo Pfeffer, "The Supreme Court as Protector of Civil Rights: Freedom of Religion," *The Annals of the American Academy of Political and Social Science* 275 (May 1951): 82.

88. This was in response to a perceived neglect in the religious education of children. For instance, a 1932 United States Office of Education found that only a small proportion of children in the nation came under the influence of the church. Protestant educators concluded that the weekday would have to be utilized for religious education; Pfeffer, *Church, State, and Freedom*, 368–69.

89. Brief for Synagogue Council for America, et al. as Amici Curiae Supporting Appellants at 12–15, *McCollum* v. *Board of Education*, 333 U.S. 203 (1948) (No. 90).

90. *McCollum* v. *Board of Education*, 333 U.S. 203 at 210–12.

91. Ibid. at 231; the released-time issue was readdressed by the Court in 1952. In *Zorach* v. *Clauson*, 343 U.S. 306 (1952), the Court upheld a similar program to that in *McCollum* except that the classes were held off campus. A more complete discussion of this case will be in the next chapter.

92. Pfeffer, "Church and State: Something Less," 3.

93. Cobb, *The Rise of Religious Liberty in America*; William Warren Sweet, *Religion in Colonial America* (New York: Charles Scribner's Sons, 1942); Stokes, *Church and State*.

94. Dreisbach, *Real Threat and Mere Shadow*, xvi.

95. Daniel L. Dreisbach, "Everson and the Command of History," in *Everson Revisited: Religion, Education, and Law at the Crossroads*, eds. Jo Renee Formicola and Hubert Morken (Landham, MD: Rowman & Littlefield Publishers, 1997), 35.

96. Quoted in Ibid., 34.

97. O'Neill, "Nonpreferential Aid," 23.

98. Edward S. Corwin, "The Supreme Court as National School Board," *Law and Contemporary Problems* 2 (1949): 16.

99. Ibid., 20.

100. See Preville, "Leo Pfeffer and the Church-State Debate," 37–53.

101. See Thomas Berg, "Anti-Catholicism and Modern Church–State Relations," *Cumberland Law Review* 33 (Summer 2002): 121–72.

102. See, for example, Steven K. Green, "Blaming Blaine: Understanding the Blaine Amendment and the No-Funding Principle," *First Amendment Law Review* 2 (2003): 107–52.

103. Cord, *Separation of Church and State*, 26.

104. Ibid., 8.

105. Malbin, *Religion and Politics*, 14.

106. Cord, *Separation of Church and State*, 23–27, 53–55.

107. Ibid., 36–46.

108. Ibid., 21–23.

109. O'Neill, "Nonpreferential Aid," 30.

110. *Wallace* v. *Jaffree*, 472 U.S. 38 (1985). The Court struck down an Alabama moment of silence statute.

111. 472 U.S. 38 at 107.

112. Dreisbach, *Real Threat and Mere Shadow*, 99.

113. Ibid., 133.

114. Ibid., 102.

115. See, for example, Steven D. Smith, *Foreordained Failure: The Quest for a Constitutional Principle of Religious Freedom* (New York: Oxford University

Press, 1995); and Justice Clarence Thomas's concurring opinions in *Van Orden v. Perry*, 545 U.S. 677 (2005), *Cutter v. Wilkinson*, 544 U.S. 709 (2005), and *Zelman v. Simmons-Harris*, 536 U.S. 639 (2002).

116. Dreisbach, *Real Threat and Mere Shadow*, 108.

117. Cord, *Separation of Church and State*, 115.

118. James H. Hutson, "Thomas Jefferson's Letter to the Danbury Baptists: A Controversy Rejoined," *The William and Mary Quarterly* 56 (October 1999): 775; see also Daniel Dreisbach, *Thomas Jefferson and the Wall of Separation between Church and State* (New York: New York University Press, 2003).

119. Corwin, "The Supreme Court as National School Board," 14.

120. Chester Antieau, et al., *Freedom From Federal Establishment: Formation and Early History of the First Amendment Religion Clauses*, (Milwaukee: Bruce Publishing Co., 1964), 122.

121. Bradley, *Church-State Relationships*, 121.

122. David Dean Bowlby, *The Garden and the Wilderness: Church and State in America to 1789* (Lanham, Md. Lexington Books, 2011), 188.

123. Ibid., 60.

124. O'Neill, "Nonpreferential Aid," 18–42; and Pfeffer, "No Law," 1–17.

125. Pfeffer, "Church and State: Something Less," 1–29. This article served as the basis for the fifth chapter of *Church, State, and Freedom*, entitled "The Meaning of the Principle."

126. Ibid., 13–15; Pfeffer, "No Law," 13.

127. Pfeffer, "No Law," 12.

128. Douglas Laycock, "Nonpreferential Aid to Religion: A False Claim About Original Intent," *William and Mary Law Review* 27 (1985–86): 881; see also, Laycock, "Original Intent and the Constitution Today," 87–112.

129. Pfeffer, "Church and State," 22–23.

130. Pfeffer, "No Law," 46.

131. Pfeffer, *Church, State, and Freedom*, 168–71.

132. Pfeffer, "Madison's 'Detached Memoranda'," 291–303.

133. Ibid., 286.

134. Pfeffer, *Church, State, and Freedom*, 169.

135. Ibid., 17.

136. Ibid.

137. Ibid., 133–34.

138. Ibid.

139. See R. Pierce Beaver, "American Missionary Efforts to Influence Government Indian Policy," *Journal of Church and State* 5 (1963): 77–94; and R. Pierce Beaver, "Church, State, and the Indians: Indian Missions in the New Nation," *Journal of Church and State* 4 (1962): 11–30.

140. Ibid., 10.

141. Singleton, "Colonial Virginia as First Amendment Matrix," 344–64.

142. Pfeffer, "Church and State," 26.

143. Laycock, "Nonpreferential Aid to Religion," 897.

144. Curry, *The First Freedoms*, 218.

145. Pfeffer, "Church and State," 26–27.

146. Levy, *The Establishment Clause*, 115.

147. Pfeffer, "Church-State and American Jewry," 180.

148. Pfeffer, *Church, State, and Freedom*, 105.

149. See, for example, H. Jefferson Powell, "The Original Understanding of Original Intent," *Harvard Law Review* 98 (March 1985): 885–948.

150. See Bernard Bailyn, *The Ideological Origins of the American Revolution* (Cambridge, Mass.: Harvard University Press, 1967); and Gordon S. Wood, *The Creation of the American Republic, 1776–1787* (Chapel Hill: University of North Carolina Press, 1969).

151. John Witte, Jr. and Joel A. Nichols, *Religion and the American Constitutional Experiment*, 4th ed. (New York: Oxford University Press, 2016), 62–63.

152. Both separationists and accommodationists have fallen for the "lure of history," according to Steve Green. Rather he argues that history is an "indispensable tool" and can "instruct and enlighten" but it "cannot provide 'answers' to modern constitutional questions" any more than it can provide 'truths'." "At best," Green concludes, "history is a handmaiden to judicial decision making, not a taskmaster." See Green, "'Bad History'," 1753.

153. Leo Pfeffer, "Religion, Education, and the Constitution," *Lawyers Guild Review* 8 (May–June 1948): 5.

154. Quoted in Brief for Appellant at 25, *Torcaso v. Watkins*, 367 U.S. 488 (1961) (No. 373) (hereinafter Torcaso Brief).

155. Quoted in Stokes and Pfeffer, *Church and State*, 45.

156. Torcaso Brief at 27.

157. Quoted in Edwin S. Gaustad, "Religion and Ratification," in *The First Freedom: Religion and the Bill of Rights*, ed. James E. Wood, Jr. (Waco, TX: J.M. Dawson Institute of Church-State Studies, Baylor University, 1990), 47.

158. *Torcaso v. Watkins*, 367 U.S. 488 at 489.

159. Ivers, *To Build a Wall*, 108.

160. Torcaso Brief at 10.

161. Ibid. at 14.

162. Ibid. at 16.

163. Ibid. at 16–20.

164. Ibid., 26.

165. Ibid. at 29–30.

166. Cohen, *Jews in Christian America*, 126.

167. That equality was central to the Jewish quest for civil liberties, see Jonathan Sarna, *American Jews and Church-State Relationships: The Search for "Equal Footing"* (New York: American Jewish Committee, Institute of Human Relations, 1989).

168. 367 U.S. 488 at 495.

169. Robert T. Miller and Ronald B. Flowers, *Toward Benevolent Neutrality: Church, State, and the Supreme Court*, 5th ed. (Waco, Tex.: Baylor University Press, 1992), 2: 736.

170. Henry J. Abraham, *Freedom and the Court: Civil Rights and Civil Liberties in the United States*, 5th ed. (New York: Oxford University Press, 1988), 280.

Chapter 3

No Aid

Leo Pfeffer and the Establishment Clause

Leo Pfeffer believed the separation principle of the unitary guarantee to be embodied in the Establishment Clause of the First Amendment. The words "Congress shall make no law respecting an establishment of religion" meant that church and state were to be separate. Religion was outside the cognizance of government, and government was to be neutral with regard to religion.[1] Pfeffer understood the separation of church and state to be unequivocal. Consequently, his jurisprudence was often described as absolutist with regard to the Establishment Clause—a characterization he did not disavow.[2]

As discussed in the previous chapter, Leo Pfeffer found a classic expression of the no-aid or separationist interpretation of the Establishment Clause in Justice Hugo Black's majority opinion in the 1947 *Everson v. Board of Education* case. Here Black stated, in part: "No tax in any amount, large or small, can be levied to support any religious activities or institutions . . . In the words of Jefferson, the clause against establishment of religion by law was intended to erect 'a wall of separation between church and state'." Despite his strict separationist or no-aid language, however, Black ruled that reimbursing parents of parochial students for their transportations costs was consistent with the Establishment Clause. This drew criticism from the four dissenting justices. Justice Wiley Rutledge, for example, noted the incongruity of the Court's rhetoric and holding, arguing that the First Amendment's purpose was to "create a complete and permanent separation of the spheres of religious activity and civil authority" and "comprehensively forbidding every form of public aid or support for religion."[3] Despite the five-to-four ruling, Pfeffer believed the majority and dissenting opinions revealed that a broad consensus had emerged on the Court embracing not only the broad reading of the Establishment Clause but also the unitary nature of the two clauses. Both Black and Rutledge, in Pfeffer's mind, agreed on both the separationist reading of the Establishment Clause as well as the notion that the Religion Clauses were "correlative and coextensive" concepts. As a result, Black's famous definition of the Establishment Clause became known as the "no-aid" principle and served as the starting point for Pfeffer's Establishment Clause jurisprudence.

The many legal issues surrounding religion and education provide an appropriate context for discussing Pfeffer's Establishment Clause jurisprudence. In fact, his career can be divided into two periods based on his litigation involving religion and education. From the beginning of his association with the American Jewish Congress in 1946 to the late 1960s, conflicts involving religion and public education were the prevalent church-state issues before the courts and occupied a significant portion of Pfeffer's attention. From the *Board of Education v. Allen* decision in 1968 on, Leo Pfeffer was immersed in the controversies surrounding aid to religious schools. In both areas, Leo Pfeffer consistently and persistently argued the absolutist position with regard to the Establishment Clause and in so doing was extremely influential in maintaining the U.S. Supreme Court's favorable disposition toward the separation of church and state as it was broadly defined in *Everson*. Whether serving as lead counsel, drafting briefs of amicus curiae, or organizing litigation strategy, Pfeffer helped shape the Court's opinion in Establishment Clause cases.

In the area of religion and public education, Pfeffer utilized four primary arguments challenging public school sponsored religious exercises, first introduced in his 1948 brief in the *McCollum v. Board of Education*. Such practices violated the no-aid provision of *Everson* and the equality of all religions, created a religiously coercive environment for impressionable children, fostered divisiveness along religious lines, and threatened to degrade religion. In the area of aid to religious schools, Pfeffer contended unfailingly that both direct and indirect aid to religious schools violated the Establishment Clause. Precipitated in part by massive federal funding programs to elementary, secondary, and higher education during the 1960s, state aid programs for public and parochial schools were manifest during this period. Leading a majority of the legal challenges to religious school aid that reached the U.S. Supreme Court, Leo Pfeffer relentlessly argued the no-aid principle on behalf of the American Jewish Congress as well as the Committee on Public Education and Religious Liberty (PEARL).[4] It was through these organizations that Pfeffer was able to orchestrate coalitions of organizations in support of successful separationist challenges before the Supreme Court. During this time, Pfeffer's arguments influenced the Court's development of the *Lemon* test, the pervasively sectarian standard, and the Court's consistent rejection of most forms of aid beyond the transportation reimbursements upheld in *Everson* and the loan of secular textbooks in *Board of Education v. Allen*. Pfeffer served as lead counsel in six of the nine aid cases decided by the Supreme Court between 1973 and 1980. As one scholar noted, "By 1980, backed by a committed organizational structure, Pfeffer had succeeded in building a corpus of case law that made it almost impossible for religious schools and parents whose children attended them to secure public financial assistance."[5]

Pfeffer's perspective was hardly uncontested. In the area of religious exercises in the public schools, the strict separationist position was challenged by those who found no objection to public institutions sponsoring "nonsectarian" religious exercises as long as dissenting students were given the opportunity to opt out and no direct coercion to participate took place. It was argued that denying such opportunities for prayer or Bible reading constituted a hostility toward religion—a troubling prospect during a post–World War II context of religious revival and Cold War angst. As the nation became increasingly pluralistic, however, even accommodationist justices on the Court had difficulty in justifying school-sponsored religious exercises. In some ways, Pfeffer's successes challenging released time, school prayer, and Bible reading were more indicative of the nation coming to terms with its religious pluralism than a victory for a particular view of the Establishment Clause.

The divide between Pfeffer's separationist philosophy and accommodationist readings of the First Amendment was more pronounced in the area of aid to public schools. Here Pfeffer's no-aid position came under constitutional attack on and off the Court by those who championed either a nonpreferentialist or neutrality approach to aid. Among their criticisms of Pfeffer's no-aid position was that it was unrealistic, hostile to religion, and led to inconsistent rulings by the Court. They argued instead that most indirect forms of indirect aid and even some direct aid that made its way to religious schools was acceptable as long as it was to serve a secular purpose and was distributed according to neutral criteria. Toward the end of Pfeffer's career, this approach was gaining currency on the Court and, in more recent years, has led to the overturning of some key aid decisions though often by the narrowest of margins.

THE SECULARIZATION OF PUBLIC EDUCATION

Leo Pfeffer's active engagement in the church-state conflicts over religion and public education can be partially understood in light of his childhood experience in the public schools.[6] The Protestant ethos that permeated his elementary school led his parents to enroll him in a yeshiva for the remainder of his elementary and secondary education. Yet this did not dissuade him from an earnest belief that public education was an indispensable tool of democracy. He, too, shared Thomas Jefferson's belief in universal education, free from sectarian control, which would provide for an educated citizenry so invaluable for the prosperity of the democratic experiment. Just as Pfeffer tied public education to the future of democracy,[7] he also saw a direct connection between public education and church-state separation. Pfeffer viewed universal education and church-state separation as two of America's greatest contributions to the world.[8] Consequently, the development of public education went hand-in-hand with the evolution of religious freedom and church-state separation. As Pfeffer put it, "The secularization of the public school is part of the evolution of the principle of separation and freedom."[9] Not surprisingly, then, Pfeffer often traced the history of public education in his briefs and scholarly writings to better contextualize the contemporary legal battles over religion and education.

Following education historian Freeman Butts, Pfeffer traced the genesis of the public school system to the Puritan communities of colonial New England. While they were community supported, the schools reflected the religious culture of the New England "Standing Order." The purpose of education was to enable the young to read the Bible and the writings of the Puritan expositors. Despite the strictly religious orientation of Puritan schools, they represented an early experiment with publicly supported education.[10] Pfeffer then noted Thomas Jefferson's later call for free, public education without sectarian influences as well as the close relationship Jefferson made between religious freedom and secular public education. Arguing that universal education was essential to the success of a democratic republic, Jefferson was active in pursuing legislation providing for a public school system in Virginia and was the founder of America's first public university, the University of Virginia. In 1779, Jefferson's bill for the More General Diffusion of Knowledge called for the establishment of a public school system in Virginia that also prohibited "religious reading, instruction or exercise shall be prescribed or practiced, inconsistent with the tenets of any religious sect or denomination."[11]

Pfeffer highlighted as well the story of Horace Mann and his efforts to eliminate "sectarianism" from public education during the mid-nineteenth century. As secretary of the Massachusetts state education board, Mann introduced "monumental" innovations to curriculum and pedagogy, but also pressed for the establishment of non-sectarian education. Pfeffer indicated that Mann believed strenuously in freedom of conscience and that non-sectarianism was necessary for an increasingly pluralistic public school setting. Pfeffer often quoted Mann's declaration that "for any human government . . . to attempt to coerce and predetermine the religious opinions of children, by law, and contrary to the will of their parents, is unspeakably more criminal than the usurpation of such control over the opinions of men."[12] Nonetheless, Pfeffer recognized that Mann's nineteenth-century understanding of non-sectarianism was a product of his time. Mann, for instance, did not perceive the reading of the King James Bible to be a sectarian exercise. Thus, while some of the more distinctly sectarian practices had been eliminated from public education during the nineteenth century, a "lowest common denominator Protestantism" prevailed in many of the nation's public schools.[13]

The Protestant ethos and religious practices in the public schools would create controversy as American society witnessed rapid changes in the mid- to late-nineteenth century. Most notable among these was the massive immigration of Catholics to America. As more Catholic student entered American public schools, opposition to these Protestant practices grew—though often Catholic opposition was met with nativist hysteria and even violence. The public schools of Cincinnati, Ohio, provided the setting for one of the most prominent battles over religion in the schools. In the 1840s, Cincinnati school officials required the reading of the Protestant King James Version of the Bible. Proponents argued the "nonsectarian" practice was to inculcate good moral behavior. Catholics opposed the practice, though it continued for more than two decades despite the fact that Cincinnati was becoming increasingly pluralistic. Catholic opposition persisted. Eventually a majority of the school board voted to ban the reading of the Bible and other "religious books" in the public schools. A lengthy legal battle ensued with the Supreme Court of Ohio ultimately siding with the school board's decision.[14] Despite their legal victory in Ohio, Catholics grew weary of battles with a recalcitrant Protestant majority and created what would become an extensive parochial school system. While efforts to gain public funds for parochial schools met with failure,[15] the practices of prayer and Bible reading in the public schools were on the decline during the last decades of the century. Pfeffer gave significant credit to the Catholic Church and Catholic parents for the secularization of public education in the nineteenth century: "The triumph of the secularization of the public school was in no small measure due to the persistence of the [Catholic] Church and the courage of Catholic parents in refusing to sacrifice their claims of conscience by yielding to a settlement that was entirely satisfactory to the Protestant majority."[16] Nonetheless, Pfeffer believed that one of the great ironies of Catholic opposition to Protestant prayers and Bible reading in the nineteenth century public schools was that he found himself most frequently in conflict with the Catholic Church in battles over religion and education in the twentieth century.

NEW BATTLES OVER RELIGIOUS EDUCATION IN THE PUBLIC SCHOOLS

The triumph of separation in the latter part of the nineteenth century gave way to a renaissance of church-state cooperation in the twentieth century. With an increasingly religious populous, the impact of two world wars, a postwar religious revival, the Cold War battle against "atheistic Communism," and the rise of Christian nationalism, religious exercises, and new modes of religious education began finding their way into public school classrooms.[17] At the same time, however, the country was becoming increasingly pluralistic. Emboldened by a seemingly sympathetic Court, minority religions raised challenges to religion in the public schools. Moreover, the forum of the debate over religion in the public schools changed as well. The U.S. Supreme Court, with the incorporation of the Free Exercise and Establishment Clauses of the First Amendment,[18] would increasingly become the arbiter of the constitutionality of religious exercises in the public schools.

Calls for providing students opportunities for religious education in the public schools increased in the early twentieth century. Finding support in a 1932 U.S. Office of Education survey indicating that children had little contact with religion at church or home, advocates of religious education called for the introduction of moral and spiritual training in the public schools as a defense against the twin enemies of communism and juvenile delinquency.[19] These advocates of public school religious education looked to plans such as the one designed by Dr. William Wirt in 1913 called "released time." Developed for the public schools of Gary, Indiana, this program allowed students, with the consent of their parents, to attend their local church or synagogue during a specified time in the school day to obtain religious instruction.[20]

A constitutional battle over a revised version of the released time program in Champaign, Illinois, culminated in 1948 in the landmark U.S. Supreme Court decision of *McCollum v. Board of Education*.[21] Released time in the Champaign program involved the releasing of children from regular instruction to attend religious education in public school classrooms provided by outside instructors. Chosen by the ecumenical Champaign Council on Religious Education, instructors were primarily Protestants and Catholics, both clergy and lay persons. Nonparticipants were removed to "study hall" or other parts of the school until the religious instruction had been completed. The constitutional challenge to the program came from an avowed atheist, Vashti McCollum, whose son, Terry, did not participate in the religious instruction. McCollum's use of the case to advocate an atheistic agenda led to the hesitancy among some in the Jewish community from joining in a challenge to the released time program, fearing it would lead to greater anti-Semitism and the association of American Jewry with atheism. To assuage these concerns, Pfeffer disassociated the participating Jewish bodies from Vashti McCollum in his brief of amicus curiae.[22]

Supporters of the released-time program argued that it not only would help eradicate religious illiteracy among school children but also would promote interfaith harmony and understanding. A religious liberty defense was made as well. Proponents claimed that if there was a First Amendment right to send children to religious schools, as the Court had affirmed in the 1925 case of *Pierce v. Society of Sisters*,[23] then there must be a free exercise right for public school children to receive religious education during the school day. Constitutional scholar Paul Kauper, for instance, suggested that to release children from public schools for religious education for one hour a week would reflect a "mere even-handed neutrality" between church and state. Not to do so, according to Kauper, was to "identify hostility with neutrality."[24]

The *McCollum* case was Pfeffer's first major involvement in church-state litigation. Not long after joining the legal staff of the Commission on Law and Social Action of the American Jewish Congress, he was asked to study the program and draft a report addressing released time's constitutionality.[25] Pfeffer provided a comprehensive analysis of the program, indicating the frequency of its practice, the extent of participation, and arguments for and against its constitutionality. While Pfeffer did not express an opinion on the program's constitutionality in his initial report, he did note that "practically all Jewish communal organizations have expressed themselves in opposition to the plan."[26] By the time he contributed to an amicus curiae brief in the *McCollum* case, Pfeffer had become firmly opposed to the program finding it to be a clear violation of the Establishment Clause. Consequently, the arguments he made challenging the program on establishment grounds would regularly reappear in subsequent cases involving religion and public education.

In his brief, Pfeffer argued that the Champaign plan violated the First Amendment as defined by the *Everson* decision. The state was clearly advancing religion, he asserted, "by permitting the intrusion of religion into the public school system by classes devoted to religious instruction or worship on public school premises."[27] Trial testimony supported this claim by revealing the highly sectarian nature of some of the religious instruction.[28] Responding to the argument that the program represented an "even-handed neutrality" between church and state, Pfeffer claimed that both the broad and narrow interpretations of the Establishment Clause were violated by released time due to the fact that the program preferred some religions over others. Even if all religions participated, he further argued, school-sponsored religious education violated the *Everson* decision's prohibition against aiding one or all religions.[29]

Nonparticipants' free exercise rights were violated as well, according to Pfeffer. Proponents had claimed the practices were voluntary since children who chose not to participate were allowed to leave the classrooms. Pfeffer countered that the compulsory school environment resulted in pressure on students to participate. Citing how Terri McCollum had regularly been singled out and ridiculed for not participating, Pfeffer concluded that "voluntary means more than just not facing punishment for not attending."[30] The impressionability of students, especially in a compulsory school environment, became a key constitutional consideration for Pfeffer: "A child does not relish being singled out as different, particularly where the difference consists of not participating in activities approved and encouraged by public authorities. The regular teacher's presence in the class established in the children's eyes that religious education was not merely socially acceptable, but approved. In a ten-year-old child fear of being singled out as a non-conformist is a potent determinant of conduct."[31] Pfeffer was also concerned that the students would interpret the teacher's presence as lending an imprimatur of authority to the teachings.[32] Pfeffer recognized the importance of the academic teaching about religion in the public schools, but he believed "inculcation" as opposed to education was what was being sponsored by released time.[33]

Pfeffer argued that religious divisiveness to be one of the "chief evils" the First Amendment was intended to avoid as well. His analysis of released time concluded that segregation of children along religious lines, combined with the often narrowly sectarian nature of released-time instruction, proved not only divisive but also harmful to children of minority faiths. Trial testimony revealed that Protestant instruction included the teaching that the Jews were responsible for the crucifixion of Christ. Pfeffer asserted that such instruction "encourages religious prejudice, and particularly contributes to anti-Semitism."[34] As a result, "Jewish groups have their opposition to the released time program on many grounds, but no consideration bulks larger in that opposition than the divisive effects of the program."[35]

In a later study entitled "Public School Sectarianism and the Jewish Child," Pfeffer tied the purposes of the Establishment Clause to the protection of religious minorities. Citing examples of persecution, violence, and harassment, Pfeffer sought to reveal how seemingly harmless public education activities such as holiday observances, released time, and Bible reading were really divisive, harmful, and unconstitutional. "The principle of separation of church and state, particularly in the field of public education," Pfeffer asserted, "is not something abstract and theoretical; it is a necessary practical guardian and protector of the welfare of American children, and particularly of children adhering to minority faiths."[36] In both this study and his *McCollum* brief, Pfeffer emphasized the problems of compulsion, impressionability, and divisiveness when public schools sponsored sectarian education and devotional exercises. These claims would continue to be at the forefront of his legal opposition to religious exercises in the public schools.

Proponents and opponents of released time anxiously awaited the judgment of the U.S. Supreme Court. Just a year earlier, the Court in *Everson*, upheld five-to-four the payment of school transportation costs to parents of parochial school children while, at the same time, articulating its belief in a high wall of separation between church and state.[37] The ambiguity of the *Everson* decision led to widespread uncertainty as to how the Court would rule in McCollum. In an 8-to-1 decision, the U.S. Supreme Court decision struck down the released-time program. Pfeffer viewed this as an important victory for several reasons. First, the Court affirmed the broad interpretation of the First Amendment as defined in *Everson*. Second, the four dissenting justices in *Everson* joined Justice Hugo Black and the majority in *McCollum* to find the released-time program unconstitutional. Third, compulsion, impressionability, and divisiveness, all raised by Pfeffer in his brief, were central to the Court's determination of unconstitutionality. In his majority opinion, Justice Hugo Black observed that "students who did not choose to take the religious instruction were not released from public school duties." This, for Black, was constitutionally significant. Consequently, he argued that "this is beyond all question a utilization of the tax-established and tax-supported public school system to aid religious groups to spread their faith."[38] The issues of impressionability and divisiveness were echoed in the concurring opinion of Justice Felix Frankfurter. According to Frankfurter, "the law of imitation operates, and non-conformity is not an outstanding characteristic of children. The result is an obvious pressure upon children to attend."[39] Frankfurter concluded that "in no activity of the state is it more vital to keep out divisive forces than in its schools, to avoid confusing, not to say fusing what the Constitution sought to keep strictly apart."[40] Oral arguments as well as the written decision in *McCollum* reveal that the majority was influenced by Pfeffer's friend-of-the-court brief. Indeed, Frankfurter acknowledged the unique evidence Pfeffer introduced regarding coercion, divisiveness, and psychological impact on children.[41]

The religious and scholarly communities were divided over the *McCollum* decision. Pfeffer understood Catholic opposition to be aimed at the strict application of the separation of church and state. Many Catholics feared that the adoption of the broad interpretation would close the door on public aid to religious schools. The decision, along with *Everson*, also sparked lively debate among legal theorists over the meaning of the First Amendment.[42] In a widely cited article entitled, "The Supreme Court as National School Board," Edward Corwin argued that Justice Black had "sold his brethren a bill of goods" by arguing that the Establishment Clause prohibited "aid to all religions."[43] Instead, Corwin advanced the narrow, nonpreferentialist reading, contending that the decision was based upon a "figure of speech." He agreed with Justice Reed who argued in his lone dissenting opinion that the separation of church and state was an "unhistorical concept." Corwin chided the Court for broadening the meaning of the Establishment Clause far beyond mere preference between religions as well as for practicing judicial activism that overturned a program "adopted by 46 states and 2,200 communities."[44]

Corwin was not alone in his criticism. Others attacked the Court arguing that the intent of the First Amendment was not to "impose neutrality between believers and unbelievers" but was a tool for ensuring the various Christian sects were treated equally. Another oft repeated criticism of the Court's decision was that the First Amendment was intended to secure "freedom of religion, not freedom from religion."[45] Political scientist Virgil Blum raised this objection while also arguing that released time had merely facilitated the free exercise rights of students. To insist on government neutrality between religion and irreligion, he observed, was to put "the government in the position of helping irreligion, while discriminating against religion." "This places government in the unwanted position of hostility to religion."[46] The hostility claim would become a common refrain of those opposed to the Court's decisions outlawing school-sponsored religious exercises as well as aid to parochial schools. So while the broad, no-aid, interpretation would largely prevail during Pfeffer's career, the accommodationist counter-arguments would persist and find a more hospitable Court in the 1980s.

Proponents of religious education seized upon a footnote in Justice Felix Frankfurter's concurring opinion in *McCollum* distinguishing between the Champaign plan and programs where the religious education was held off campus.[47] Consequently, the breadth of the *McCollum* decision was called into question when the Court addressed another religious education plan four years later in *Zorach v. Clauson*.[48] In *Zorach*, the Court considered a modified released-time policy in New York that sought to overcome the constitutional infirmities found in *McCollum*. The primary change was that the religious education would take place off campus. This, supporters believed, would diminish the role of the public schools in administering or promoting the religious education program, other than maintaining enrollment cards and confirming attendance.

Despite these constitutional safeguards, parents Tessi Zorach and Esta Gluck challenged the legality of the New York City program on several grounds. First, they argued that the program involved the "machinery" of the public schools including the indirect involvement of principles, teachers, and staff to coordinate participation and supervise attendance. Second, since the program took place at times associated with the school day, sectarian religious instruction was being assisted by the compulsory school system. Third, the program created pressure, if not coercion, on students to participate. And fourth, the program created divisiveness along religious lines. In *Church, State and Freedom*, Pfeffer included affidavits provided to the Court that illustrated not only that the New York regulations were not being complied with but also that the plaintiff's complaint of the divisive and coercive effects of the program were real.[49]

Upon the strength of the victory in *McCollum*, Pfeffer was able to persuade the major American Jewish organizations to sponsor a lawsuit challenging the practice of "dismissed time" in *Zorach*. Nonetheless, lower courts upheld the New York program. Since no religious instruction was held in public school classrooms, and the public schools did not promote the programs, the New York trial and appellate courts concluded that the program did not result in state sponsorship of religious exercises in violation of the Establishment Clause.[50]

Zorach v. Clausen eventually reached the U.S. Supreme Court, and Pfeffer, in his brief of amicus curiae, argued that the change in venue did not mitigate the constitutional problems of which the released-time program ran afoul in *McCollum*. According to Pfeffer, it was clear that the *McCollum* ruling was "intended to and did invalidate any released time program which involved the use of the tax-established and tax-supported, compulsory, public school machinery as aid in recruiting children for religious instruction."[51] Pfeffer took special aim at the accommodationist justification for the New York program that government may aid or accommodate religion as long as it was done on a nonpreferential basis. Pfeffer responded that nonpreferentialism was rejected by the *Everson* and *McCollum* decisions for a broader reading of the First Amendment. If the nonpreferentialist interpretation prevailed, he argued, then it "would take an Amendment designed to prevent certain legislative action and convert it into an affirmative grant of legislative power."[52] Moreover, he argued that the released-time programs would violate even a nonpreferentialist reading of the Constitution since they favored some religions over others.[53] The contention here was that in practice only mainstream religions, and at that, primarily Christians, sought public school-sponsored religious education. This led Pfeffer to conclude in his brief: "Preferential treatment is an inevitable consequence of sectarian intrusion upon the public school system." Since *McCollum* had been previously defended on nonpreferentialist grounds, Pfeffer argued that "no adequate reason has been presented for this Court to repudiate its interpretation of the First Amendment in the *Everson* and *McCollum* cases."[54]

Fundamentally, released-time programs, whether on or off campus, involved the public school personnel and machinery to an unconstitutional degree. Moreover, Pfeffer argued that the change of location did not eliminate the compulsion placed on children to attend. While he agreed that children have a free exercise right to religious education, Pfeffer asserted that it did not follow that the government must sponsor it. He concluded that "the crucial aspect of released time is not the release of children wishing to partake of religious instruction, but the non-release of those not wishing to do so."[55]

Pfeffer's constitutional challenges to the contrary, Justice William O. Douglas, in writing for a 6-to-3 majority, found the distinctions between the released-time and dismissed-time programs to be constitutionally significant. Furthermore, he found that holding the religious education off-campus substantially reduced the coercion to participate. Pfeffer had claimed, in both the *McCollum* and *Zorach* briefs, that opposition to such programs was born not out of hostility toward religion but out of a desire to preserve the integrity of public education and the Constitution. Nevertheless, Douglas warned that not allowing for an accommodation such as this would manifest a hostility toward religion.[56] "We are a religious people whose institutions presuppose a supreme being" Douglas concluded. "When the state encourages religious instruction or cooperates with religious authorities by adjusting the schedule of public events to sectarian needs, it follows the best of our traditions."[57]

Douglas's language appeared to be a reversal from the absolutist language of the *Everson* and *McCollum* decisions. For those who viewed the prohibitions of the Establishment Clause less broadly than did Pfeffer, *Zorach* was celebrated as a victory.[58] Indeed, accommodationists would seize upon Douglas's language in future litigation over the role of religion in public life. The notion that a strict or absolutist application of the Establishment Clause manifests hostility to religion would gain renewed strength due to Douglas's opinion as well. Overall, the decision left the position of the Court on church and state unclear. For instance, dissenting opinions were registered by the author of the majority opinion in *Everson* and *McCollum*, Justice Hugo Black, as well as Justices Felix Frankfurter and Robert Jackson. Like Leo Pfeffer, Black saw no meaningful difference between the Champaign and New York City plans. While the classes were held off-campus in *Zorach*, Black argued that the state still used the "compelling classroom hours of its compulsory school machinery so as to channel children into sectarian classes . . . This is not separation, but combination of church and state."[59]

Pfeffer speculated that the *Zorach* decision was a compromise resulting from the political climate of the early 1950s. The combined pressures the Red Scare, a growing interest in public religion, as well as the Catholic Church's vocal criticism of the *McCollum* decision likely influenced justices in *Zorach*. This is a broad claim, but one seemingly supported by the *New York Time*'s editorial, "Time Off For Religion." While recognizing the potential abuses of released time, the editorial went on to conclude: "In this time of so much moral bankruptcy, with the demonstrated need for religious and ethical training, we feel the door cannot be closed to a program . . . that offers promise of strengthening the religious and moral fiber of our youth."[60]

Although he lost the case, Pfeffer took comfort in the fact that the Court reaffirmed the broad interpretation of the First Amendment. In his opinion, Douglas addressed the meaning of the First Amendment: "There cannot be the slightest doubt that the First Amendment reflects the philosophy that Church and State should be separated. And so far as interference with the 'free exercise' of religion and an 'establishment' of religion are concerned, the separation must be complete and unequivocal."[61] Thus, while the decision was a setback for absolutists, such as Pfeffer, the Court refused to repudiate the separationist philosophy of the Establishment Clause. Nor did he view the Court's decision as a legitimation of the nonpreferentialist interpretation of the First Amendment. The broad interpretation of the First Amendment, Pfeffer believed, remained intact.[62]

While released time involved efforts to include religious education in the public schools, other legal battles emerged over efforts to bar certain subjects, such as evolution, from the public school curriculum. During the fundamentalist-modernist debates of the 1920s, some states passed laws outlawing the teaching of evolution in public institutions. The most famous of these was the 1925 Tennessee law that "prohibited the teaching of Evolution Theory in all the Universities, Normals, and all other Public Schools of Tennessee."[63] The ensuing case involved John T. Scopes, a science teacher who was fined $100 for violating the statute. The subsequent trial became a media spectacle drawing national attention to the small town of Dayton, Tennessee. Americans followed with interest the legal clashes between national figures William Jennings Bryan and Clarence Darrow. While Scopes's conviction was eventually upheld by the Tennessee Supreme Court, the "Scopes Monkey Trial" failed the resolve the cultural, theological, and religious tensions between largely urban progressives who embraced modern scientific theories and rural traditionalists who saw them as threats to their theological and cultural views. Nor, as subsequent civil liberties cases would attest, did it resolve tensions between individual rights and local control of education.[64]

Long after the Scopes trial, a number of anti-evolution laws, while largely unenforced, remained on the books in some Southern states. Typical of these was an Arkansas statute forbidding in state-supported schools the teaching of "the theory or doctrine that mankind ascended or descended from a lower order of animals."[65] Sixteen years after *Zorach*, in the 1968 case *Epperson v. Arkansas*,[66] Pfeffer filed an amicus curiae brief on behalf of Susan Epperson, a public school teacher at Central High School in Little Rock, Arkansas, who challenged the anti-evolution statute. While Epperson and her lawyers opposed the law solely on free speech grounds, Pfeffer argued that it violated the Establishment Clause as well. In Pfeffer's reasoning, a statute violates the separation of church and state if it penalizes teachers of secular subjects for teaching a widely held scientific explanation for the origins of humans because such a teaching was inconsistent with some religious beliefs regarding creation. Such a law gave aid and advancement to religion and also preferred one or some religions over other religions. "We submit," Pfeffer argued in his brief, "that the sole purpose of the Arkansas anti-evolution statute is to use the State's coercive power to protect and aid those sects that adhere to a literal interpretation of Genesis and hold heretical any theory that man may have evolved from a lower order of animals."[67]

The *Epperson* case is significant not only because it provides another example of how Pfeffer interpreted the Establishment Clause but also because it reveals the influence of Pfeffer's arguments on the Court. Specifically, Pfeffer's brief on behalf of the American Jewish Congress, followed closely by Justice Abe Fortas in his majority opinion, was the only brief presented to the Court challenging the statute on Establishment Clause grounds. Advocating the *Everson* no-aid principle, Fortas declared that "there can be no doubt that the First Amendment does not permit the State to require that teaching and learning must be tailored to the principles or prohibitions of any religious sect or dogma."[68] While affirming as "absolute" the inability of government to aid or oppose religion, Fortas asserted that the First Amendment "forbids alike the preference of a religious doctrine or the prohibition of theory which is deemed antagonistic to a particular dogma."[69] Fortas also echoed Pfeffer's use of legislative history to emphasize the purely religious nature of the statute against claims that the central issue was the state's right to determine curriculum. According to Fortas, "It is clear that fundamentalist sectarian conviction was and is the law's reason for existence."[70] Importantly, Fortas, as Pfeffer urged, struck down the statute not only on establishment but also free exercise grounds. The causal relationship of the two clauses for which Pfeffer tirelessly argued was thus evidenced in Fortas' decision. According to Fortas, "The law must be stricken because of its conflict with the constitutional prohibition of state laws respecting an establishment of religion or prohibiting the free exercise thereof. The overriding fact is that Arkansas' law selects from the body of knowledge a particular segment which it proscribes for the sole reason that it is deemed to conflict with a particular religious doctrine; that is, with a particular interpretation of the Book of Genesis by a particular religious group."[71]

Opponents of evolution would subsequently initiate a new approach to the battle over public school curriculum. "Balanced treatment" statutes were devised, during the late 1970s and early 1980s, declaring wherever evolution was taught, equal time should be given to creationism. In order to provide the statutes with sufficient secularity, proponents began calling the alternative curriculum "creation science." Portrayed as the study of the scientific evidences for creation, creation science and the balanced treatment statutes were defended on the grounds of academic freedom. Statutes typically required that if either evolution or creation science were taught, the other must be taught as well. Yet these canopies of secularity were not sufficient to protect a Louisiana balanced treatment statute from being ruled unconstitutional in 1987. In *Edwards v. Aguillard*,[72] the Court relied in part on the Louisiana statutes' legislative history and motivation, finding that the "preeminent purpose" of the balanced-time statute "was clearly to address the religious viewpoint that a supernatural being created humankind."[73] Statutes such as these had also been justified on the grounds that evolution was a part of the religion of "Secular Humanism" which, it was alleged, was being taught in the schools. While Pfeffer was not directly involved in the *Aguillard* case, he did provide commentary on the case arguing that this legislative remedy would still run afoul of a proper understanding of the First Amendment. According to Pfeffer: "It would seem that if 'Secular Humanism,' whatever that may mean, is a religion, then the appropriate judicial remedy is an injunction against it being taught in the public schools rather than giving equal time to conventional religious instruction, for that would compound the wrong rather than eliminate it."[74]

RELIGIOUS EXERCISES IN THE PUBLIC SCHOOLS: PRAYER AND BIBLE READING

After *Zorach*, the U.S. Supreme Court took a ten-year hiatus from deciding cases involving religion and public education. During this time, Pfeffer was reluctant to challenge religious exercises in the public schools until public opinion had shifted more on released time. As a strategic matter, Pfeffer was concerned that the Catholic Church, in particular, had successfully portrayed the decision negatively to the public and had put separationists on the defensive. He was also skeptical that the courts were prepared yet to strike down prayer and Bible reading on First Amendment grounds.[75] Nevertheless, Pfeffer, with the ACLU's urging, submitted an amicus curiae brief in the 1956 case, *Doremus v. Board of Education*. Here official classroom Bible reading was being practiced in the public schools of New Jersey. Based on *Everson* and *McCollum*, Pfeffer filed a brief of amicus curiae on behalf of the plaintiffs challenging the claim that the practices were voluntary and nonsectarian. The Court threw out the case, however, arguing that the plaintiff did not have standing to sue.[76]

A similar fate met a 1954 Bible distribution case sponsored by Pfeffer.[77] Before the New Jersey Supreme Court, Pfeffer successfully challenged the practice of Bible distribution in the public schools by the Gideons International Missionary Society. Due to the Protestant and evangelistic nature of the Gideons's practices, both Catholics and Jews opposed the Bible distribution in the public schools. Representing both Catholic and Jewish interests, Pfeffer challenged the claim that the Gideon Bible was a nonsectarian book. Introducing social scientific evidence, namely the psychological impact Bible distribution had on public school children, Pfeffer concluded that the Gideons's practice was harmful to children of religious minorities and to the aims and purposes of public education.[78] The Gideons's subsequent appeal to the U.S. Supreme Court was unsuccessful.

Pfeffer later speculated that the Court's reluctance to hear *Doremus* and *Tudor* was influenced largely by the political climate of the day. The heightened nationalism of the Cold War, along with a rise in public religion, conspired against a declaration from the nation's highest tribunal that might be interpreted as being anti-religious, or, in the least, against the nation's customs. With regard to *Doremus*, Pfeffer concluded: "It (the Court) invoked a technicality to avoid a decision until the times were more propitious for the decision it wished to give."[79] At the same time, the Court was not willing to overturn the well-established precedent of previous church-state cases. Of *Tudor*, Pfeffer explained: "There was no way in which its constitutionality could be upheld without repudiating all that had been said and held in the *Everson* and *McCollum* decisions."[80]

Pfeffer's reading of the Court's actions in these two cases is substantiated by historian Naomi Cohen. Cohen indicated that the Court was unwilling, during this particular period of American history, to ignite the passions of the American people with a controversial church-state decision. Thus, the status of Black's and Pfeffer's broad interpretation remained unchanged with *Doremus* and *Tudor*. According to Cohen, "the Court preferred not to deal with the volatile issue, but neither was it prepared to backtrack on *McCollum*."[81]

Eventually, the opportunity for Leo Pfeffer to rearticulate his understanding of the Establishment Clause as it related to prayer and Bible reading would occur in two of the Court's most controversial decisions of the 1960s. Concurrent with the calls for religious education in the early twentieth century, came a resurgence of religious exercises in the public school classrooms such as teacher-led prayer and Bible reading. Their inclusion in some classrooms around the country[82] provided yet another area of church-state controversy, and for Leo Pfeffer, another opportunity to present to the Court his understanding of the First Amendment.

In 1951, the New York State Board of Regents composed a "denominationally neutral" prayer to be recited voluntarily by classes at the beginning of each school day.[83] Accompanying the prayer proposal was a policy statement that justified the practice as consistent with the religious heritage of the American people. It also served to teach "obedience to the law" and to protect against abandonment of students' "inherited faiths."[84] Support for the Regent's prayer included prominent Protestant ministers Norman Vincent Peale and Charles H. Tuttle as well as several leading Catholic clergy. Opposition was voiced by a number of mainline Protestant church leaders and the *Christian Century* editorialized that the prayers would likely be "ineffectual" and would "deteriorate quickly into an empty formality."[85]

Despite the widespread controversy it would create, the Regent's prayer, by 1958, was only practiced in approximately ten percent of the New York school districts. All of these allowed students to leave the classroom during the prayer if their parents were opposed to their participation. In the New Hyde Park school district, only about 29 of 4,000 students formally requested nonparticipation rights. Nevertheless, in 1958, a group of New Hype Park parents filed suit charging the program to be unconstitutional.[86]

Both the trial and New York appellate courts upheld the prayer policy due to several factors. First, they accepted the argument that they prayers were "nonsectarian." Second, they were satisfied that the public schools had taken measures to ensure that students could opt-out of the prayers. Third, they found longstanding nature of the practices undercut due process objections. Fourth, the courts, echoing the *Zorach* decision, reiterated the nation's religious heritage and found school prayer, like dismissed time, consistent with that heritage. Finally, denial of the prayer practice, the court determined, would "manifest hostility to religion."[87]

While the American Civil Liberties Union sponsored the plaintiffs' challenging the Regent's prayer, it had looked to Pfeffer for legal support. Pfeffer was initially reluctant to participate. As with *Doremus*, he did not believe *Engel* was the best case to the American Jewish Congress to take on religious exercises. And, like *Doremus*, Pfeffer wasn't convinced the relatively innocuous Regent's prayer would generate the same constitutional objections needed to be successful.[88] At one point, Pfeffer surprisingly described the prayer as "the most inoffensive . . . most innocuous religious practice imaginable."[89] Once the case reached the U.S. Supreme Court, however, Pfeffer decided to file a separate brief of amicus curiae challenging the constitutionality of the Regents' prayer. Arguing that the New York practice violated the Establishment Clause, Pfeffer's brief attacked four basic assumptions upon which the lower courts had based their rulings. He first challenged the finding that the prayers were non-sectarian. The prayer's acknowledgment of God and recognition of dependence upon God, he argued, "constitute a preference of theistic religions over non-theistic ones,"[90] and also preferred those religions that approved of such practices to those religions that found them objectionable.[91] Stating that "what is non-denominational to the majority frequently is sectarian to the minority," Pfeffer rejected the notion of non-sectarianism in public prayers.[92]

The Regents' prayer also represented an unconstitutional aid to religion. According to Pfeffer, if the prayers had truly been non-sectarian, they would still be unconstitutional because the state must be, according to *Everson* and *McCollum*, not only impartial but neutral with regard to religion and irreligion. School-sponsored prayer was clearly an advancement of religion on behalf of the state.[93] Pfeffer challenged the lower court's claim that sufficient safeguards had been enacted in order that the practices would be truly voluntary as well. As he had done in his *McCollum* brief, Pfeffer asserted that the problem of compulsion was heightened by the impressionability of school-aged children. Citing evidence that psychological or nonphysical coercion was no less a violation of the Establishment Clause, as was physical coercion, Pfeffer argued that the state must not force or influence religious obligations.[94]

The Establishment Clause, as Pfeffer understood it, commanded a comprehensive prohibition of school-sponsored religious exercises in the public schools, not just a consideration of whether such exercises were voluntary or nonsectarian. Again, he made the distinction between government compulsion to participate in secular, as opposed to religious activities:

> The distinction is a critical one. For if the act is secular it is within the constitutional competence of the State, and therefore the sole question remaining is whether a particular religiously motivated person has a constitutional right under the free exercise clause to be excused from participating therein. On the other hand, if the conduct is religious, then it is outside the competence and jurisdiction of the State or its instrumentalities, and even if participation were not compulsory the conduct would be unconstitutional.[95]

Since the prayer was school sponsored, Pfeffer argued that it violated both clauses of the First Amendment. The contention that the prayers had the secular purpose of teaching morality and good citizenship was thus irrelevant. For Pfeffer, to allow the state to use religious means to achieve secular ends would render the First Amendment meaningless. It also would have the consequence of mandating "not only that religion could constitutionally be taught in the public schools, but also that tax-raised funds could be used to finance religion and religious education."[96]

The long history of prayers in school made the practice no less a violation of the Constitution, according to Pfeffer. The ever-expanding pluralism of America's classrooms made the issue an especially sensitive one to religious minorities. Pfeffer believed that children of minority faiths, or those of no faith, were put in the compromising position of being identified as nonconformists or participating in religious exercises at variance with what they or their parents believed. For Pfeffer, the First Amendment was intended to protect religious minorities from such a dilemma.[97]

Pfeffer also rejected the argument that outlawing school-sponsored prayers reflected hostility toward religion. He suggested instead that removing religious exercises from the control and sponsorship of government actually served to protect religion. For Pfeffer, the state should not be telling children when and how to pray. Plus, he argued that a ban on school-sponsored religious exercises would not exclude individual prayers or Bible reading during school hours as long as they do not interfere with the regular school-day activities and instruction.[98]

Writing for the 6-to-1 majority in the 1962 decision, Justice Hugo Black found the New York Regents' prayer unconstitutional. This was a surprise to Pfeffer, many Court observers, and the American public. It was clear to Black, author of the *Everson* and *McCollum* majority decisions, that school-sponsored prayer was a religious exercise sponsored by the state in violation of the establishment of religion. Holding that the Establishment Clause, in the least, meant that the government had no business composing prayers,[99] Black rejected the arguments that the prayer was nonsectarian and participation was voluntary. Recognizing the coercive nature of the practices, Black declared: "When the power, prestige and financial support of government is placed behind a particular religious belief, the indirect coercive pressure upon religious minorities to conform to the prevailing officially approved religion is plain."[100]

As Pfeffer had carefully articulated in his amicus brief, the principles of separation and freedom meant that assertions of sectarianism or compulsion were not in themselves constitutionally determinative. Similarly, Black found that "neither the fact that the prayer may be denominationally neutral nor the fact that its observance on the part of the students is voluntary can serve to free it from the limitations of the Establishment Clause." Using historical evidence to support his absolutist language, Black concluded that religion was "too personal, too sacred," and "too holy" to be controlled by government.[101]

Black denied the claim that excluding school prayer manifested a hostility toward religion. He responded that it was neither "sacrilegious nor antireligious" to leave prayers and their composition up to individuals and their ministers.[102] Importantly, Black concluded his decision by affirming that the Establishment Clause went beyond the establishment of one particular sect. This endorsement of the broad principles underlying the First Amendment, which Pfeffer continuously put before the Court as lead counsel, in friend-of-the-court briefs, or behind the scenes as a legal strategist, was a rejection of non-preferentialist jurisprudence.[103]

The public outcry condemning the *Engel* decision was intense and widespread. Pfeffer noted some of the most hyperbolic criticism came from Southern congressmen perhaps "embittered at the Court because of its decision outlawing racial segregation in the public schools." Illustrative of this was Alabama Representative George Andrews who said that "they put the Negroes in the schools and now they've driven God out." Senator Sam Ervin lamented that "the Supreme Court has made God unconstitutional." Yet criticism of the decision was bipartisan and spanned the theological spectrum. Herbert Hoover described the decision as a "denigration of one of the most sacred of American heritages," while Evangelist Billy Graham feared the decision was "another step toward the secularization of the United States." "The framers of the Constitution," Graham declared, "meant we were to have freedom of religion, not freedom from religion."[104]

Pfeffer found it perplexing that some of the most outspoken criticism came from the Catholic Church, considering the past discrimination Catholic children had faced in public schools. In Pfeffer's opinion, this represented a complete reversal of the Church's previous opposition to religious exercises in the public schools. Having given American Catholics most of the credit for opposing sectarian religious exercises in the schools in the nineteenth century, Pfeffer regretted the Catholic Church's strident opposition to the *Engel* decision.[105] Tensions between the two groups heightened when an editorial in the Jesuit periodical *America*, entitled "To Our Jewish Friends," warned that there was a "long range objective" to persuade the Court to "make decisions in consonance with the principle of church and state as that principle has been interpreted in absolutist terms by Leo Pfeffer." "It would be most unfortunate," the editorial warned, "if the entire Jewish community were to be blamed for the unrelenting pressure tactics of a small but overly vocal segment within it."[106] Hinting that an anti-Semitic backlash might result, the editorial, as a whole "reeked of patient tolerance and overbearing superiority," according to one historian.[107] *America* was criticized by a number of religious publications, including the *Christian Century* which chastised the magazine's editorial for "trying to bully the Jews." In response, the *Christian Century* expressed hope that "the American Jewish Congress and its distinguished counsel will persist in using all legal means to uphold liberties which they will continue to share will all Americans."[108]

For many religious conservatives, the *Engel* decision continues to be a touchstone event in a perceived downward spiral of morality in America. Their concerns, in part, have provided the motivation for over 200 school prayer amendment proposals introduced in Congress. The *Engel* decision sparked a lively debate within the Jewish community as well between separationist advocates like Pfeffer and those who feared that the broad reading of the Establishment Clause had gone too far. Opposition to the decision as well as Jewish strict separationist advocacy came from Erwin Griswold, dean of the Harvard Law School. He, according to Naomi Cohen, sent a clear message: "Christians had moved over and made ample room for non-Christian minorities. For the minorities to expect the extirpation of all vestiges of a public, Christian flavored religion was both unnatural and wrong."[109] Jewish commitment to strict separation drew a rebuke from noted sociologist well Herberg who criticized the "doctrinaire" separationist position as "short sighted and self-defeating."[110] Such criticism didn't deter Pfeffer who continued to argue the separation of church and state before the U.S. Supreme

Court, pushing it to draw its conclusions in line with his own understanding of the Establishment Clause.

Public outcry was surprisingly minimal when the Court struck down the practice of Bible reading in the public schools just one year later. In *Abington v. Schempp*[111] and its companion case, *Murray v. Curlett*, the Court ruled on a Pennsylvania statute that required the reading of at least ten verses of the King James version of the Bible at the beginning of the school day and a Maryland law that required daily Bible reading or the recitation of the Lord's prayer in public school classrooms. Along with classroom prayer, Bible reading enjoyed a renewed emphasis in post–World War II America and was perceived by some as a way of bolstering the moral fiber of American youth in light of the twin threats of communism and secularism.[112]

Invited by the ACLU to join in the legal strategy in *Schempp*, Pfeffer prepared an amicus curiae brief, but only after the litigation had progressed successfully did he involve the American Jewish Congress.[113] Pfeffer's arguments followed along the same lines as his *Engel* brief. He repeated, for example, his challenges to the claims that the practices were nonsectarian. "Even if the state-sponsored Bible reading and Lord's prayer recitation were equally acceptable to all major faiths," Pfeffer contended, "they would still be unconstitutional under the principles espoused in the *Everson*, *McCollum*, *Zorach*, and *Engel* cases." These decisions demanded government neutrality not only among religions, but between religion and nonreligion, Pfeffer continued, and in *Engel* "the non-sectarian nature of the prayer did not salvage its constitutionality." For Pfeffer, the issue of constitutionality went beyond considerations of voluntarism and sectarianism. Accordingly, he concluded that "the issue is not compulsion, but state aid to religion."[114]

The free exercise justifications for the practices were challenged by Pfeffer as well. Essentially, he argued that a free exercise right to state-sponsored religious exercises did not exist. A free exercise claim would be relevant if the state forced an individual to participate in a secular activity against his or her religious conscience. However, "if the conduct is religious," Pfeffer urged, "then it is outside the competence and jurisdiction of the State or its instrumentalities" and constitutes a violation of the Establishment Clause.[115] Faced again with the contention that the activities inculcated moral and ethical virtues, Pfeffer reiterated his belief that the Establishment Clause required government to use only secular means and seek only secular ends. Aiding religion in order to achieve secular goals was no less constitutional than seeking a distinctly religious goal. According to Pfeffer, "Invalidation of the regulations here challenged would place the responsibility for religious exercises where it properly belongs—the home, the church, the synagogue and on the individual conscience."[116]

In a robust endorsement of the broad interpretation of the First Amendment, the U.S. Supreme Court ruled classroom prayer and Bible reading unconstitutional. Justice Tom Clark, in writing for the majority, argued that the Court had "rejected unequivocally" the position that the First Amendment bans only the preferential treatment of one religion over others.[117] Tracing the eight previous Establishment Clause cases before the Court, Justice Clark noted that the Court had gone much further: "The Establishment Clause has been directly considered by this Court eight times in the past score of years and, with only one Justice dissenting on the point, it has consistently held that the clause withdrew all legislative power respecting religious belief or the expression thereof."[118] The Court had reiterated a doctrine of "wholesome neutrality," Clark concluded, which was the result of the "double aspect" of the two clauses of the First Amendment.[119] Not since the *McCollum* decision had the unitary guarantee of being so explicitly affirmed.

In identifying the reach of the two clauses, Clark utilized a test which Pfeffer had expressed in both his *Engel* and *Schempp* briefs. According to Clark, "the distinction between the two clauses is apparent—a violation of the Free Exercise Clause is predicated on coercion while the Establishment Clause violation need not be so attended."[120] Pfeffer had argued this same distinction in his brief: "If the conduct is religious, then it is outside the competence and jurisdiction of the state, and even if participation were not compulsory the conduct would be unconstitutional."[121] Stating the same principle another way, Pfeffer urged that the government's ends must be solely secular and, in achieving them, its means must be secular as well. Justice Clark took these two expressions of the Establishment Clause's prohibitions and fashioned a two part question: "What are the purpose and primary effect of the enactment? If either is the advancement or inhibition of religion then the enactment exceeds the scope of legislative power as circumscribed by the Constitution."[122] Subsequently, the secular purpose and primary effect queries became the first two parts of the tripartite "*Lemon* test" which became the Court's primary evaluative tool in determining violations of the Establishment Clause.[123]

The significance of the *Engel* and *Schempp* decisions went beyond the origins of the *Lemon* test. As political scientist Gregg Ivers has suggested, "The Court essentially redefined religious pluralism." "One cannot overestimate the influence that *Engel* and *Schempp* had on the development of church-state law," Ivers continued, "or the extent to which these decisions shook the foundations of the majoritarian civic—and religious—culture."[124] Indeed, the Court's reaffirmation of the broad interpretation of the First Amendment in these cases, as well as in *Torcaso v. Watkins*,[125] redefined the constitutional debate over the First Amendment. This broader consequence of the *Engel-Schempp* decisions was recognized by Pfeffer as well. He viewed the decisions as having marked the end of a dominant Protestant-Catholic ethos in America, and the beginning of an era of religious pluralism. Under this new paradigm, Pfeffer concluded that "all creeds are equal participants in American society."[126]

This may have been a victory for religious pluralism, but opponents of the school prayer and Bible reading decisions were undeterred. Of the more than 200 school prayer amendment proposals that have been submitted to Congress since the *Engel* decision, the most serious effort was launched by Congressman Frank Becker of New York in 1964. Becker's resolution read, in part, "Nothing in this Constitution shall be deemed to prohibit the offering, reading from or listening to prayers or Biblical scriptures, if participation therein is on a voluntary basis, in any governmental or public school, institution, or place. . . . Nothing in this Constitution shall be deemed to prohibit making reference to belief in, reliance upon, or invoking the aid of God or a Supreme Being in any governmental or public document, proceeding, activity, currency, school [or] institution." Becker successfully secured the support needed to hold hearings before the House Judiciary Committee.[127]

Leo Pfeffer was among those invited to give statements before the Committee on the proposed amendment. Pfeffer's statement identified a number of "false concepts" he believed undergirded the Becker Amendment. He first provided an extensive history of the school prayer debate to challenge the claim that opposition to school prayers was of recent vintage. Second, he challenged the privileging of a single God or Scriptures in the language of the amendment. This he found contrary to the historical record as well. Instead, Pfeffer asserted that there is a long history of "violence and persecution over what is the true word of God." Third, he contradicted the notion that the practices were voluntary just because a child could opt out of the practice. This, Pfeffer called a "delusion" and cited concerns of student impressionability that had been raised in prior cases. Finally, Pfeffer dismissed the argument that opposition to the school prayer amendment was primarily coming from atheists and secularists. Citing opposition to the amendment by the National Council of Churches as well as a number of leading ministers, Pfeffer suggested to the committee that opposition to school-sponsored prayers was widespread among the religious community.[128] Beyond these arguments, much of his testimony focused on how such an amendment would undermine the principles of the First Amendment. After several days of testimony, the Judiciary Committee would eventually take no action on the proposal.[129]

During the period of the *Engel* and *Schempp* cases, Leo Pfeffer was actively litigating a case in Dade County, Florida challenging a variety of religious exercises in the Miami public schools. In fact, Pfeffer believed the Miami case, *Chamberlin v. Dade County*,[130] to be a better test case than either

Engel or *Schempp* because of the wide variety of unconstitutional practices involved. Classroom Bible reading and prayers, religious holiday observances, religious oaths for teachers, and required religious census of students were some of the practices. Buoyed by the prospect of such a good test case, Pfeffer initiated litigation on behalf of the American Jewish Congress challenging all of these practices on constitutional grounds. In doing so, he found himself in conflict with the Miami Jewish community who feared anti-Semitic backlash. Pfeffer and the American Jewish Congress chose to proceed with the litigation which was perceived by some in the Miami Jewish community as high handed and arrogant. As one critic complained, "That whole affair was just another case of Leo Pfeffer having to demonstrate the he knew better than anyone what was right for Jews."[131] These tensions led the Anti-Defamation League to issue a memorandum seeking to reassure the Miami Jewish community that its regional office was "doing whatever it can to ease the strain or conflict to rebuild the friendly relationships which have been weakened as a result of the trial." Such direct and indirect criticism did not sit well with Pfeffer who found the ADL's memorandum to undermine his efforts and question his integrity. In a letter to Sol Rabkin of the ADL, he complained: "Purely as it affect me personally and in my personal capacity, I consider this the most dishonest, unethical, and unprofessional conduct that I have experienced in my fifteen years in Jewish community relations work."[132]

Despite these conflicts, Pfeffer challenged in his brief the assertions that the practices were voluntary and that no compulsion was involved. In doing so, he reiterated the claim that the Establishment Clause does not depend upon a showing of compulsion to be unconstitutional.[133] The lower courts found all of the practices unconstitutional except for the prayer and Bible recitations. Because of the subsequent holdings in *Engel* and *Schempp*, the U.S. Supreme Court vacated the state courts' decisions upholding prayer and Bible reading, while upholding the ruling on the other practices.

With few exceptions, Pfeffer was on the winning side of Supreme Court cases involving religion and public education. And the U.S. Supreme Court, under the leadership of Earl Warren during the 1960s, was willing to perpetuate the interpretation of the First Amendment articulated by Justice Black in the *Everson* and *McCollum* decisions. Even in the *Zorach* case, the Court, while upholding the dismissed-time statute, reiterated the broad interpretation of the First Amendment. Yet Pfeffer's influence went beyond wins and losses. He orchestrated a number of the Establishment Clause challenges to religious exercises in the public schools during this period and his influence can be witnessed in the justices' separationist opinions. Many of these arguments would be utilized by an emboldened Pfeffer when challenging aid to religious schools in future years.

PUBLIC FUNDS FOR RELIGIOUS SCHOOLS

From 1968 on, Leo Pfeffer was actively involved in challenging public aid to religious schools. Warning that aid to "parochial" schools "represents the most serious threat to the principle of separation of church and state in the history of our nation,"[134] Pfeffer believed that not only the judicial interpretation of the Establishment Clause was at stake, but also fate of the public schools. For much of Leo Pfeffer's career, his struggles against public funds for religious schools appeared to be a battle with the Catholic Church. As noted above, the Catholic parochial school system was formed in the mid-nineteenth century out of protest to the Protestant religious exercises in the public schools as well as a desire to provide Catholic children with a religious education. With the growth of the Catholic parochial school system came calls for public support. Battles over aid to the growing parochial school system ensued.

At the national level, Senator James G. Blaine introduced a constitutional amendment declaring: "No state shall make any law respecting an establishment of religion or prohibiting the free exercise thereof; and no money raised by taxation in any State for the support of public schools, or derived from any public fund therefore, nor any public lands devoted thereto, shall ever be under the control of any religious sect or denomination."[135] While the so-called Blaine Amendment passed the House, it failed to receive the necessary two-thirds vote in the Senate. Nevertheless, more than thirty states adopted similar provisions in their constitutions.

As discussed in the previous chapter, the extent to which anti-Catholicism was responsible for these no-aid provisions has been the source of scholarly and legal debate in recent years.[136] Constitutional scholar Philip Hamburger has argued that no-aid separationism found its origins not in the Jefferson-Madison tradition, but rather late nineteenth-century anti-Catholicism. According to Hamburger, the threat posed by a growing Catholic population led to a coalition of nativists, theological liberals, and secularists that sought constitutional amendments banning aid to parochial schools.[137] U.S. Supreme Court justice Clarence Thomas, in his opinion in the 2000 *Mitchell v. Helms* opinion upholding aid to religious schools, likewise argued that the Blaine Amendments arose during a period of "pervasive anti-Catholicism" and concluded that the no-aid position was "a doctrine born of bigotry."[138] To be sure, nativist sentiments fostered support for the no-ad measures. Some Protestant angst over Catholicism was influenced by the fact the church had frequently allied itself with more authoritarian governments in Europe and stood against most liberalizing movements. Facing anti-ecclesiastical threats from nationalism, liberalism, and socialism, the Catholic Church's response included Papal pronouncements that attacked the separation of church and state as well as the "absurd proposition" that "liberty of conscience must be maintained for everyone."[139]

Nonetheless, the support for the no-aid separationist position during this period is more a more nuanced story than simply anti-Catholicism. Scholars have demonstrated that the no-aid tradition long predated these cultural conflicts and that many Catholics had articulated their support for Jefferson's wall of separation during the nineteenth century.[140] Others have argued that it is more likely that separation provided the "rationale or excuse for anti-Catholicism" rather than nativism "strengthening popular convictions about separation."[141] "The fact that that nativist groups hijacked the no-funding principle," one constitutional historian concluded, "does not invalidate the concept or mean that all advocates of the no-funding principle supported nativist goals."[142] Nonetheless, with both the increased secularization of public education and the concerted effort to restrict public funds from private schools, the late nineteenth century has been called the "high water mark" of church-state separation. Whether influenced by nativism or not, these developments were proof to Leo Pfeffer that by the late nineteenth century, "the American people had accepted a much broader concept of separation," especially as it related to religion and education.[143]

With a resurgence of nativism in the early twentieth century, though, parochial school leaders were forced to shift to a defensive posture. Some states went beyond merely blocking aid to parochial schools to challenging their right to exist. In 1922, the Oregon legislature, for example, passed the Compulsory Education Act that required all children to attend public schools. A private military academy and a Catholic grade school run by the Society of Sisters of the Holy Name of Jesus challenged the statute based on the Due Process Clause of the Fourteenth Amendment. In *Pierce v. Society of Sisters*, a unanimous U.S. Supreme Court struck down the Oregon statute as violating the liberty of parents to choose where to send their children for education.[144] Referred to as "the Magna Carta of the parochial school system", *Pierce* ensured the right of both private secular and religious schools to exist.

Emboldened by this legal affirmation, parochial schools renewed their efforts to gain public financial support. The extensive parochial school system was an economically challenging endeavor especially since these schools often served an urban working class constituency. As a result, proponents of parochial school aid made several claims. Among these was that state support of a variety of educational endeavors, private or public, religious or nonreligious, was consistent with the religious pluralism of American society. They also argued that parochial schools served an important civic duty by providing education in secular subjects. Moreover, they contended that parents of parochial school students are double taxed, since they paid taxes to support the public schools along with paying tuition to parochial schools.[145]

Ultimately, "parochiaid" proponents argued for a narrow reading of the Establishment Clause that would not prohibit aid to religious institutions as long as it was available on a nondiscriminatory basis.

While legislatures and the courts remained unwilling to provide direct funds to parochial schools, other forms of aid, many argued, found acceptance based upon a "child-benefit" rationale. Introduced in the *Cochran v. Board of Education* decision in 1930, the theory held, in this case, that the beneficiaries of a state textbook loan program were not the religious schools, but rather, the children.[146] While *Cochran* was not decided on First Amendment grounds, it provided impetus for those who would seek greater public support for parochial schools. Consequently, the child-benefit theory provided a rationale for the U.S. Supreme Court's upholding state reimbursement of transportation costs in *Everson* in 1947 and the loan of secular textbooks in *Board of Education v. Allen* in 1968.[147]

Discussed at length in earlier chapters, *Everson v. Board of Education* involved the constitutionality of a New Jersey state statute authorizing the reimbursement of transportation costs to parents of parochial school children. Justice Hugo Black's declaration that "no tax in any amount, large or small, can be levied to support any religious activities or institutions, whatever they may be called, or whatever form they adopt to teach or practice religion,"[148] became for Pfeffer the starting point of his constitutional challenges to religious school aid. The irony of the *Everson* decision for many was that, despite its broad interpretation of the First Amendment and its seemingly absolutist language with regard to the no-aid principle, the Court found state payment of parochial students' bus fares to be constitutional. Utilizing the reasoning of the child-benefit theory, the Court justified the practice on the grounds that they, like other public welfare benefits, such as police or fire protection, were "indisputably marked off from the religious function" of the schools.[149] Leo Pfeffer strenuously challenged the child-benefit argument because he feared almost any aid could be justified under its reasoning. Describing it as a "legal fiction," Pfeffer argued that the theory was created in order to circumvent the restrictions of the Establishment Clause. Noting that most state courts had rejected the child-benefit theory, Pfeffer concluded that "it permits and sanctions government action through indirection which would be unconstitutional if it were direct."[150]

The debate over public funds for religious schools was of fundamental importance to Leo Pfeffer because it had ramifications for the very meaning of the First Amendment. More constitutionally significant than the child-benefit theory, he believed, was the justification for parochial school aid based on a narrow or non-preferentialist reading of the First Amendment. For Pfeffer, this nonpreferentialist approach subordinated the Establishment Clause to the Free Exercise Clause.[151] "If the Establishment Clause is so interpreted," Pfeffer warned, "it appears to present no barrier to governmental aid to church schools as long as all religious groups are treated equally without preference or discrimination."[152] Advocates of this position were emboldened by the Court's released-time decision in *Zorach*, Pfeffer surmised, as some viewed it as a repudiation of the *Everson-McCollum* no-aid interpretation.

In his legal briefs and other writings on aid to parochial schools, Pfeffer consistently rejected this understanding of the First Amendment. Claiming that "the struggle for religious liberty and the separation of church and state in America is largely a history of the struggle against compulsory taxation for religious purposes," Pfeffer concluded that the First Amendment banned state financing of religious schools whether direct or indirect.[153] Subordinating the Establishment Clause to the Free Exercise Clause, moreover, ran counter to the philosophical and historical roots of the unitary guarantee and was a fundamental misunderstanding of the Court's ruling in *Zorach*. According to Pfeffer, the Establishment Clause had little meaning under such a reading of the First Amendment.

In a number of publications, Leo Pfeffer presented arguments against state aid that provided the framework of his own advocacy and which appeared, in one form or another, in subsequent briefs, testimony, and publications. Along with the argument that such aid violated the separation of church and state, Pfeffer affirmed the legitimacy of parochial schools but challenged the claim that they had a free exercise right to taxpayer funds.[154] Pfeffer was careful to clarify that such a position was not born out of hostility to religious schools, as many aid proponents claimed: "America has always been friendly to religion but it has always barred governmental involvement in religious affairs and the use of governmental funds for religious purposes, and has never considered the bar a manifestation of unfriendliness."[155] Nonetheless, Pfeffer did fear that public funding would have a disastrous effect on public education. Pfeffer believed that as public funds became available to religious schools, the funding and student-pool for public schools would be lessened. For Pfeffer, "the inevitable result would be the fragmentation and destruction of the public school system."[156]

Pfeffer also challenged the argument that parents of parochial school children were double-taxed, since they had to pay taxes to support public schools while also paying tuition to private schools. Pfeffer declared that "the double taxation argument is fallaciously based on the premise that the public education of children is a benefit only to their parents . . . this is not the theory of the American program of public education."[157] Emphasizing the connection between public education and democracy, Pfeffer explained that all citizens benefit from public education whether they have children or not and whether they choose to send them to public schools or not.[158]

Pfeffer was equally concerned for the impact aid to religious schools would have on religion as well. History had also proven, Pfeffer asserted, that state financing of religion intensified religious rivalry and conflict. "Religio/political parties" would be formed to secure funding for their religious persuasion, he claimed. Pfeffer frequently asserted that aid to parochial schools constituted "taxation without representation." Unlike public schools, parochial schools were not subject to local and popular control. Thus, taxpayers would have no input as to how their tax moneys were spent at religious schools. Conversely, Pfeffer warned that with public funds would come government interference and surveillance.[159] In order to protect the integrity of religious schools, then, public funds should be prohibited.

The free exercise claim for funding of religious schools was unpersuasive to Pfeffer as well. He asserted that while there may be a free exercise right to send one's children to parochial schools, it did not follow that the state must fund the schools. According to Pfeffer, "The very raison d'être of parochial schools is to enable children to obtain all their education—secular as well as sacred—in a framework of religion, and that is why the same Constitution that secures the right to maintain such schools forbids the government to finance them."[160] Moreover, Pfeffer sought to turn upside down the claim by many parochial school apologists that denial of such funding was discriminatory. Instead, he claimed that discrimination was practiced by parochial schools which based admission on religious affiliation and academic attainment.[161] Pfeffer did not question the right of religious schools to have admission requirements. Rather, he believed the government should not finance schools with exclusive policies. Moreover, Pfeffer feared that granting funds to parochial schools for even basic services, such as textbooks and transportation costs, justified on the child-benefit theory, would open the door to other types of aid and eventually direct subsidization.[162]

By the 1970s, the fight for aid to religious schools was no longer undertaken primarily by the Catholic Church. The growth of Protestant Christian schools witnessed a marked increase in the 1960s and 1970s as racial integration of the public schools took place. For Pfeffer, this was no coincidence as he believed that opposition to integration was a key motivating factor in the creation of Christian academies. Often small and limited in funds, these Protestant schools, commonly established by churches historically opposed to Catholic schools receiving public aid, joined the efforts of proponents to gain state aid.[163] For Pfeffer, this added a whole new dimension to the constitutional debate. The funding of Christian day schools, he argued, constituted the state financing of racial segregation. Pfeffer feared the egalitarian, multiethnic, and pluralistic nature of the public schools would be lost: "In a constitutional democracy, public education must be universal and egalitarian. It cannot afford to divide its community into superior and inferior groups, racial or religious. The *McCollum* and *Brown* decisions are two sides of the same coin."[164]

The 1960s witnessed massive federal spending for education. This too set the stage for Pfeffer's active legal involvement in issues of aid to religious schools. In January 1965, President Lyndon Johnson submitted the Elementary and Secondary Education Act to Congress. The Act, for the first time, provided over a billion dollars of federal funds to the nation's elementary and secondary schools. Title II of the Act provided textbooks and other instructional materials to "private" schools. The allocations to "private" schools provided optimism for proponents of aid to parochial schools. To opponents, the provision was troubling.[165]

Testifying before the U.S. House of Representatives' Subcommittee on Education and Labor, Pfeffer sought clarification of the word "private" in the Act. He testified that if "private" schools meant non-religious elementary and secondary schools, then constitutional problems would not exist. Nevertheless, he found that "the legislative history of the testimony given here by these remarks of the members of the committee, leaves no doubt what the bill intends is primarily religious schools and not secular public and non-private elementary schools."[166] Pfeffer consequently challenged the constitutionality of Title II, arguing as well that the provisions of textbooks and instructional equipment went beyond the findings of the 1930 *Cochran* case which upheld, on due process grounds, a Louisiana statute that allowed the state to supply free textbooks to children in private as well as public schools. Similar objections were raised by Pfeffer against Title III which provided for the loan of textbooks and library materials from public to private schools and Title IV which required representation of private schools on local committees that oversaw the distribution of the Act's funds.[167]

Pfeffer's fundamental argument was that, in each instance, the primary beneficiaries of the provisions were the religious schools and not the children. Essentially, the provisions permitted "the actual channeling of both money and equipment to parochial schools." "Here I cannot see where this can be utilized under the child-benefit or welfare theory."[168] These provisions provided impermissible aid to religion as well as violated the constitutionally mandated neutrality on the part of government. Pfeffer's testimony notwithstanding, the term "private" remained in the statute thus retaining the ambiguity as to what schools were to receive federal aid. It would be up to the courts to decide the constitutionality of these provisions.

In 1968, Pfeffer argued the case of *Flast v. Cohen*.[169] Pfeffer was selected to serve as lead counsel to represent Florence Flast, president of the United Parents Association, challenging the 1923 Supreme Court case of *Frothingham v. Mellon* which held that individuals could not challenge the constitutionality of Congressional appropriation bills purely on the basis that they were taxpayers. Pfeffer viewed this de minimis rule as a key obstacle to challenging parochiaid. The suit also challenged the Elementary and Secondary Act as violating the Establishment Clause. Pfeffer argued that the designation of "private" schools in the Act in reality meant religious schools. Consequently, any funding for these schools would violate the Establishment Clause. The federal district court circumvented the Establishment Clause issue raised by Pfeffer and upheld *Frothingham's* applicability to Establishment Clause challenges.[170]

The U.S. Supreme Court agreed to hear the case on appeal and, in his brief for appellants, Pfeffer argued that the factors which dictated judicial restraint in *Frothingham* were not controlling the *Flast* case. Specifically, he found the de minimus rule of *Frothingham* to be irrelevant with regard to Establishment Clause issues. Calling the de minimus a common law, not a constitutional question, Pfeffer concluded that "no constitutional barrier precludes acceptance of jurisdiction of a citizen-taxpayer's suit challenging an expenditure of Federal funds as violative of the Establishment and Free Exercise provisions of the First Amendment."[171] Addressing the concern that allowing taxpayer suits would encourage the filing of frivolous lawsuits, Pfeffer contended that if the price of protecting a fundamental freedom is "suffering a multitude of meritless suits, the bargain may nevertheless be very much worthwhile."[172] Upholding the narrow *Frothingham* rule, then, would mean that "fundamental freedoms will go violated without an eligible protagonist."[173] The U.S. Supreme Court granted decided the case in Pfeffer's favor. While avoiding the Establishment Clause challenge, the Court did rule, eight-to-one, that taxpayers had a right to challenge the constitutionality of federal expenditures that violate the religion clauses if there is a "logical nexus between the status asserted and the claim sought to be adjudicated."[174]

The *Flast* decision proved to be one of the most significant decisions of Pfeffer's career because it allowed for more widespread taxpayer challenges to federal funding of religious schools. *Flast* also motivated Pfeffer's formation of the New York Committee for Public Education as well as the National Coalition for Public Education and Religious Liberty (PEARL). New York PEARL and National PEARL included representatives from separationist organizations and other like-minded individuals and served to facilitate taxpayer suits against state aid. Rather than duplicating efforts and costs among separationist organizations, PEARL would serve as "a centralizing force in church-state litigation."[175] With Pfeffer as general counsel, PEARL became the lead plaintiff in a number of landmark Supreme Court cases involving public aid to religious schools.[176]

Board of Education v. Allen

PEARL was also formed in response to the *Board of Education v. Allen* decision in 1968.[177] *Allen* involved a New York law that required the free loan of textbooks to all students, of both public and private schools, grades seven through twelve. The New York program was justified constitutionally by the child-benefit theory of the *Cochran* and *Everson* decisions. On behalf of the American Jewish Congress, Pfeffer filed a friend-of-the-court brief challenging the constitutionality of the New York statute. At the heart of Pfeffer's brief was a challenge to the child-benefit rationale which he believed undergirded not only the New York law but also the Elementary and Secondary Education Act of 1965. Using *Everson* as his guide, Pfeffer argued that the child-benefit theory did not warrant the use of public funds for religious schools. Instead, he asserted that the language of *Everson* was very clear, in that it did not allow the secular expenses of religious schools to be paid by taxpayers. Pfeffer feared the child-benefit rationale would justify the financing of all aspects of parochial education except for explicitly religious instruction.[178]

In writing for a six member majority, Justice Byron White upheld the New York statute based on the child-benefit theory. Despite the Court's affirmation of the broad interpretation of the First Amendment in previous cases, White was able to persuade a majority of the justices that the loan of textbooks was a reasonable accommodation that did not vitiate the prohibitions of the Establishment Clause. In general, White found aid that related to the secular instruction in parochial schools may be acceptable. Utilizing the secular purpose and effect tests from *Schempp*, he ruled the loan, as opposed to the grant, of secular textbooks to have a genuine secular legislative purpose and a primary effect that neither advanced nor inhibited religion.[179] According to White, "the law merely makes available to all children the benefits of a general program to lend books free of charge. . . . Thus no funds or books are furnished to the parochial schools, and the financial benefit is to parents and children, not to schools."[180]

Justices Hugo Black and William Douglas registered dissenting opinions. They both distinguished between providing transportation costs, which they viewed as a welfare benefit like police or fire protection, and providing textbooks which they found unconstitutional. Black, who had written the majority opinion in *Everson*, reaffirmed his adherence to the no-aid principle: "I still subscribe to the belief that tax-raised funds cannot constitutionally be used to support religious schools, buy their school books, erect their buildings, pay their teachers, or pay any other of their maintenance expenses, even to the extent of one penny."[181] Books, to Black, were "not difficult to distinguish . . . from bus fares" and can be used to assist in "the teaching and propagation of sectarian religious viewpoints." White, in response, agreed that "books are different from buses," but countered that New York was authorizing the purchase of secular, not religious, books.[182]

To Pfeffer, the *Allen* decision was potentially devastating and the child-benefit rationale, on which it was based, was especially pernicious: "Since everything that goes on in both private and public schools is presumably for the benefit of the children, practically everything (exclusive of religious 'benefit') in the private schools can be financed with public funds, as is everything in the public schools."[183] Equally troubling to Pfeffer was White's contention that the secular and religious functions of parochial schools could be distinguished. This, Pfeffer feared, affirmed the contention of pro-aid proponents that since parochial schools provided instruction in secular subjects, they were entitled to a wide array of public support. Declaring that the American people wanted high-quality education and that they continued to rely on private schools to help achieve that, White had concluded "that parochial schools are performing, in additional to their sectarian function, the task of secular education."[184] Affirmation of the secular role of religious education led Pfeffer to conclude that "the pro-aid groups could hardly have expected more." And, as Pfeffer feared, the *Allen* decision "opened a floodgate of State bills for the financing of private operations."[185] To counter this trend, Pfeffer would, in subsequent cases, concentrate on proving that religion permeated the curriculum and atmosphere of private religious schools. Consequently, any aid to such schools would run the risk of violating the First Amendment.

Lemon v. Kurtzman

The *Allen* decision reflected the Court's struggle, as in *Everson*, to decide how to apply the separationist principle to aid cases.[186] Pfeffer was aware the Court would unlikely revisit issues of transportation costs and loan of secular textbooks, so he focused his energies on challenging new forms of aid, including the contracting of educational services by the state with parochial school teachers. In 1971, the Court heard the companion cases of *Earley v. DiCenso* and *Lemon v. Kurtzman.*[187] The *Earley* case involved a Rhode Island plan in which parochial school teachers teaching secular subjects in schools serving a low socioeconomic community would receive 15 percent of their annual salary from the state. The *Lemon* case involved a Pennsylvania statute that authorized the state to pay parochial schools for teaching certain secular subjects. On behalf of the American Jewish lobbies and the American Civil Liberties Union, Pfeffer served as co-counsel in both cases and attacked in his briefs the constitutionality of the use of taxpayer funds to pay a percentage of parochial school teachers' salaries for teaching secular subjects. As he had earlier testified before the Rhode Island legislature against the 15 percent plan, Pfeffer believed that such payments violated the Establishment Clause because they constituted a subsidy by the state to parochial schools.[188]

Adopted just nine days after the *Allen* decision, the Pennsylvania program had been justified on the basis that only the teaching of secular subjects was being subsidized and that the state superintendent of public instruction had to approve all instructional material. It was argued that the program did not violate the no-aid state constitutional prohibitions since Pennsylvania was merely contracting with parochial schools secular instruction services not unlike the purchase of maintenance supplies or other secular services. Pfeffer argued that these provisions did not adequately protect the plans from the prohibitions of the Establishment Clause. Before submitting the statutes to the no-aid test of *Everson* and the purpose and effect tests of *Schempp*, Pfeffer challenged the idea that the curriculum in a religious school could be divided between religious and secular. In doing so, he introduced evidence that religion permeated the curriculum of the parochial school. For instance, he cited Joseph Fichter's 1958 study, *Parochial Schools: A Sociological Study*,[189] in which Fichter concluded that "in the parochial school religion permeates the whole curriculum and is not confined to a single half-hour period of the day." He found similar evidence in the Providence, Rhode Island *Handbook of School Regulations.* Pfeffer cited the Handbook's claim that "religious formation is not confined to formal courses; nor is it restricted to a single subject area."[190]

Yet even if there was a logical division between the secular and religious elements of parochial school instruction, Pfeffer argued that the Rhode Island and Pennsylvania practices were unconstitutional. Looking to the legislative history behind the Pennsylvania program, Pfeffer contended that it had a religious purpose since it was "one of the many increasingly successful efforts throughout the nation to siphon off public funds for non-public schools." The statute also advanced religion, Pfeffer believed, since it amounted to a direct subsidy to the parochial school: "The school receives public funds for continuing to do what it has always been doing and what it has legally been required to do."[191]

In addition to these Establishment clause concerns, Pfeffer contended that the parochial schools were "playing a substantial, though unintended role" in preserving racial segregation. The state was facilitating this by potentially making it "economically feasible for white middle-income parents to send their children to non-public schools."[192] The claim that parochiaid undermined integration of the public schools would be utilized by Pfeffer in subsequent briefs.

Pfeffer borrowed from the Court's recent decision in *Walz v. Tax Commission*,[193] upholding tax exemption for churches, to fashion another test to determine violations of the Establishment Clause. In *Walz*, the Court determined that laws fostering an "excessive entanglement" between church and state unconstitutional. Consequently, Pfeffer argued that the continued "policing and surveillance" of school authorities to ensure that public funds were going to purely secular instruction, at issue in *Lemon*, led to an impermissible excessive entanglement. "But in seeking to avoid the Scylla of sectarianism," Pfeffer explained, "the statutory plan is necessarily engulfed in the Charybdis of entanglement."[194]

It was the excessive entanglement consideration that provided the basis for the Court's determination that the Pennsylvania and Rhode Island plans were unconstitutional. Chief Justice Warren Burger, in writing for the majority, concluded that "the government's post-audit power to inspect and evaluate a church-related school's financial records and to determine which expenditures are religious and which are secular creates an intimate and continuing relationship between church and state."[195] Unlike textbooks, on-going surveillance would also be required to ensure that teachers were not inculcating or advancing religion. "We simply recognize that a dedicated religious person teaching in a school affiliated with his or her own faith . . . will inevitably experience great difficulty in remaining religiously neutral."[196] Burger also placed under the excessive entanglement prohibition the problem of divisiveness. He suggested that the Rhode Island and Pennsylvania state program's divisive political potential led to excessive entanglement arguing that "political division along religious lines was one of the principal evils against which the First Amendment was intended to protect."[197] By placing the issue of divisiveness under the excessive entanglement test, Burger gave expression to one of the primary constitutional arguments Pfeffer had been making since his brief in *McCollum*. Moreover, with the addition of the excessive entanglement test to the purpose and effect tests of *Schempp*, the Court, in effect, adopted what became known as the tripartite "Lemon Test" to determine violations of the Establishment Clause. Declaring that laws must have a secular purpose, must have a primary effect that neither advances nor inhibits religion, and must not foster an excessive entanglement between church and state, the *Lemon* Test became the primarily evaluative tool the Court would use to determine Establishment Clause violations.

The excessive entanglement consideration became an especially effective, yet controversial, tool in challenging school aid statutes. Opponents of the excessive entanglement test believed it created an untenable Catch-22 for those seeking to provide resources for parochial schools. If safeguards are put in place to ensure religion is not advanced by state aid, they argued, then the plan risks violating the excessive entanglement prohibition. Separationists like Pfeffer were unsympathetic. They viewed with suspicion any aid and believed the three-part *Lemon* test created for them an effective barrier to unconstitutional aid. Proponents of aid would find a glimmer of hope in Burger's decisions when he noted that the line between permissible and impermissible aid was not bright. According to Burger, this "blurred, indistinct, and variable barrier," was often the judgment of the Court based upon the "nature of the institution, type of aid, and kind of aid provided."[198]

Pfeffer viewed *Lemon* as a significant victory for separationists and of its significance, he stated: "The world of aid on the elementary and secondary school levels had come to an end not with a whimper but with a great big bang. . . . What was surprising about the *Lemon* opinion was not White's partial dissent—but rather the Court's opinion should be written by the conservative Burger and concurred with by all the other members of the Court."[199] In future years, however, Burger and future chief justice William Rehnquist became vocal opponents to the Court's strict adherence to the wall of separation, especially as it restricted aid to religious schools. Convincing the Court to strike down forms of parochiaid would become a greater challenge for Pfeffer as the make-up of the Court changed and some centrist justices began to vote with accommodationist justices in aid cases. Pfeffer's confidence, then, was somewhat misplaced. While *Lemon* seemingly provided clearer direction to lower courts on Establishment Clause issues, "fundamental disagreements existed about the practical implications of the Establishment Clause."[200] Nonetheless, at least during the 1970s, the *Lemon* test proved to be an effective barrier to most forms of aid beyond transportation funds and the loan of secular textbooks. This useful tool was largely the result of Pfeffer's strategic advocacy on church-state issues. "The Court's adaptation of the Lemon Test and its subsequent use in almost all establishment clause litigation were achievements for which Pfeffer," Gregg Ivers has argued, "could claim substantial credit."[201]

PEARL v. Nyquist

The *Lemon* decision certainly did not dissuade proponents of school aid from introducing new aid schemes. As Pfeffer indicated, states passed slightly altered statutes faster than the courts could strike them down:

> A game plan emerged. Pass a law providing aid to parochial schools and start paying immediately or as quickly as possible. Continue paying until the Supreme Court finally declares the law unconstitutional. It may take a year or more before a suit is started to challenge a law, and perhaps another two years until the case gets to the Supreme Court. In the meantime, keep paying. When the law is finally struck down by the Supreme Court, rush some variation through the legislature and start over again. This pattern was followed in New York, Pennsylvania, Ohio, and Connecticut, among others.[202]

These actions were described by Pfeffer as a "chess game with the Constitution" and one he criticized as a lack of respect for court precedent.[203] Through organizations, such as PEARL and the American Jewish Congress, Pfeffer responded to these plans with lawsuits challenging their constitutionality. Such was the case involving a New York statute which had been passed within a year after the *Lemon* decision. The *PEARL v. Nyquist* case was the culmination of an effort in New York to find constitutional parochiaid measures. After failing to repeal the state's Blaine Amendment, aid proponents pushed for more "direct and substantial aid" for parochial schools.[204] The statute provided three types of aid for nonpublic elementary and secondary schools. The first part provided direct grants to nonpublic schools for the maintenance of facilities that serve a "high-concentration" of low-income students. The second provision entailed the granting of tuition reimbursements of up to $100 per student to parents who earned less than $5,000 a year. The third allowed for tax deductions for parents of nonpublic school students depending on the family's annual income.[205]

Filing suit on behalf of PEARL and several other organizations, Pfeffer challenged the constitutionality of all three parts of the New York statute and presented oral arguments before the U.S. Supreme Court. Pfeffer asserted in his brief for appellants that the statute fundamentally ran afoul of the *Everson* no-aid test as well as the *Lemon* test. The secular considerations of children's health and safety notwithstanding, Pfeffer believed maintenance grants to be an unconstitutional government support of religion. He argued that because the state required nonpublic schools to be safe, it did not follow that the Establishment Clause allowed the state subsidize them to ensure safety.[206] This logic, Pfeffer contended, would justify state funds for the maintenance of churches and Sunday schools. Furthermore, he found no safeguard to prevent expenditures related to the operation of "school buildings as are used exclusively for sectarian instruction and religious worship." If any such safeguard did exist, then it would most likely result in the excessive entanglement of government and religion.[207]

Tuition reimbursements to parents of low-income students were prohibited by the Establishment Clause as well. The fact that the grants were given to parents did not avoid Establishment Clause objections according to Pfeffer. Anticipating future debates over school vouchers, Pfeffer argued that the ability to divert funds had constitutional significance. No matter how it was distributed, tax payer funds were ending up at religious schools. "The crux of the matter is that, whether characterized as 'conduit,' 'channel,' or another synonym, tuition grants have no meaning except as a 'transfer (of) part of (government) revenue.'"[208] Moreover, he found the tax deduction constitutionally indistinguishable from the tax reimbursement or a tax credit. "It is not constitutionally material that the payments are made to the parents in reimbursement for tuition already paid rather than in advance for tuition to be paid."[209]

In his complaint, Pfeffer had created a profile of sectarian non-public schools. Sectarian schools were identified as those that (1) imposed religious restrictions on admissions; (2) required attendance of pupils at religious activities; (3) required obedience by students to the doctrines and dogmas of a particular faith; (4) required pupils to attend instruction in the theology or doctrine or a particular faith; (5) were an integral part of the religious mission of the church sponsoring it; (6) had as a substantial purpose in the inculcation of religious values; (7) imposed religious restrictions on faculty appointments; and (8) imposed religious restrictions on what or how the faculty taught. This profile was adopted by the Court in *Nyquist* and subsequently utilized by the Court in aid to religious school cases.[210] Presumably, if the school in question fit the profile, the standard for what constituted permissible aid was much higher than for a school with only a marginal religious affiliation or orientation.

A majority of the Court again found Pfeffer's arguments convincing as Justice Lewis Powell, writing for a 6-to-3 majority, found all three provisions of the statute unconstitutional. Applying the *Lemon* Test, the Court found the stated secular purpose of the law, to promote "pluralism and diversity among public and non-public schools," satisfactory. The effect of the law, however, advanced religion as it "subsidized and advanced the religious mission of public schools." Powell's line of reasoning was similar to that of Pfeffer. He found that the maintenance grants could be used for the upkeep of facilities used exclusively for religious practices and would thereby violate the Constitution: "If the state may not erect buildings in which religious activities are to take place, it may not maintain such buildings or renovate them when they fall into disrepair."[211] Similarly, the Court found that tuition grants violated the Establishment Clause irrespective of who received them. As Pfeffer had argued, the Court found a "practical similarity between New York's tax and tuition reimbursement programs." Powell concluded that "neither form of aid is sufficiently restricted to assure that it would not have the impermissible effect of advancing the sectarian activities of religious schools."[212]

Chief Justice Burger, joined in part by Justices White and Rehnquist, concurred with the majority that the maintenance grants were direct aid forbidden by the Constitution. Nevertheless, he argued in his dissent that tuition reimbursements and tax deductions were not violations of the Establishment Clause. Burger contended that *Everson*, *Allen*, and other Establishment Clause cases did not prohibit indirect aid as long as it was a "program of general welfare under which benefits are distributed to private individuals." Moreover, Burger argued that "while there is not straight line running though our decisions interpreting" the Religion Clauses, the "balance between the policies of free exercise and establishment of religion tips in favor of the former when the legislation moves away from direct aid to religious institutions and takes on the character of general aid to individual families."[213] The tax benefits in *Nyquist* were indistinguishable from the transportation funds in *Everson* or the textbooks in *Allen*, Burger concluded because they merely sought to "equalize the costs incurred by parents in obtaining an education for their children." Echoing an exchange he had with Leo Pfeffer during oral arguments, Burger suggested that the tax benefits were not different than the G.I. Bill and similar educational benefits given to veterans attending religious colleges and universities. For Burger, the fact that most of the private schools that stood to benefit from the program were religious was "irrelevant."[214]

Yet, for Powell and the majority, the effect of the aid was not neutralized because it was given to the parents. Neither was the effect of a tax credit diminished because it is given to the parent after the tuition had been paid. The problem was that, unlike transportation reimbursements and textbook loans, there were no provisions in the law to ensure that the tuition was not used to further the religious mission of the participating sectarian schools. This was the weakness of the tax credit plan as well because the practical effect was that the "qualifying parent under either program receives the same form of encouragement and reward for sending his children to non-public schools." Powell also dismissed the argument that the tax benefits were constitutionally equivalent to church tax deductions upheld in *Walz*. In *Walz*, denying tax deductions to churches and religious institutions increased entanglement between church and state while prohibiting tax credits and deductions for private school tuition diminished entanglement. Powell and the majority found the free exercise right to religious education unpersuasive as well concluding that it does not follow that the free exercise requires what no-establishment prohibits.[215]

Nyquist was a victory for Pfeffer and other no-aid advocates, but distinctions between direct and indirect aid raised in the dissents would gain greater support over time. Two of the dissenters, Burger and Rehnquist, had voted with the majority in *Lemon*, but dissented in *Nyquist* and would, as Pfeffer would later put it, "become a majority when Lewis F. Powell deserted and Reagan appointed Sandra Day O'Connor."[216] Burger's argument that general welfare benefits distributed to individuals would be embraced by a majority of the Court in more recent years. As will be discussed below, the *Nyquist* barrier to aid would be knocked down in as the Court embraced an equal treatment approach to aid cases.

Meek v. Pittenger

Two years after *Nyquist*, the Court addressed yet another Pennsylvania plan intended to provide assistance for the state's parochial schools. The Pennsylvania statute provided for the loan of textbooks, auxiliary services (counseling, testing, psychological and other diagnostic services), instructional materials, and equipment (maps, films, charts, and projectors).[217]

The district court in Pennsylvania upheld much of the plan but not the loan of instructional equipment since it could be "diverted to religious purposes." Emboldened by previous victories before the Court,[218] Pfeffer appealed to the U.S. Supreme Court challenging all aspects of the program, including the loan of textbooks to children of nonpublic schools. Citing numerous examples of administrative entanglement involved in the state's loaning textbooks to children in religious schools, Pfeffer encouraged the Court to reconsider the *Allen* decision. Noting Justice Hugo Black's dissent in *Allen*, Pfeffer held that *Allen* went beyond *Everson* and thus violated the no-aid test.[219]

Provision of auxiliary services was equally unconstitutional according to Pfeffer. Even if the direct payment of money was not involved, the provision of diagnostic and remedial services administered by state personnel would require continuing surveillance by the state to make sure the programs were not used to advance a religious message. For Pfeffer, this was a clear violation of the excessive entanglement test. Fundamentally, Pfeffer argued that Pennsylvania's provision of services to religious schools "propels the State into partnership with the Church."[220] Pfeffer did recognize that the state had a legitimate secular purpose in providing diagnostic and aptitude examinations to children. The crux of the problem for him was that the services were held on religious school grounds. Even if public school teachers were brought in to provide these services, Pfeffer argued, the pervasive religious nature of the school would make the program unconstitutional. He suggested instead that the children should receive the services off campus. Moreover, the state's payment was an indirect subsidy to the religious school, since it was now free of the financial burden of providing auxiliary services.[221]

The loan of instructional equipment ran afoul of the excessive entanglement inquiry as well according to Pfeffer. Surveillance was required to ensure that the maps, globes, and other equipment were not used to teach religion. Much like his challenge to the loan of textbooks, Pfeffer found little difference between the loan of equipment and a cash payment for the equipment or even a tuition reimbursement to parents to enable them to purchase the materials. "In short," Pfeffer concluded, "it constitutes a State subsidy for the operation of religious schools" especially since the equipment would be in possession of the parochial school in perpetuity.[222]

A divided Court struck down all parts of the Pennsylvania plan except for the loan of textbooks. Relying on *Allen*, the Court emphasized that the loan of textbooks was to children and not to the schools. This is distinguished from the direct loan of instructional material and equipment to the religious school which "has the unconstitutional primary effect of advancing religion because of the predominantly religious character of the schools."[223] The Court distinguished appropriations for instructional materials as well from "secular and nonideological services" such as bus transportation, school lunches and public health facilities.[224] Regarding the auxiliary services, the Court agreed with Pfeffer's contention that the secular and nonideological nature of the services notwithstanding, the subsidization of state personnel in religious schools would inevitably result in excessive entanglement between church and state.[225]

While Pfeffer was unable to convince the Court to reconsider the loan of secular textbooks, *Meek* reveals that the excessive entanglement prong of the *Lemon* test had become an effective weapon in his attacks on aid to religious schools. Proponents of aid had learned to craft their proposals to provide sufficiently secular purposes and ends[226] but found it much more difficult to satisfy the excessive entanglement prohibitions. For some Court observers, however, the excessive entanglement prong had led the Court not to a position of neutrality between government and religion but rather to one of hostility. In fact, it was the application of excessive entanglement that generated much of Chief Justice Burger's ire in his dissenting opinion. He was particularly critical of the Court's denial of auxiliary services based upon what he called the "Court's extravagant suggestion of potential entanglement."[227] Burger found that the state was merely attempting "to provide—through the services of its own state-selected professionals—the remedial assistance necessary for all its children." To deny this was not only discriminatory toward religious institutions but also children "who have the misfortune to have to cope with the learning process under extraordinary heavy physical and psychological burdens." Repeating his dissent in *Nyquist*, Burger viewed these as general welfare benefits that did not contravene the First Amendment.[228]

In *Religion, State and the Burger Court*, Pfeffer noted that the separationist justices in *Nyquist* and *Meek* would later regret the inclusion of "footnote 49" in the *Nyquist* decision. There, Justice Powell distinguished the tax benefits in *Nyquist* from traditional tax deductions, like those given for charitable purposes. Pfeffer argued that this footnote would "haunt" the Court in later cases, such as *Mueller v. Allen*, where tax deductions for parochial school tuition were upheld.[229] Interestingly, what Pfeffer did not note in his book is that, on at least two occasions during oral arguments in *Nyquist*, he conceded that "a fairly good case could be made of the constitutionality of tax deductions for tuition paid to parochial schools."[230]

Wolman v. Walter

Increasingly vocal discontent with the extent of the Court's prohibitions of aid to parochial schools may provide some explanation for the complex and confusing 1977 decision, *Wolman v. Walter*.[231] *Wolman* involved an Ohio statute providing a variety of forms of aid to nonpublic schools, including textbook loans, supplying standardized tests and scoring services, instructional equipment, diagnostic services performed by public school employees on campus, and remedial instruction held off campus. As the Court's decision indicated, the Ohio statute was written specifically with the *Meek* decision in mind. To Pfeffer, this was an example of the attempt of proponents of aid to parochial schools to circumvent the Constitution: "What we are witnessing is a sort of historic game of chess played between ingenious lawyers and legislators on one side and this Court on the other side of the chessboard of the Establishment Clause, with each move by the former checked by the latter, but the game continuing in the hope that a successful move will ultimately be found."[232] Pfeffer submitted a brief of amicus curiae in opposition to the Ohio plan arguing again that any aid beyond transportation and textbooks was unconstitutional in light of the previous decisions of the Court.[233] The fatal flaw of the Ohio program for Pfeffer was the inability to distinguish aid supporting secular and religious instruction in the parochial school context.

In a 5-to-4 decision, "shifting majorities" upheld much of the plan. Not only were textbooks affirmed but so, too, was the funding of certain diagnostic services such as hearing and speech tests. Other services, which required more adult-student contact, such as counseling and remedial instruction, were upheld as long as they were offered off-campus. Alternatively, field trips were associated with instructional materials such as maps and charts and were held unconstitutional since "the public school authorities will be unable to adequately insure secular use of the field trip funds without close supervision of the nonpublic teachers."[234] The complexity of the *Wolman* decision left the aid issue unsettled. Since Warren Burger had become chief justice in 1969, the Court had largely held to the constitutional interpretation of the previous Warren Court. This was illustrated by the fact that Pfeffer was victorious in most of the challenges to parochial school aid during this period. By the late 1970s, however, the membership of the Court seemed more inclined to uphold more forms of aid. On aid to religious schools, in particular, a discernible division in the Court became apparent. Justices Byron White, William Rehnquist, and Chief Justice Warren Burger were more willing to grant accommodations to religion. This was in contrast to the predictable objections of Harry Blackmun, William Brennan, Thurgood Marshall, and John Paul Stevens. Thus, decisions often came down to the swing votes of Potter Stewart and Lewis Powell during this period. The shift in Stewart's and Powell's voting patterns during this time led Pfeffer to later describe the *Wolman* decision as the beginning of the Court's unfriendliness to legal challenges to aid to religious schools.[235]

PEARL v. Regan

Pfeffer's fear that an accommodationist majority was emerging in the Court was realized in the 1980 *PEARL v. Regan* decision upholding a New York statute that provided funds to religious schools for the grading of state-prepared tests.[236] In his brief challenging the New York plan before the U.S. Supreme Court, Pfeffer argued that it unconstitutionally advanced religion. The fact that the services were state-mandated was irrelevant, he held, especially since the services were educational and not health or welfare benefits. Moreover, the subsidy went directly to the schools and not indirectly through parents or children which would invalidate the program even under a child-benefit rationale.[237]

Pfeffer's argument centered on the fact that direct funding to the schools would inevitably lead to excessive entanglement between church and state. He urged that guarding against the potential misuse of funds would require continued monitoring by the state of the nonpublic school. Furthermore, he warned that a favorable ruling in *Regan* would contradict the prohibition against direct aid that had enjoyed a broad consensus on the Court in past cases. Even in *Wolman*, no funds went directly to the religious school but were either nonmonetary diagnostic services or were remedial services held off campus.[238] The potential political divisiveness resulting from the direct subsidization of religious schools was equally problematic to Pfeffer: "It is both unconstitutional and inequitable to compel all persons regardless of religion to pay taxes used to finance the operations of schools from which some of them are excluded because of their religion."[239]

In a 5-to-4 decision, however, the accommodationist justices were joined by Justices Stewart and Powell and rebuffed Pfeffer's contentions. Justice Byron White held that the payment for the grading of standardized tests by parochial school teachers was little different from that upheld in *Wolman*. Essentially, White was convinced that enough safeguards had been set in place to ensure that the funds went solely for the secular purpose of evaluating state-mandated examinations. As in *Wolman*, White argued, "the District Court was correct in concluding that there was no substantial risk that the examinations could be used for religious education purposes." Thus *Wolman* was controlling, White believed, even though the state was sending money directly to the schools to finance the evaluation of exams. White rejected any constitutional distinction between the two cases: "We decline to embrace a formalistic dichotomy that bears so little relationship either to common sense or to the realities of school finance."[240]

Dissenting justices Blackmun and Stevens disagreed and expressed concern that *Regan* allowed, for the first time, the direct subsidization of religious schools by the state.[241] Justice Blackmun chided the majority, particularly justices Stewart and Powell, and implied their votes with the majority were influenced by public opinion. "I am able to attribute this defection only to a concern about the continuing and emotional controversy," he argued, "and to a persuasion that a good faith attempt on the part of a state legislature is worth a nod of approval."[242] Blackmun failed to see how *Wolman* and *Regan* could be reconciled. For Blackmun, *Meek* and *Wolman* had largely settled the aid issue by determining that "direct aid to the educational function of religious schools necessarily advances the sectarian enterprise as a whole."[243] Justice Stevens, in a separate dissenting opinion, complained that the majority in *Regan* was "groping for a rationale" to justify aid. Instead, he suggested that the Court abandon "the entire enterprise of trying to justify various types of subsidies to nonpublic schools" but rather "resurrect" the "high and impregnable 'wall between church and state' constructed by the Framers of the First Amendment."[244]

In reflecting on the *Regan* decision, Pfeffer feared that it marked "the beginning of a new era" in which "accommodation rather than separation becomes the paramount concern in deciding church-state cases."[245] After a decade of helping shape the Court's opinion on the Establishment Clause as it related to aid toreligious schools, Pfeffer found the Court less willing to apply the no-aid principle by prohibiting aid to religious schools beyond the limits already set by previous cases.[246] The future seemed even more foreboding to Pfeffer with the prospect of judicial appointments by the conservative President Ronald Reagan in the 1980s.[247]

Mueller v. Allen

Described by Pfeffer as the "most serious assault upon the principles stated in the Court's decisions from *Lemon-DiCenso* on," the 1983 case of *Mueller v. Allen* opened wider the door for state funding of religious schools. At issue was a Minnesota law which provided a tuition-based income tax deduction to parents of children in elementary and secondary schools. The deduction was allowable irrespective of whether the children attended public or private schools.[248]

Pfeffer contended, in a brief of amicus curiae, that the deduction failed all three prongs of the *Lemon* test and was virtually indistinguishable from the tax credit ruled unconstitutional in *Nyquist*.[249] Again a slim majority of five justices found the Minnesota plan constitutional. In his majority decision, Justice William Rehnquist, the leading advocate on the Court of the narrow or accommodationist reading of the Establishment Clause, upheld the deduction's constitutionality. First, Rehnquist argued that the program had a valid secular purpose of "ensuring that the state's citizenry is well educated." Second, he concluded that the statute did not advance religion since the deduction was one of many allowed under Minnesota tax laws and, more significantly, it was available for educational expenses incurred by all parents "whether their students attended public or private schools."[250] For Pfeffer, Rehnquist's argument was chimerical, since almost no public schools charge tuition. Similarly, Justice Thurgood Marshall argued, on behalf of the dissenting justices, that the deduction was "constitutionally infirm," since a "tax deduction has a primary effect that advances religion if it is provided to offset expenditures which are not restricted to the secular activities of parochial schools."[251] Marshall also challenged the argument that the deduction was available to all parents. Rather he argued that the deduction was only available to "parents whose children attend schools that charge tuition, which are comprised almost entirely of sectarian schools." "More importantly," Marshall went on to conclude, "the assistance that flows to parochial schools as a result of the tax benefit is not restricted, and cannot be restricted, to the secular functions of those schools."[252]

By the 1980s, Pfeffer's activities slowed due to illness and age. Thus, *Mueller v. Allen* was the last major parochiaid case in which Pfeffer directly participated through either a brief of amicus curiae or brief for plaintiffs. Pfeffer proved to be right in placing high significance on the *Mueller* case. It has, consequently, provided the constitutional bases for a variety of subsequent tax deduction and credit plans, as well as current school choice voucher proposals.

AID TO RELIGIOUS HIGHER EDUCATION

Leo Pfeffer fought for the Court to adopt just as rigorous an application of the Establishment Clause to religiously affiliated colleges and universities as he did in cases involving aid to religiously affiliated elementary and secondary schools. Consequently, Leo Pfeffer was no less active in the aid to higher education battles than he had been in grade school cases. In part, he feared that if the Court adopted a less rigorous reading of the Establishment Clause in higher education cases, its rationales could be used to justify increased aid at the elementary and secondary level. He challenged aid to religious colleges and universities as a violation of the Establishment Clause, especially if the institution was "pervasively sectarian." Despite Pfeffer's advocacy, the Court allowed for a more porous wall between church and state when it came to public aid for religiously affiliated higher education.

Horace Mann v. Board of Public Works

In 1966, Pfeffer led a group of Maryland taxpayers and the Horace Mann League[253] challenging a $2.5 million grant by the state of Maryland to four religiously affiliated colleges for the construction of buildings.[254] Two of the colleges were affiliated with the Catholic Church. The two other schools were Protestant, with one affiliated with the Methodist Church and the other with the United Church of Christ. Pfeffer argued that it would violate the Establishment Clause for the state to fund colleges that engaged in religious activities, including religious education and worship. Pfeffer's legal brief emphasized the sectarian nature of the colleges by examining their close ties to their denominations. At the heart of Pfeffer's First Amendment challenge to the Maryland grants was his assertion that it seeks "to make the propagation of religion public business supported in part at taxpayers' expense."[255]

The Maryland Circuit Court focused on testimony and evidence that sought to determine the extent of sectarianism in the colleges. Evidence included an analysis of college catalogues and student handbooks as well as the testimony of faculty and administration. Much like his profile of religiously affiliated elementary and secondary schools adopted by the Supreme Court, Pfeffer introduced six criteria to determine the level of religious affiliation of colleges: (1) The stated purposes of the college; (2) the college personnel, which includes the governing board, the administrative officers, the faculty, and the student body; (3) the college's relationship with religious organizations and groups; (4) the place of religion in the college's program; (5) the result of "outcome" of the college program; (6) the work and image of the college in the community. While factual proof indicated the sectarian nature of some of the colleges, the circuit court judge ruled that the benefit to religion from the grants was incidental and the purpose and effect of the grants was sufficiently secular.[256]

Leo Pfeffer found a more favorable result upon appeal to the Maryland state Court of Appeals. Here the court gave significant weight to Pfeffer's criteria in determining the sectarianism of a college.[257] Consequently, the court determined that the grants to the two Catholic colleges and the grant to the Methodist college were unconstitutional aid to religion. Due to the marginal relationship Hood College had to the United Church of Christ, the court ruled its grant constitutional. In rendering its decision, the court noted the predominantly religious purpose and atmosphere of the Catholic colleges, the high-percentage of Catholic faculty and student body, the Catholic-oriented curriculum, and the ownership, control, and governance of the Catholic colleges by orders of nuns.[258] The schools made an unsuccessful attempt to appeal the decision to the U. S. Supreme Court.

Tilton v. Richardson

A similar case reached the nation's highest court just a few years later. *Tilton v. Richardson*[259] was decided on the same day as *Lemon v. Kurtzman* and proved to be the landmark decision involving aid to religiously affiliated higher education. The genesis of *Tilton* can be found in 1968 when fifteen Connecticut taxpayers challenged the constitutionality of Title I of the Higher Education Facilities Act of 1963. Title I provided federal grants for the construction of buildings on college campuses. The funds were available to religiously affiliated schools as long as they were used for secular instruction only. After a twenty-year period, however, the buildings could be used for any purpose. Under the Act, four Catholic colleges received funds for the construction of buildings on their campuses including a library, a fine arts building, a science building, and a language laboratory.[260]

Pfeffer served as lead counsel for the plaintiffs in a suit sponsored jointly by the American Civil Liberties Union and the American Jewish Congress. The plaintiffs' argument was primarily aimed at the Higher Education Facilities Act, claiming it represented an impermissible aid to religion in violation of the Establishment Clause defined in *Everson* and subsequent cases. In making their argument before the District Court, the plaintiffs scrutinized the Catholic colleges in light of the criteria set forth in the *Horace Mann* case.[261] The defendants argued that the *Horace Mann* criteria were too arbitrary and that the colleges were fulfilling their chartered function as recognized by the state. The Higher Education Facilities Act was defended as having a legitimate secular purpose and effect as well. These arguments found favorable reception in the District Court which held that the plaintiffs were overzealous in their application of the *Schempp* purpose and effect tests.[262]

Leo Pfeffer appealed the decision to the U.S. Supreme Court which agreed to hear oral arguments in June 1970. In his brief for appellants, Pfeffer first clarified that he did not oppose the construction grants to all church-related colleges. Rather, it was to those distinctly sectarian colleges, as identified by the Horace Mann criteria, whose receipt of funds raised constitutional questions. Pfeffer explained that "the issue before the Court is not whether church-related colleges may receive government funds, but whether sectarian colleges as we use the term, may do so." Funding pervasively sectarian higher education violated the no-aid principle no less than tax support for parochial schools according to Pfeffer. "The principle that government may not subsidize an institution whose purpose and practice is to propagate religion," Pfeffer asserted, dates back "to the earliest days of our history as a nation."[263]

Pfeffer argued that the Higher Education Facilities Act was not immune to constitutional challenge despite the condition that the construction grants may not subsidize the building of facilities used for religious purposes. If the reasoning behind the Act was accepted, Pfeffer argued, "then a church could receive a grant from the government provided it was to fix the 'furnace room.'"[264] Moreover, Pfeffer found the Act to violate the purpose and effect tests. For example, construction grants had a religious purpose if the buildings were to increase enrollment. Likewise, the primary effect was violated because of the religious orientation of the schools. It is "unrealistic, even at the college level," Pfeffer argued, "to create an island of secularity surrounded by a sea of sectarianism."[265] As he asserted in the aid to parochial school cases, Pfeffer found the Act violated the excessive entanglement test due to the state involvement required to ensure the secular use of the construction grants.[266] Pfeffer further argued that using compulsory tax funds for religious purposes was equally violative of the Free Exercise Clause. In making this argument, Pfeffer likened the educational grants to the Virginia Assessment Bill against which James Madison fought in colonial Virginia. A "large part of the struggle for religious freedom," Pfeffer concluded, "was a struggle against compulsory taxation" for religious purposes.[267]

In ruling for a 5-to-4 majority, Chief Justice Warren Burger upheld the constitutionality of construction grants, although he struck down the provision opening the buildings to sectarian use after twenty years. He found the purpose of the Higher Education Facilities Act: to assist institutions of higher education in accommodating the rapidly growing numbers of youth who aspire to a higher education, to be sufficiently secular. He also rejected the argument that the primary effect of the Act was to advance religion: "The Act itself was carefully drafted to ensure that the federally subsidized facilities would be devoted to the secular and not the religious function of the recipient institutions."[268] Burger further questioned the use of Pfeffer's "hypothetical profile" rather than the actual facts of the case to determine constitutionality. Arguing that the colleges in question to have an "atmosphere of academic freedom rather than religious indoctrination,"[269] Burger drew a number of distinctions between religious colleges, on the one hand, and religious elementary and secondary schools, on the other:

> There is substance to the contention that college students are less impressionable and less susceptible to religious indoctrination. Common observation would seem to support that view, and Congress may well have entertained it. . . . Furthermore, by their very nature, college and postgraduate courses tend to limit the opportunities for sectarian influence by virtue of their own internal disciplines. Many church-related colleges are characterized by a high degree of academic freedom and seek to evoke free and critical responses from their students.[270]

Based on this assessment, Burger held that the colleges did not risk the "intensive government surveillance" that would result on the elementary and secondary level. Thus, the "resulting entanglements between government and religion" were lessened.[271] Neither does the college setting promote the political divisiveness as does lower educational settings, Burger held, due to the "diversity" of the "student constituency" which "is not local but diverse and widely dispersed."[272] Burger's final remarks were addressed to the free exercise claims. These he rejected because of the lack of coercion "directed at the practice or exercise of their religious beliefs." He also found the tax moneys expended to be indistinguishable from the loan of textbooks in *Allen* or the tax exemption granted in *Walz*.[273]

Describing the majority's decision as a "radical departure from Madison's Remonstrance," Justice William Douglas's dissent decried the move away from the traditional understanding of the First Amendment.[274] He, like Pfeffer, believed the broad prohibitions of *Everson* should be controlling in *Tilton*. His contention, as was Pfeffer's in numerous aid cases, was that money could be diverted to or freed for religious purposes: "The parochial school operates on one budget. Money not spent for one purpose becomes available for other purposes. Thus the fact that there are no religious observances in federally financed facilities is not controlling because required religious observances will take place in other buildings."[275] Thus, Douglas echoed the fundamental convictions of Leo Pfeffer regarding state funding of religious institutions. No matter how cloaked in a secular purpose, funds, other than safety or welfare benefits, are unconstitutional because the government is aiding or advancing religion. Pfeffer found this strict prohibition to be not only historically relevant but also served to protect against compulsory taxation for religious purposes.

Pfeffer would later write that while a "reasonable" argument could be made in support of Chief Justice Burgers' distinction between colleges and elementary/secondary schools, "there is, nevertheless, considerable difficulty with this line of reasoning." Pfeffer was unconvinced, for example, that college students were necessarily any less vulnerable to religious indoctrination. Neither was he satisfied that religious inculcation would be relegated to religious or other non-publicly funded buildings on campus. "It hardly makes sense," he concluded, "to predicate constitutionality on the fact that the nonsectarian Dr. Jekyll controls and manages the science building but the Reverend Mr. Hyde is in charge of the building in which philosophy or history is taught."[276]

Tilton remained the landmark decision involving aid to religious higher education, despite efforts by Pfeffer and other separationist attorneys to persuade the Court to overrule its decision. Two years after *Tilton* was handed down, the Court ruled that the state of South Carolina could issue bonds to the Baptist College of Charleston for capital improvements as long as the buildings were not used for religious instruction or worship.[277] Despite the close denominational control of the school, the Court determined that it was not pervasively sectarian since non-Baptists served on the faculty and there was not a religious requirement for admission. The Court found the Baptist

College of Charleston to be similar to the Catholic colleges in *Tilton*. "There is no basis to conclude that the College's operations are oriented significantly towards sectarian rather than secular education," the Court concluded.[278]

Roemer v. Board of Public Works

In 1976, Pfeffer filed a brief of amicus curiae challenging a Maryland law that would provide unspecified annual subsidies to private colleges in the state as long as the colleges were not pervasively sectarian and used the funds for only secular purposes.[279] Pervasively sectarian institutions, such as those exclusively awarding theological degrees, were ineligible for program funds. Eligible schools had to file annual reports that demonstrated the funds were used exclusively for secular purposes. Five colleges received $525,000 from the program, prompting a lawsuit challenging its constitutionality. Despite the fact that the funds were given annually and that the schools were given relative freedom in utilizing them, the majority found the program constitutional. Justice Blackmun, writing a plurality opinion, found the recipient schools to sufficiently distinguish their religious and secular education. The Court also found the nature of the institutions mitigated the need for ongoing and pervasive surveillance from the state. Excessive entanglement was unlikely to result, according to Blackmun, because "there is no danger, or at least a substantially reduced danger, that an ostensibly secular activity—the study of biology, the learning of a foreign language, an athletic event—will actually be infused with religious content or significance."[280]

To Pfeffer's dismay, *Roemer v. Board of Public Works* went well beyond the holding in *Tilton* and seemed difficult to reconcile with either the primary effect or excessive entanglement prongs of the *Lemon* test. Direct subsidies to pervasively religious colleges had been approved with little guarantee the funds would not advance the religious mission of the schools. Pfeffer would later speculate that the decision was a compromise between a contingent on the Court that did not want to abandon the *Lemon* test and those that would allow more public aid for religious schools.[281]

Pfeffer objected to the legal reasoning on which the *Tilton*, *Hunt*, and *Roemer* decisions were based, finding it at odds with court precedent and the Establishment Clause's no-aid requirement. Moreover, he found the constitutional safeguards to be largely indefensible:

> To an objective observer, one not influenced by either pro- or anti-religious predilections, the reasoning underlying the *Roemer* opinion and to a somewhat lesser but nevertheless substantial extent the *Tilton* and *Hunt* decisions, if taken seriously, approach sheer nonsense. Nothing in this decision prevents a sectarian college from transferring to the chapel account the amount budgeted for

> building a new gymnasium and simultaneously seeking federal funds to finance the construction of a gymnasium, and in all of them the Court held that this did not matter. The net result is to require church-related colleges that might seek government funds to engage the services not only of a competent lawyer but of a public accountant as well.[282]

The Court's willingness to extend greater leeway in the granting of state funds for religiously affiliated colleges and universities than to elementary and secondary schools was based on the nature of higher education and the differences in age and impressionability of the students. Pfeffer likewise recognized these differences and would not disallow all aid to church-related colleges.[283] Yet, unlike the Supreme Court, Pfeffer would bar all aid to colleges that manifested a pervasively religious atmosphere or had a distinct religious mission. For Pfeffer, the high wall of separation commanded by the Establishment Clause of the First Amendment applied no less to institutions of higher learning than to elementary and secondary schools.

THE ACCOMMODATIONIST ADVANCE

The emerging accommodationist sympathies of the Court worried Pfeffer as his career drew to a close. With the advent of the 1980s, the Burger Court "began handing down decisions pointing in the direction exactly opposite to that of the preceding decade." For Pfeffer, this was due in large part to Justice Lewis F. Powell's "conversion from absolutism to accommodationism." Pfeffer claimed he experienced a "period of despondency" fearful that the Court would undo all that he and other strict separationists "had strived for in the seventies would be vitiated case by case in the eighties." Pfeffer's "period of acute despondency" ended, however, when he realized that much of what he had accomplished had not been undone. The Court continued to strike down tax credits for parochial school tuition, banned funding of religious instruction, and continued to take a dim view of school-sponsored religious exercise. In 1985, Pfeffer would write optimistically that "the situation is not as tragic as we strict separationists have thought it to be."[284]

Pfeffer had further reason for optimism after the Court handed down the *Grand Rapids School District v. Ball*[285] and *Aguillard v. Felton*[286] decisions in 1985. Grand Rapids involved a "Shared-Time" program that paid private school teachers to teach secular subjects in private school classrooms leased by the state. It also involved a "Community Education" program where public school teachers were sent into private schools to teach certain secular subjects. In a five-to-four ruling, the U.S. Supreme Court ruled that both programs violated the Establishment Clause by having the primary effect of advancing religion. Due to the pervasively sectarian nature of the schools, the Court determined that the teacher might "subtly or overtly" proselytize students in the institution's faith at taxpayer expense. State-supported secular instruction in sectarian schools would also create the impression that the state endorses religion. And by saving religious schools the cost of some secular instruction, the state in effect funded religious schools.[287]

In *Aguilar v. Felton*, the Court invalidated, in another five-to-four decision, a New York plan to pay public school teachers to offer remedial education in parochial schools. This plan put in place safeguards to protect against the advancement of religion, but the majority found that it violated the excessive entanglement prong of the *Lemon* Test nonetheless. The Court concluded that "the scope and duration of New York City's Title I program would require a permanent and pervasive state presence in the sectarian schools receiving aid."[288] The Court was closely divided, but Pfeffer no doubt felt vindicated by the outcome of these decisions. Pfeffer's past arguments that the religious context of the school was significant as the impressionability of students and the risk of excessive entanglement between church and state were key factors in the Court's reasoning.

It would not be until after his death in 1993 that Leo Pfeffer's worst fears would be realized, at least on the aid to religious schools front. An increasingly accommodationist Court began to undermine if not overturn some of the key aid decisions of the Pfeffer era. Increasingly critical of the *Lemon* Test, especially its excessive entanglement prong, as too restrictive a barrier to state aid, the emerging accommodationist majority on the Court adopted instead a neutrality or equal treatment approach to aid cases. This test essentially holds that public funding of religious institutions is constitutionally satisfactory as long as "neutral criteria" are used in determining eligibility for the aid.

The strict separationist or no-aid interpretation drew increased criticism not just on the Court but in scholarly legal circles as well. Robert Cord not only challenged the separationist historical narrative but also he and other critics claimed that the Court's adherence to a strict separation of church and state, as applied through the no-aid and *Lemon* tests, have led to decisions that are inconsistent and restrictive of religious freedom. Taking aim in particular at the Court's aid decisions during the 1970s, critics such as Jesse Choper similarly claimed:

> For example, a provision of therapeutic and diagnostic health services to parochial school pupils by public employees is invalid if provided *in* the parochial school, but not if offered at a neutral site, even if in a mobile unit adjacent to the parochial school. Reimbursement to parochial schools for the expense of administering teacher-prepared tests required by state law is invalid, but the state may reimburse parochial schools for the expense of administering state-prepared

> tests. The state may lend school textbooks to parochial school pupils because, the Court has explained, the books can be checked in advance for religious content and are "self-policing"; but the state may not lend other seemingly self-policing instructional items such as tape recorders and maps. The state may pay the cost of bus transportation to parochial schools, which the Court has ruled are "permeated" with religion; but the state is forbidden to pay for field trip transportation visits. . . . I hope that these illustrations are sufficiently striking to demonstrate the unpredictability of the Court's approach.[289]

To Pfeffer's detractors, these inconsistencies lie in the faulty logic of the strict separationist position, especially as it is adjudicated through the no-aid and *Lemon* tests. The separationist approach drew Chief Justice Rehnquist's ire as well in his *Wallace v. Jaffree* dissent when he declared that "the *Everson* 'wall' has proved all but useless as a guide to sound constitutional adjudication."[290] As a result, Leo Pfeffer was implicated in the seemingly unprincipled and ad hoc nature of these judgments.

Leo Pfeffer believed any incongruity among the Court's decisions could be partially blamed on the political pressures on the Court. Vocal discontent regarding the extent of the Court's prohibitions of aid to parochial schools in *Meek v. Pittenger*[291] played a role in the complex and confusing case of *Wolman v. Walter*.[292] In *Meek*, the Court struck down all forms of auxiliary and diagnostic services as well as instructional materials and equipment provided by a Pennsylvania statute. By contrast, the Court in *Wolman* upheld specific diagnostic services and off-campus services such as counseling and remedial instruction. Along with political pressures were the sheer number of parochiaid proposals, many of which were written in an attempt to circumvent the strictures of the three-part *Lemon* test. Described by Pfeffer as "a chess game with the Constitution," proponents of religious school aid regularly submitted slightly altered statutes after previous proposals had been found unconstitutional.[293] Furthermore, Pfeffer explained the Court's inconsistencies on the basis of its changing makeup in the late 1970s. Some of the new members of the Court interpreted the prohibitions of the Establishment Clause less strictly than their predecessors. Writing in the early 1980s, Pfeffer feared that the Court had embarked on a new period in which "accommodation" as opposed to "separation" had become the preeminent constitutional consideration.[294]

While Pfeffer found greater continuity than discontinuity in the Court's Establishment Clause decisions, his arguments did not always enjoy support from a majority of the justices. Pfeffer's application of the no-aid principle was consistent. During the numerous religious school aid cases during the 1970s, Pfeffer unfailingly challenged any aid beyond reimbursement of transportation costs and the loan of secular textbooks for children in religious schools.[295] Responding to Justice William Rehnquist's dissenting opinion in *Wallace v. Jaffree*, Pfeffer stated: "Thus, what Justice Rehnquist has shown is that if the Court had only always ruled in my favor, its position would have been fully consistent. I doubt that this is the lesson Justice Rehnquist would want us to draw."[296] Furthermore, Pfeffer insisted that inconsistencies did not lead to the repudiation of the broad interpretation of the First Amendment as an appropriate adjudicative norm. It was not the theory behind the Amendment, nor the tests the Court utilized, Pfeffer argued, but rather the political pressures and competing ideologies upon and within the Court that created the "tortuous journey" the Court had taken in deciding religious school aid cases.[297]

Some scholars have recently challenged the notion that the Burger and Rehnquist Courts' Establishment Clause rulings have been inconsistent or that any consistency would be necessarily attributable to the separationist philosophy. Rather, it was the Court's "fact and context based approach" particularly of the less ideological swing voters on the Court that explains the seeming differences not only between religious exercise and aid cases but also among the aid cases themselves. During the Burger Court, it was Blackmun, Powell, and Stewart, who, according to historian Emma Long, "tended to focus on the facts of each case" and seemed to be more concerned with "consistency in approach rather than results."[298] This, she argues, was a similar approach of Justices O'Connor and Kennedy during the Rehnquist Court who often were the swing voters in civil liberties cases. Indeed, Long quotes Justice Powell in his *Wolman v. Walter* opinion in which he explains that the Court's decisions "have sought to establish principles that preserve the cherished safeguard of the Establishment Clause without resort to blind absolutism."[299] The context and facts of each case were central to understanding aid decisions as well, according to Long. Rather than an inflexible tool that led to incongruous decisions, the *Lemon* Test was a "balancing test" to which the unique facts of each case could be applied.[300]

SUMMARY

Leo Pfeffer's involvement in landmark cases concerning religious exercises in the public schools reflects his consistent application of the Establishment Clause's separation doctrine. Pfeffer believed that any sponsorship or endorsement of religious exercises by the state was unconstitutional. Thus, Pfeffer found public school prayer and Bible reading, as well as religious education, gave the imprimatur of state endorsement to majoritarian religious practices. He also believed the First Amendment had been set in place to free the religious minority from choosing between his or her faith and acceptance in a majoritarian religious culture. Consequently, Pfeffer argued before the courts that public school-sponsored religious exercises and education did not only violate the separation of church and state but also the free exercise rights of religious minorities. In doing so, Pfeffer provided psychological and other social scientific data to prove the harmful and divisive nature of state-endorsed public school religious exercises.

Pfeffer was extensively involved in challenging state aid to religious schools as well. He served in numerous parochiaid cases as counsel, strategist, or author of a friend-of-the-court brief arguing against the constitutionality of aid beyond health and welfare benefits. Utilizing the no-aid dictum of the *Everson v. Board of Education* case as well as the *Lemon* test, Pfeffer was largely successful in challenging aid to religious schools beyond transportation costs and textbooks.

Pfeffer's challenges to aid to religiously affiliated higher education indicate again his strict application of the Establishment Clause. He contested public aid to any college manifesting a meaningful religious orientation. However, he was less successful in blocking aid to religious institutions of higher learning than he was on the elementary and secondary levels. In *Tilton v. Richardson* and *Roemer v. Board of Works of Maryland* the Court approved funds to church-related colleges despite the religious atmosphere of the institutions in question. The decisions, however, did not necessarily indicate the Court's adoption of a new interpretation of the Establishment Clause. Rather, the Court applied the *Lemon* test less stridently than would have Pfeffer. A legitimate secular purpose and effect, mandated by the broad interpretation of the First Amendment, remained the Court's constitutional evaluative tool.

Tangible evidence of Pfeffer's influence on the Court can be found in several Court decisions. Justice Felix Frankfurter, in *McCollum v. Board of Education*,[301] adopted Pfeffer's social scientific evidence of the effect school-sponsored religious education and exercises had on children of minority faiths. Likewise, the Court adopted Pfeffer's profile of a religiously affiliated college in cases involving state aid to religious higher education. In *Epperson v. Arkansas*,[302] Pfeffer filed the only brief arguing against the constitutionality of an anti-evolution statute based on Establishment Clause grounds. The Court's subsequent ruling of unconstitutionality was based on the Establishment Clause and followed closely Pfeffer's argumentation.

Not all of Pfeffer's influence is as clearly identifiable. Often the court's reasoning followed closely to that which Pfeffer argued, but without citing him explicitly. When the Court, for example, introduced the purpose and effect tests of what would become the *Lemon* test in *Abington v. Schempp*,[303] it echoed what Pfeffer had been arguing in his legal briefs; namely, that the government's ends must be secular and, in achieving them, its means must be secular as well.

Personnel changes on the U.S. Supreme Court over the past thirty years have led to a more accommodationist shift in its aid decisions as a slim majority of justices adopted a neutrality or equal treatment approach particularly in aid cases. As a result, the Court has reversed some decisions of the Pfeffer era and has marginalized some of the strictures of the Establishment Clause approach Pfeffer advocated. This trend in part was based upon a contested perception that the separationist philosophy led to inconsistent decision making by the Court. Others have argued that the strict separationist philosophy as well as the separationist decisions of the Court during the Pfeffer-era manifested hostility to religion and have marginalized religion in the public square. Such claims are difficult to reconcile with Leo Pfeffer's commitment to rigorous free exercise protections. His broad reading of the Free Exercise Clause will be the focus of the next chapter.

NOTES

1. Pfeffer's concept of neutrality was based upon his belief that Establishment Clause guaranteed a secular state that neither aided nor inhibited religion.

2. See "The Establishment Clause: An Absolutist's Defense," *Notre Dame Journal of Law, Ethics and Public Policy* 4 (1990): 699–729.

3. *Everson v. Board of Education*, 330 U.S. 1 (1947) at 31–32.

4. Pfeffer played a major role in forming two PEARLs. The New York Committee on Public Education and Religious Liberty and the National Coalition for Public Education and Religious Liberty. Members of the National PEARL included: American Association of School Administrators, American Civil Liberties Union, American Ethical Union, American Humanist Association, American Jewish Congress, Americans United for Separation of Church and State, Anti-Defamation League of B'nai B'rith, Baptist Joint Committee on Public Affairs, Board of Church and Society of the United Methodist Church, Central Conference of American Rabbis, National Association of Catholic Laity, National Council of Jewish Women, National Education Association, Preserve our Public Schools, Union of American Hebrew Congregations, and the Unitarian Universalist Association. PEARL provided Pfeffer greater flexibility than his role with the American Jewish Congress to organize and lead broad coalitions of religious, educational, and civil liberties organizations against parochiaid measures.

5. Ivers, *To Build A Wall*, 185; In an earlier study analyzing church-state litigation, Frank Sorauf concluded that "Leo Pfeffer was the dominant, driving force among separationist attorneys in these cases and in the entire universe of church-state litigation in the 1950s and 1960s." Sorauf, *The Wall of Separation*, 159.

6. See Chapter 2.

7. The significance of public education to Leo Pfeffer was evident in his response to its critics: "Now this is grave (attacks on public education) not only because the public schools hold a precious spot in our tradition, but because the

principle upon which the public schools system is based is the principle upon which our entire democracy is based, and an attack upon the principle of public education is an attack upon the principle as it relates to our entire democratic way of life"; Pfeffer, "Church and State, 33.

8. Pfeffer, "Religion, Education, and the Constitution," 1.

9. Pfeffer, *Church, State, and Freedom*, 321.

10. R. Freeman Butts, *The American Tradition in Religion and Education* (Boston, MA: Beacon Press, 1950); for the early development of public education and their democratizing role, see Johann N. Neem, *Democracy's Schools: The Rise of Public Education in America* (Baltimore: Johns Hopkins University Press, 2017).

11. Thomas Jefferson's "Bill for the More General Diffusion of Knowledge," quoted in Pfeffer, *Church, State, and Freedom*, 327; see also Robert M. Healey, *Jefferson on Religion and Public Education* (New Haven, CT: Yale University Press, 1962); a recent study over the tensions over the role of religion in the development of the public education, seek Colin Macleod, *Have a Little Faith: Religion, Democracy, and the American Public School* (Chicago: University of Chicago Press, 2016).

12. Horace Mann, "Twelfth Annual Report to the Massachusetts Board of Education" (1848), printed in the *Republic and the School: Horace Mann on the Education of Free Men*, ed. Lawrence A. Cremin (New York: Teachers College, Columbia University, 1957), 77.

13. Miller and Flowers, *Toward Benevolent Neutrality*, 1: 263.

14. See Tracy Fessenden, "The Nineteenth-Century Bible Wars the Separation of Church and State," *Church History* 75 (December 2005): 784–811.

15. By 1870, most state constitutions prohibited funds for parochial schools and most state courts ruled correspondingly; James E. Wood, Jr., "Religion and Education in American Church–State Relations," in *Religion, the State and Education*, ed. James E. Wood, Jr. (Waco, TX: J.M. Dawson Institute of Church–State Studies, Baylor University, 1984), 30.

16. Pfeffer, *Church, State, and Freedom*, 335.

17. See Miller, *Piety along the Potomac*; see also Kevin M. Kruse, *One Nation Under God: How Corporate America Invented Christian America* (New York: Basic Books, 2015).

18. *Cantwell v. Connecticut*, 310 U.S. 296 (1940); *Everson v. Board of Education*, 330 U.S. 1 (1947).

19. Miller and Flowers, *Toward Benevolent Neutrality*, 1: 263.

20. Pfeffer, *Church, State, and Freedom*, 369.

21. *McCollum v. Board of Education*, 333 U.S. 203 (1948).

22. Pfeffer, "An Autobiographical Sketch," 492–93. See Vashti McCollum, *One Woman's Fight* (Boston, MA: Beacon Press, 1951).

23. *Pierce v. Society of Sisters*, 269 U.S. 510 (1925).

24. Paul G. Kauper, "*Church, State, and Freedom*: A Review," *Michigan Law Review* 52 (1954): 842.

25. Leo Pfeffer, "Preliminary Report on Released Time," Memorandum to Alexander Pekelis, October 31, 1945, p. 3; "Legal and Constitutional Aspects

of Released Time," Paper presented at Conference on Religious Instruction and the Public School, National Jewish Community Relations Advisory Council and Synagogue Council of America, New York City, November 11, 1946.

26. Ibid.

27. Brief for Synagogue Council for America, et al. as Amici Curiae Supporting Appellants at 12, *McCollum v. Board of Education*, 333 U.S. 203 (1948) (No. 90) (hereinafter *McCollum* Brief).

28. In *Church, State, and Freedom*, Pfeffer devoted significant attention to the released time issue and the *McCollum* case. This included excerpts from trial testimony and exhibits; see *Church, State, and Freedom*, 401–10.

29. 330 U.S. 1 at 15.

30. *McCollum* Brief at 19.

31. Ibid., at 22.

32. Ibid., at 40.

33. Ibid., at 36.

34. Pfeffer, *Church, State, and Freedom*, 389.

35. *McCollum* Brief at 3.

36. Leo Pfeffer, "Public School Sectarianism and the Jewish Child: A Report of Experiences." Paper prepared for the Commission on Law and Social Action of the American Jewish Congress, May 1957, 2–4.

37. *Everson v. Board of Education*, 333 U.S. 1 (1947).

38. *McCollum v. Board of Education*, 333 U.S. 203 at 209–10.

39. Ibid., at 227.

40. Ibid., at 231.

41. Cohen, *Jews in Christian America*, 143; Frommer, "The American Jewish Congress," 211.

42. See for example, Kauper, "*Church, State, and Freedom*," 829–49; Leo Pfeffer, "Released Time and Religious Liberty: A Reply," *Michigan Law Review* 53 (1954): 91–98; and Paul G. Kauper, "Released Time and Religious Liberty: A Further Reply," *Michigan Law Review* 53 (1954): 223–35; Justice Black's separationist history of the Establishment Clause faced criticism from some constitutional scholars during this period, including Erwin N. Griswold's, "Absolute is in the Dark," *Utah Law Review* 8 (1963): 167–82.

43. Corwin, "The Supreme Court as National School Board," 16.

44. Ibid., 21.

45. Donald E. Boles, *The Two Swords: Commentaries and Cases in Religion and Education* (Ames, IA: Iowa State University Press, 1967), 44; see especially articles in *Law and Contemporary Problems* 14 (Winter 1949).

46. Virgil Blum, "Review of *Church, State, and Freedom* by Leo Pfeffer," *The Georgetown Law Journal* 43 (1954–55): 147.

47. "We do not consider, as indeed we could not, school programs not before us which, though colloquially characterized as 'released time,' present situations differing in aspects that may well be constitutionally crucial"; 333 U.S. 203 at 231.

48. *Zorach v. Clausen*, 343 U.S. 306 (1952).

49. Pfeffer, *Church, State, and Freedom*, 417–29.

50. *Zorach v. Clausen*, 198 Misc. N.Y. 631 (1950) at 637–40; Ivers, *To Build a Wall*, 88–89.

51. Brief for Appellant at 30, *Zorach v. Clauson*, 343 U.S. 306 (1952) (No. 431).

52. Ibid. at 59.

53. *McCollum* Brief at 18.

54. Ibid. at 34.

55. Ibid. at 63.

56. 343 U.S. 306 at 315.

57. Ibid. at 313–14.

58. See "A Matter of Tradition," *Commonweal* (16 May 1952).

59. 343 U.S. 306 at 317.

60. "Editorial: Time Off for Religion," *New Times York* (April 30, 1952), in *Religious Liberty In the Supreme Court: The Cases That Define the Debate over Church and State*, ed. Terry Eastland (Grand Rapids, MI: William B. Eerdmans Publishing Co., 1993), 116–17.

61. *McCollum* Brief at 312.

62. Leo Pfeffer, "Religion, the Public Schools, and the Jewish Community: A Thirteen Year Review." Paper presented at Conference of Synagogue Council of America and National Jewish Community Relations Advisory Council, New York City, December 13, 1959, p. 10.

63. Quoted in Pfeffer, *God, Caesar and the Constitution*, 221.

64. See, especially, Edward J. Larson, *Summer for the Gods: The Scopes Trial and America's Continuing Debate over Science and Religion* (New York: Basic Books, 2006).

65. *Epperson v. Arkansas*, 393 U.S. 97 (1968) at 98–99.

66. 393 U.S. 97 (1968).

67. Leo Pfeffer, "Brief of Amicus Curiae," *Epperson v. Arkansas*, 393 U.S. 97 (1968): 4–15; "An Autobiographical Sketch," 512.

68. 393 U.S. 97 at 106.

69. Ibid., at 106–07.

70. Ibid., at 108. The case was a bit of an anomaly in that the evolution bill, on the books since 1928, had never been enforced. Moreover, Susan Epperson, by the time the case reached the Supreme Court, had moved to another state. See, also, Jonathan L. Thorndike, *Epperson v. Arkansas: The Evolution-Creationism Debate* (Berkeley Heights, N.J.: Enslow Publishers, 1999).

71. 393 U.S. 97 at 103.

72. *Edwards v. Aguillard*, 482 U.S. 578 (1987).

73. Ibid., at 591.

74. Ibid., Leo Pfeffer, *Religion, the State, and the Burger Court* (Buffalo, NY: Prometheus Books, 1984), 73–74. A more recent manifestation of the creationism debate is the Intelligent Design movement. This theory claims that the nature of biological life has been designed and ordered by a supernatural intelligence. Advocates of this perspective argue that their claims are rooted in scientific inquiry and make no religious claims regarding the intelligence behind the natural world. As a result, Intelligent Design proponents contend that it would be constitutional to include ID

as a competing theory to evolution in biology courses. Nevertheless, this theory has been met with skepticism by most scientists and a number of scholars and jurists as well. See Matthew J. Braver, Barbara Forrest, and Steve G. Gey, "Is It Science Yet?: Intelligent Design, Creationism, and the Constitution," *Washington University Law Quarterly* 83 (2005): 1–149; see also *Kitzmiller v. Dover Area School District*, 400 F. Supp. 2d 707 (M.D. Pa. 2005).

75. Ivers, *To Build a Wall*, 116–18.

76. *Doremus v. Board of Education*, 342 U.S. 429 (1952).

77. *Tudor v. Board of Education* 348 U.S. 816 (1954).

78. Pfeffer, "An Autobiographical Sketch," 513; see also Leo Pfeffer, "The Gideons' March on the Schools," *Congress Weekly* 20 (October 5, 1953): 7–9.

79. Pfeffer, *God, Caesar, and the Constitution*, 195.

80. Ibid., 194.

81. Cohen, *Jews in Christian America*, 190; Pfeffer was initially hesitant to push the Doremus case as well feeling that the timing and nature of the case was not right; Ivers, *To Build a Wall*, 16–17.

82. See Richard B. Dierenfield, *Religion in American Public Schools* (Washington, DC: Public Affairs Press, 1962) and Bruce J. Dierenfield, *The Battle Over School Prayer: How Engel v. Vitale Changed America* (Lawrence: University Press of Kansas, 2007).

83. The text of the prayer was: "Almighty God, we acknowledge our dependence upon Thee, and we beg Thy blessings upon us, our parents, our teachers and our Country."

84. Pfeffer, *Church, State, and Freedom*, 461–62.

85. Quoted in *Church, State, and Freedom*, 462.

86. *Engel v. Vitale*, 370 U.S. 421 (1962) at 423; for extended discussion on the school prayer issue and the *Engel* case, see John Herbert Laubach, *School Prayers: Congress, the Courts, and the Public Schools* (Washington, DC: Public Affairs Press, 1969); Robert S. Alley, *School Prayer: The Court, the Congress, and the First Amendment* (Buffalo, NY: Prometheus Books, 1994); William O. Douglas, *The Bible and the Schools* (Boston, MA: Little, Brown and Company, 1966); Robert Michaelsen, *Piety in the Public School: Trends and Issues in the Relationship between Religion in the Public School in the United States* (New York: Macmillan Company, 1970); and William K. Muir, Jr. *Prayer in the Public Schools: Law and Attitude Change* (Chicago: University of Chicago Press, 1967).

87. Pfeffer, *Church, State, and Freedom*, 463.

88. Ivers, *To Build a Wall*, 126.

89. Quoted in Cohen, *Jews in Christian America*, 167.

90. This argument was based on his brief and the Court's decision in *Torcaso v. Watkins*; see Chapter 2.

91. Engel Brief at 9–10.

92. Ibid., at 11.

93. Ibid., at 12–13.

94. Ibid., at 19–21; in stating this position, Pfeffer utilized his study of the effects of religious exercises in the public schools on Jewish children he had developed for the *McCollum* case; see "Public School Sectarianism and the Jewish Child," 2–4.

95. Engel Brief at 17.

96. Leo Pfeffer, "Court, Constitution, and Prayer," *Rutgers Law Review* 16 (Summer 1962): 747.

97. Engel Brief at 23.

98. Pfeffer, "Court, Constitution, and Prayer," 750.

99. *Engel v. Vitale*, 370 U.S. 41 (1962) at 425.

100. Ibid., at 431.

101. Ibid., at 430–32.

102. Ibid., at 436.

103. Discussion of the nature of Pfeffer's legal activity in these various capacities can be found in Ivers, *To Build a Wall*; Cohen, *Jews in Christian America*; and Sorauf, *The Wall of Separation.*

104. Quoted in Pfeffer, *Church, State, and Freedom*, 466.

105. Leo Pfeffer, "State Sponsored Prayer," *Commonweal* 76 (July 27, 1962): 417–19.

106. "Editorial: To Our Jewish Friends," *America* 107 (September 1, 1962): 665–66

107. Cohen, *Jews in Christian America*, 172.

108. Quoted in Pfeffer, *Church, State, and Freedom*, 468.

109. Cohen, *Jews in Christian America*, 185.

110. Sarna and Dalin, *Religion and State in the American*, 250–51.

111. *Abington v. Schempp*, 374 U.S. 203 (1963).

112. James E. Wood, Jr., "Religion and America's Public Schools," in *Reflections on Church and State*, ed. James E. Wood, Jr. (Waco, TX: J.M. Dawson Institute of Church–State Studies, 1995), 132–33; for a comprehensive discussion of the issue of Bible reading in the public schools published during this period, see Donald E. Boles, *The Bible, Religion, and the Public Schools* (Ames: Iowa State University Press, 1964).

113. Ivers, *To Build a Wall*, 131.

114. Schempp Brief. at 11–15.

115. Ibid., at 16–17.

116. Ibid., at 37.

117. *Abington v. Schempp*, 374 U.S. 203 at 216.

118. Ibid., at 222.

119. Ibid., at 222, 217.

120. Ibid., at 223.

121. Schempp Brief at 17.

122. 374 U.S. 203 at 222.

123. In *Walz v. Tax Commission* (397 U.S. 664 (1970)), it was argued that a statute must not only have a secular purpose and a primary effect that neither advances nor inhibits religion, but also it must not foster "excessive entanglement" between church and state. Excessive entanglement was added to the purpose and effect tests of *Schempp* to form the three-part *Lemon* test that was first fully applied in the *Lemon v. Kurtzman* case involving public aid to religious schools in 1971. Naturally Pfeffer found the *Lemon* test to be an appropriate rearticulation of the no-aid test of *Everson*

and consistent with his understanding of the Establishment Clause since it reflected much of the constitutional considerations he put before the Court.

124. Ivers, *To Build A Wall*, 113.

125. *Torcaso v. Watkins*, 306 U.S. 488 (1961); see chapter Three.

126. Leo Pfeffer, "From Religious Monism to Pluralism," *Congress Bi-Weekly* 31 (February 10, 1964): 7; "A Momentous Year in Church and State: 1963," *Journal of Church and State* 6 (Winter 1964): 36.

127. Pfeffer, *God, Caesar, and the Constitution*, 213–15.

128. Leo Pfeffer, "The First Amendment to the United States Constitution with Respect to Bible Reading and Prayers in Public Schools (H.J. Res. 693)." Statement and Testimony submitted to U.S. House Committee on the Judiciary, Washington, DC (April 30, 1964): 2–9; see also Leo Pfeffer, "The Becker Amendment," *Journal of Church and State* 6 (Autumn 1964): 344–51.

129. Pfeffer, *Church, State, and Freedom*, 477.

130. *Chamberlin v. Dade County Board of Public Instruction*, 307 U.S. 402 (1964).

131. Quoted in Ivers, *To Build a Wall*, 134.

132. Leo Pfeffer to Sol Rabkin, August 17, 1960, Leo Pfeffer Papers, Box 12, Folder 1, George Arendts Research Library, Syracuse University.

133. Jurisdictional Statement at 18–20, *Chamberlin v. Dade County Board of Public Instruction*, 377 U.S. 402 (1964).

134. Leo Pfeffer, "Federal Funds for Parochial Schools? No," *Notre Dame Lawyer* 37 (March 1962): 309–22.

135. Quoted in Pfeffer, *Church, State, and Freedom*, 148.

136. Hamburger, *Separation of Church and State*; and Green, "'Blaming Blaine'; see also See Miller and Flowers, *Toward Benevolent Neutrality*, 617; Edwin Gaustad, "Church, State, and Education in Historical Perspective," in *Religion, the State and Education*, ed. James E. Wood, Jr. (Waco, TX: J.M. Dawson Institute of Church–State Studies, Baylor University Press, 1984), 20; Wood, "Religion and Education in American," 27–28; for a history of parochial schools, see Harold A. Buetow, *Of Singular Benefit: The Story of Catholic Education in the United States* (New York: Macmillan Company, 1970) and Neil G. McCluskey, *Catholic Education in America* (New York: Teacher's College, Columbia University, 1964).

137. Hamburger, *Separation of Church and State*, 287.

138. *Mitchell v. Helms*, 530 U.S. 793 (2000) at 829.

139. R. R. Palmer and Joel Colton, *A History of the Modern World Since 1815* (New York: Alfred A. Knopf, 1984), 598–601; Marc D. Stern, "Blaine Amendments, Anti-Catholicism, and Catholic Dogma," *First Amendment Law Review* 2 (Winter 2003): 172–74.

140. T. Jeremy Gunn, "The Separation of Church and State Versus Religion in the Public Square: The Contested History of the Establishment Clause," in *No Establishment of Religion: America's Original Contribution to Religious Liberty*, 3rd ed., eds. T. Jeremy Gunn and John Witte, Jr. (New York: Oxford University Press, 2012), 32.

141. William R. Hutchison, "Book Review: Philip Hamburger, Separation of Church and State," *Law and History Review* 23 (Spring 2005): 201.

142. Green, "'Blaming Blaine'," 113.

143. Pfeffer, "Religion, Education and the Constitution," 7.

144. *Pierce v. Society of Sisters*, 268 U.S. 510 (1925).

145. Pfeffer, *Church, State, and Freedom*, 522–24; see S. J. Virgil Blum, *Freedom in Education: Federal Aid for All Children* (Garden City, NY: Doubleday and Co., Inc., 1965); Robert F. Drinan, *Religion, the Courts, and Public Policy* (New York: McGraw-Hill, 1963); and Legal Department, National Catholic Welfare Conference, "The Constitutionality of the Inclusion of Church-Related Schools in Federal Aid to Education," *Georgetown Law Journal* 50 (1961).

146. *Cochran v. Louisiana State Board of Education*, 281 U.S. 370 (1930).

147. 330 U.S. 1 (1947); 392 U.S. 236 (1968).

148. Ibid., at 15–16.

149. Ibid., at 18.

150. Leo Pfeffer, "Child-Benefit Theory: A Legal Fiction," *Church and State* 19 (April 1966): 7.

151. Major advocates of this position, especially as it related to aid to parochial schools, included O'Neill, "Nonpreferential Aid," 18–42; and Blum, *Freedom in Education*.

152. Pfeffer, "Federal Funds," 313.

153. Ibid., 310–12.

154. *Pierce v. Society of Sisters*, 268 U.S. 510 (1925)

155. Pfeffer, "Federal Funds," 313.

156. Pfeffer, *Church, State, and Freedom*, 525; Pfeffer presented these arguments on numerous occasions in both written and oral fashion; see "An Analysis of Federal Aid to Parochial Schools," *Journal of Church and State* 3 (November 1961): 137–48; "Federal Funds," 309–22; "The Price We Pay," 38–42; "The Case Against Parochiaid," *Church and State* 30 (April 1977): 14–17; "Aid to Elementary and Secondary Education (H.R. 2361 and 2362)." Testimony at Hearings of General Subcommittee on Education, U.S. House Committee on Education and Labor, Washington, DC, February 2, 1965; and "Parochiaid: The Courts, the Legislature, and the Executive"; paper presented at the National Conference on School Finance, National Education Association, New York City, 27 March 1972.

157. Pfeffer, *Church, State, and Freedom*, 524.

158. Ibid., 526.

159. Pfeffer, "Federal Funds," 319–22.

160. Pfeffer, "The Price We Pay," 40; "Federal Funds," 315.

161. Pfeffer, "Public Funds for Parochial Schools," 319–20.

162. Ibid.

163. Miller and Flowers, *Toward Benevolent Neutrality*, 620; Randall Ballmer has argued that changing conservative evangelical views on aid to private schools and opposition to integration was a large factor in the formation of the Religious Right. See Randall Ballmer, "The Real Origins of the Religious Right," *Politico Magazine* (May 27, 2014).

164. Leo Pfeffer, "The Uneasy Trinity: Church, State, and Constitution," *The Civil Liberties Review* 2 (Winter 1975): 158; see *Religion, State and the Burger Court*,

16–17; *God, Caesar and the Constitution*, 244–50; and Pfeffer's brief in *Sloan v. Lemon*, 413 U.S. 825 (1973).

165. Emma Long, *The Church–State Debate: Religion, Education and the Establishment Clause in Post War America* (London: Bloomsbury Academic, 2012), 27–29.

166. Leo Pfeffer, "Aid to Elementary and Secondary Education (H.R. 2361 and 2362)," Testimony at Hearings of General Subcommittee on Education, U.S. House Committee on Education and Labor, Washington, DC, 2 February 1965, p. 1607.

167. Ibid.

168. Ibid., 1610; although he found the child-benefit theory to be constitutionally questionable, Pfeffer interpreted its utilization by the courts narrowly. In other words, the only constitutional child-benefit was transportation costs. Welfare benefits, whose constitutionality he did not question, generally referred to public services such as police and fire protection.

169. *Flast v. Cohen*, 392 U.S. 83 (1968).

170. *Frothingham v. Mellon*, 262 U.S. 447 (1923).

171. Brief for Appellants at 8, *Flast v. Gardner*, 392 U.S. 97 (1968).

172. Ibid., at 36.

173. Ibid., at 7.

174. 392 U.S. 83 at 102.

175. Ivers, *To Build a Wall*, 185.

176. Pfeffer, "An Autobiographical Sketch," 521; *Religion, State and the Burger Court*, 25–26.

177. *Board of Education v. Allen*, 392 U.S. 236 (1968).

178. Brief for American Jewish as Amicus Curiae Supporting Appellants at 32–35, *Board of Education v. Allen*, 392 U.S. 236 (1968) (No. 660).

179. 392 U.S. 236 at 242–49.

180. Ibid., at 243–44.

181. Ibid., at 253–54.

182. Ibid., at 244–45.

183. Pfeffer, *God, Caesar, and the Constitution*, 273–74.

184. 392 U.S. 236 at 248.

185. Pfeffer, *God, Caesar, and the Constitution*, 276.

186. Long, *The Church–State Debate*, 30–31.

187. 403 U.S. 602 (1971). While co-counsel in both cases, Pfeffer handled the appeal in the *Earley* case and submitted a brief of amicus curiae in the *Lemon* case.

188. Brief for American Association of School Administrators, et al. of Amici Curiae in Support of Appellants at 5–6, *Lemon v. Kurtzman*, 403 U.S. 602 (1971) (No. 89) (hereinafter *Lemon* Brief); not only did he file a brief on behalf of the American Jewish Congress, the American Jewish Committee, and the Anti-Defamation League, but also Pfeffer mobilized a group of public education lobbies and drafted a brief on their behalf; see Ivers, *To Build a Wall*, 179.

189. Joseph H. Fichter, *Parochial Schools: A Sociological Study* (Notre Dame, IN: University of Notre Dame Press, 1958), 86.

190. See Brief of Amicus Curiae, *Earley v. DiCenso,* 403 U.S. 602 (1971) (No. 569); and *Lemon v. Kurtzman*, 402 U.S. 602 (1971), 26–30; this and other evidence

was frequently utilized by Pfeffer to reflect the pervasive religious character of parochial schools and of the continuing adherence to the teachings of Pope Pius XI's 1929 Encyclical, *On Christian Education of Youth*, in which he declared that "the only school approved by the Church is one where . . . the Catholic religion permeates the entire atmosphere [and where] all teaching and the whole organization of the school and its teachers, syllabus and textbooks in every branch [are] regulated by the Christian spirit"; see Pfeffer, *Church, State and Freedom*, 510–11; Pfeffer, *God, Caesar, and the Constitution*, 231–35.

191. Lemon Brief at 3–9.

192. Ibid.

193. *Walz v. Tax Commission* 397 U.S. 664 (1970).

194. Lemon Brief at 32.

195. 403 U.S. 602 (1971) at 621–22.

196. Ibid., at 618.

197. Ibid., at 622.

198. Long, *The Church–State Debate*, 35.

199. Pfeffer, *Religion, State, and the Burger Court*, 27.

200. Long, *The Church–State Debate*, 36.

201. Ivers, *To Build a Wall*, 180.

202. Pfeffer, *God, Caesar, and the Constitution*, 282.

203. Leo Pfeffer, "Aid to Parochial Schools: A Chess Game with the Constitution," *Reform Judaism* 1 (October 1972): 5.

204. Sorauf, *The Wall of Separation*, 331–33.

205. *PEARL v. Nyquist*, 413 U.S. 756 (1973) at 761–69.

206. Brief for Appellants at 8, *PEARL v. Nyquist*, 413 U.S. 756 (1973) (No. 72-694).

207. Ibid., at 25–26.

208. Ibid., at 26.

209. Ibid., at 32.

210. 413 U.S. 756 at 76768; see also Pfeffer, *Religion, State and the Burger Court*, 31.

211. 413 U.S. 756 at 777.

212. Ibid., at 794. The same year as *Nyquist*, Pfeffer led successful challenges to two other aid plans. In *Levitt v. PEARL* 413 U.S. 472 (1973), the U.S. Supreme Court, in an 8-to-1 decision, ruled unlawful a New York plan that provided reimbursements to private schools for administering state mandated tests. In a 6-to-3 vote, the Court ruled, in *Sloan v. Lemon* 413 U.S. 825 1973), that a Pennsylvania plan providing partial tuition reimbursements to parents of parochial school children was unconstitutional.

213. 413 U.S. 756 at 799–802.

214. Ibid., at 802–03.

215. Ibid., at 789–94.

216. Pfeffer, *Religion, State, and the Burger Court*, 30.

217. *Meek v. Pittenger*, 421 U.S. 349 (1975) at 351–55.

218. Since *Lemon*, the court had also struck down various forms of aid including another Pennsylvania tuition reimbursement plan in *Sloan v. Lemon* and a New York

plan which would pay nonpublic schools for mandated services such as standardized tests as well as teacher-prepared tests in *Levitt v.* PEARL. These victories, along with *Lemon* and *Nyquist*, encouraged Pfeffer to challenge even the loan of textbooks which had been upheld in *Board of Education v. Allen*.

219. Brief for Appellants at 23, *Meek v. Pittenger*, 421 U.S. 349 (1975) (No. 73-1765) (hereinafter *Meek* Brief).

220. Ibid., at 15–20.

221. Ibid.

222. Ibid., at 26–27.

223. 421 U.S. 349 at 363.

224. Ibid., at 364.

225. Ibid., at 368–70.

226. For instance, the stated purpose of the Pennsylvania plan in *Meek v. Pittenger* was "that every school child in the Commonwealth will equitably share in the benefits of auxiliary services, textbooks, and instructional material provided free of charge to children attending public schools"; Ibid., at 351–52.

227. 421 U.S. 349 at 385.

228. Ibid. at 386.

229. Pfeffer, *Religion, State and the Burger Court*, 32.

230. Transcript of Oral Argument, *Committee for Public Education and Religious Liberty vs. Nyquist*, 16 April 1973, 72–694.

231. *Wolman v. Walter,* 433 U.S. 229 (1977).

232. Pfeffer, "The Case Against Parochiaid," 15; "Aid to Parochial Schools," 5.

233. Brief of Amicus Curiae for PEARL Supporting Appellants, *Wolman v. Walter*, 433 U.S. 229 (1977) (No. 76-496).

234. 433 U.S. 229 at 254.

235. Pfeffer, *Religion, State and the Burger Court*, 53.

236. *PEARL v. Regan*, 444 U.S. 646 (1980).

237. Brief for Appellants at 9-11, *PEARL v. Regan*, 444 U.S. 646 (1980) (No. 78-1369).

238. Ibid., at 13–16.

239. Ibid., at 25.

240. *PEARL v. Regan*, 444 U.S. 646 at 658.

241. Ibid., at 663–71.

242. Ibid., at 664.

243. Ibid., at 666.

244. Ibid. at 671.

245. Pfeffer, *Religion, State and the Burger Court*, 39.

246. Ibid.

247. Reagan's Attorney General Edwin Meese was a prominent advocate and popularizer of the philosophy of original intent from which he developed a nonpreferentialist reading of the First Amendment.

248. *Mueller v. Allen*, 463 U.S. 388 (1983) at 390–93.

249. Brief of Amicus Curiae, *Mueller v. Allen*, 463 U.S. 388 (1983) (No. 82-195).

250. 463 U.S. 388 at 396–402.

251. Ibid., at 414.
252. Ibid.
253. An educational organization committed to the ideals of the nineteenth century educator, Horace Mann.
254. The colleges were the Methodist Western Maryland, given $500,000 for the construction of a science wing and dining hall; Roman Catholic St. Joseph College and College of Notre Dame, receiving $750,000 each for the construction of science buildings; and the United Church of Christ Hood College, which received $500,000 for the construction of dormitory and classroom buildings; see *Horace Mann League v. Board of Public Works*, 242 Md. 645, 220 A.2d 51, cert. denied, appeal dismissed, 385 U.S. 97 (1966); see also, Preville, "Catholic Colleges, the Courts, and the Constitution," 197.
255. Jurisdictional Statement at 7, *Horace Mann League v. Board of Public Works of Maryland*, 385 U.S. 97 (1966).
256. Preville, "Catholic Colleges, the Courts, and the Constitution," 198–200.
257. Ibid., 200.
258. Ibid., 200–01.
259. *Tilton v. Richardson*, 403 U.S. 672 (1971).
260. The colleges were Sacred Heart University, Annhurst College, Fairfield University, and Albertus Magnus College.
261. Preville, "Catholic Colleges and the Supreme Court," 296–99.
262. Ibid., 299–300.
263. Brief for Appellants at 14-17, *Tilton v. Richardson*, 403 U.S. 672 (1971) (No. 153) (hereinafter *Tilton* Brief).
264. Ibid., at 28.
265. Ibid., at 39.
266. Ibid., at 42.
267. Ibid., at 50.
268. 403 U.S. 672 (1971) at 679.
269. Ibid., at 681–82.
270. Ibid., at 686.
271. Ibid., at 687.
272. Ibid., at 689.
273. Ibid.
274. Ibid., at 697.
275. Ibid., at 693.
276. Pfeffer, *Religion, State and the Burger Court*, 54.
277. *Hunt v. McNair*, 413 U.S. 734 (1973).
278. Ibid., at 744.
279. *Roemer v. Board of Public Works of Maryland*, 426 U.S. 736 (1976).
280. Ibid., at 742–64; see also J. David Holcomb, "Religion and Higher Education," in *Church–State Issues in America Today: Religion, Family, and Education* Vol. 2, eds. Ann W. Duncan and Steven L. Jones (Westport, CT: Greenwood, 2008), 158–59.
281. Pfeffer, *Religion, State and the Burger Court*, 54.
282. Ibid., 56.

283. *Tilton* Brief at 14.

284. Pfeffer, "Autobiographical Sketch," 530–31; *Religion, State, and Burger Court*, xiii–xiv.

285. 473 U.S. 373 (1985).

286. Ibid.

287. Ibid., at 384–98.

288. Ibid., at 473.

289. Jesse H. Choper, "The Religion Clauses of the First Amendment: Reconciling the Conflict," *University of Pittsburgh Law Review* 41 (Summer 1980): 680–81; see also Michael W. McConnell, "Religious Freedom at a Crossroads," in *The Bill of Rights in the Modern State*, eds. Geoffrey R. Stone, Richard A. Epstein, and Cass R. Sunstein (Chicago: The University of Chicago Press, 1992), 119–20.

290. 472 U.S. 38 (1985) at 107.

291. *Meek v. Pittenger*, 421 U.S. 349 (1975).

292. *Wolman v. Walter*, 433 U.S. 229 (1977).

293. Pfeffer, "Aid to Parochial Schools," 5; "The Case Against Parochiaid," 15.

294. Pfeffer, *Religion, State and the Burger Court*, 39.

295. This is not to suggest that Pfeffer found these practices, upheld in the *Everson* and *Board of Education v. Allen* cases, to be consistent with the broad reading of the First Amendment. He challenged, for instance, the child-benefit theory on which the transportation costs were justified ("The Child-Benefit Theory") and used other cases to contest the constitutionality of textbook loans (see *Meek* Brief). See also Chapter Four of this dissertation, 125–56.

296. Pfeffer, "The Establishment Clause," 728.

297. Norman Redlich, "Separation of Church and State: The Burger Court's Tortuous Journey," *Notre Dame Law Review* 60 (1985): 1094–149.

298. Long, *The Church–State Debate*, 196–99.

299. Ibid., 200.

300. Ibid., 198.

301. *McCollum v. Board of Education*, 333 U.S. 203 (1948).

302. *Epperson v. Arkansas*, 393 U.S. 97 (1968).

303. *Abington v. Schempp*, 374 U.S. 203 (1963).

Chapter 4

The Clash of Conflicting Interests

Leo Pfeffer and the Free Exercise of Religion

While Leo Pfeffer is better known for his Establishment Clause advocacy, he was actively engaged in key free exercise disputes throughout his career. Championing an expansive reading of the Free Exercise Clause, Pfeffer believed the free exercise of religion meant more than the right to worship or to hold particular religious beliefs. Religiously motivated advocacy and conduct were protected by the First Amendment as well. "The free exercise of religion protected by the First Amendment extends far beyond the freedom of worship," Pfeffer once declared, "it includes the right to believe, to practice, to preach, and to teach."[1] Pfeffer further claimed that the First Amendment "secures freedom from religion no less than freedom of religion," and, taken together with the Free Speech and Article VI's No Religious Test clauses, the Free Exercise Clause also protects nonbelief, disbelief, and religious dissent. "There is little doubt," Pfeffer frequently asserted that both religion clauses were "intended to have . . . a broad and comprehensive meaning."[2] Nonetheless, Pfeffer acknowledged that religious freedom, like all freedoms, was not absolute. "While the Free Exercise Clause extends beyond merely freedom to believe," he explained, "it does not preclude, among many others, prosecution for tax evasion, perjury, or endangering human life."[3]

Despite Pfeffer's broad reading of the Free Exercise Clause, he did recognize the potential conflicts between an individual's conscience and the state's duty to protect the health, safety, and welfare of society. Pfeffer described this as the "clash of conflicting interests" that determine the limits of the free exercise of religion under the First Amendment.[4] In light of this, one might assume that Leo Pfeffer, in holding to a high wall of separation between church and state, would oppose granting a religious exemption from secular laws. In other words, if the state was to show no preference or to provide aid, or to sponsor religion, then would not allowing an exemption for religious reasons violate the separation of church and state? Not to Pfeffer. He argued that not all religious exemptions were *de facto* violations of the Establishment Clause. Nonetheless, Pfeffer frequently faced criticism that his broad reading of both religion clauses would inevitably lead to conflict or tension between the two. Many of these argued that a broad reading of the Free Exercise clause was irreconcilable with a broad reading of the Establishment Clause. Indeed, some specifically identified the "strict separationist" approach advocated by Pfeffer as having exacerbated what they perceived to be a tension between the two clauses.[5] Pfeffer deflected this argument claiming that the tension between the two clauses was "more apparent than real." Rarely did religious freedom cases involve just one clause or the other. In fact, he argued that the U.S. Supreme Court has rarely had to choose between what religious freedom demands and church-state separation forbids.[6]

In defense of religious minorities, Sabbatarians, conscientious objectors, and other nonmainstream faiths, Pfeffer sought to protect religious conscience and ensure equality for religious minorities. Consequently, Pfeffer submitted briefs in landmark free exercise cases supporting the granting of exemptions from neutral, secular laws when they infringed on the rights of an individual's conscience. For much of his career, Pfeffer's position on free exercise generally found favorable reception in the U.S. Supreme Court. As will be shown below, the Court, from *Cantwell v. Connecticut* (1940)[7] to *Wisconsin v. Yoder* (1973)[8] embraced an increasingly broad reading of the Free Exercise Clause. During this time, the Court adopted the compelling state interest test that required the state to prove an overriding interest before burdening religious exercise.[9] Pfeffer viewed this test as an important bulwark of protection for religious freedom, particularly for people of minority or nonmainstream faiths.

In the clash of conflicting interests, however, the Court neither always granted exemptions nor applied the broad reading of the Free Exercise Clause. And toward the end of Pfeffer's career, a plurality of the Court returned to a narrower approach to free exercise disputes. Nonetheless, an examination of Leo Pfeffer's free exercise litigation and writings reflects an expansive view of the Free Exercise Clause motivated by his commitment to religious equality, pluralism, and the integrity of religious faith.

FREE EXERCISE OF NONMAINSTREAM FAITHS

The American understanding of religious liberty has been largely defined by marginalized and nonconventional religions seeking legitimation in society. Mainstream American religions generally have the political means and social prestige to avoid discrimination. Minority religions, however, have often looked to the courts to protect their First Amendment rights.[10] While the First Amendment has resulted in broad religious freedom and the religious pluralism of American society suggests a high degree of tolerance of theological diversity and experimentation, minority religions, especially those whose beliefs run counter to societal norms or mores, have often faced legal obstacles and social hostility. As scholars have noted, "The history of the development of free exercise doctrine has been one of an expansion of the concept of what is religious and what constitutes religiously motivated conduct deserving protection."[11]

Legal contests have arisen when a particular religious group's teachings or practices have conflicted with national secular values. Cases involving the Mormon practice of polygamy, the Jehovah's Witnesses' methods of evangelism, or the healing practices of Christian Scientists are clear examples of these clashes. According to Leo Pfeffer:

> Broad as are the tolerances of law and public opinion for religious movements, they are not unlimited, and the ensuing tensions may reach the point of traumatic crisis. . . . When, by reason of change either in the group's position or in national secular norms, the threat disappears or becomes manageable, the legitimation of the group and its acceptance by the general community are practically automatic and generally simultaneous.[12]

These conflicts raised issues not only of legitimation but also the nature and extent of the free exercise of religion.

During his career, Leo Pfeffer was an outspoken defender of new and unorthodox religions. His motivation can be found not only in his identity as a religious minority but also in his interpretation of the First Amendment. The principles of freedom, separation, equality, and pluralism were all central to his legal advocacy on behalf of nonmainstream religions. For Pfeffer, the religion clauses worked in tandem to prohibit the state from discriminating against a particular religion as well as prefer one religion over another. All religions were equal before the law, and the state, by its secular nature, was barred from making any theological judgments. Moreover, the constitutional protection of religious minorities resulted in religious pluralism, which, according to Pfeffer, was beneficial to the American democratic experiment. Pfeffer also tied the religious freedom of other religious groups to the welfare of Judaism. "One thing I feel certain: intolerance is contagious, and a threat to religious freedom of any group, including those whose beliefs are repugnant to us, is a threat to us as Jews and commands our concern."[13]

In the nineteenth century, members of the Church of Jesus Christ of Latter-day Saints were the subject of the U.S. Supreme Court's first major free exercise decision. These followers of Joseph Smith faced persecution and harassment during their early history, due, in part, to their theological endorsement of polygamy. While not widely practiced by Mormons, polygamy became a tenet of the Mormon faith and was practiced by leaders such as Brigham Young. This unorthodox practice was labeled as immoral by much of the American public and was outlawed in a number of states. In 1862, Congress passed the Morrill Act prohibiting plural marriages at the federal level.[14] A conflict thus emerged between the interest of the state to avowedly preserve the monogamous family versus the free exercise rights of Mormons to teach and practice polygamy. In 1878, the Court upheld the conviction of a Mormon, George Reynolds, who had been accused of practicing polygamy. Despite the Mormons' claim that polygamy was a central theological conviction, the Supreme Court denied Reynolds's free exercise claim by declaring that the Act was within "the legislative practice." Polygamy had been viewed as immoral and patriarchal, so Congress had the right, according to the Court, to criminalize its practice. In deciding *Reynolds v. United States*[15] the Court adopted the belief-action dichotomy in determining free exercise contests. Simply stated, the Court held that while religious belief was absolute, action based on that belief was not. As Justice Morrison Waite stated in his majority opinion: "Laws are made for the government of actions, and while they cannot interfere with mere religious belief and opinions, they may with practices."[16] Pfeffer interpreted the *Reynolds* decision to say that while the government had no legal interest in the theology of a religious group, it did have the right to intervene when a group's practices threatened a secular interest.

Twelve years later, the Court's decision in *Davis v. Beason* proved to be even more problematic for members of the Mormon faith. In 1882, Congress had passed the Edmunds Act making polygamy a felony and requiring voters to declare an oath denying they engaged in the practice. A subsequent Idaho territorial statute went further by requiring oath takers to deny membership in organizations that advocated polygamy. Some accounts indicate that as many as 1300 Mormons were prosecuted under these anti-polygamy statutes. Among these was Samuel Davis who, while not personally practicing polygamy, was found in violation of the Utah statute for swearing a false oath.[17] Davis challenged his indictment as a violation of the free exercise of religion and appealed to the U.S. Supreme Court after losing at the territorial court level. A unanimous U.S. Supreme Court denied Davis's religious freedom claim. In his opinion for the Court, Justice Stephen Field argued that the Free Exercise Clause did not exempt claimants from behavior that was "inimical to the peace, good order, and morals of society."[18] Congress continued its campaign against polygamy by revoking the charter of the Mormon Church and declaring its property forfeited.[19] The Court would subsequently uphold Congress's actions in *Church of Latter-Day Saints v. United States*, 136 U.S. 1 (1890). The continued legal pressure led the Mormon Church to abandon the teaching of polygamy just months later. Pfeffer noted that the Court, in *Davis*, went beyond the rationale of even the belief-action test. Mere association with a church that advocated polygamy was enough to run afoul of the law. And while the Court did not challenge the legitimacy of the Mormon religion in *Reynolds*, Pfeffer concluded that "it adjudicated the non-legitimacy of the Mormons as a religious movement."[20]

Pfeffer found the belief-action test of *Reynolds* to be an inadequate protection of free-exercise rights. According to Pfeffer,

> This belief-yes-action-no rule, however, proves unsatisfactory for a number of reasons. In the first place, it is directly contrary to the written rule, which protects the free *exercise* of religion, a word that surely connotes action. In the second place, if only belief is encompassed, the amendment offers little help to the nonbeliever, for, as the common law adage had it, the Devil himself knows not the thought of man, and all the nonbeliever need do is to keep his thoughts to himself.[21]

With no burden placed upon the state to justify restrictions on free exercise, it is no surprise that the belief–action test proved inadequate in protecting religious liberty. As one observer noted: "Every case that applied this standard of reviews found for the government."[22]

Another nonmainstream faith, the Jehovah's Witnesses, played a prominent role in a number of foundational free exercise and free speech decisions in the first half of the twentieth century. Organized in the late 1870s, these millenarian prophets often found themselves in conflict with local authorities due to their unorthodox teachings and aggressive forms of evangelism. Along with their refusal to hold political office, vote, or serve in the military, the Jehovah's Witnesses refused to salute the flag or receive blood transfusions.[23] Two prominent U.S. Supreme Court cases developed out of the Jehovah's Witnesses' refusal to salute the flag. During the outbreak of World War II, the refusal of Jehovah's Witness children in public schools to participate in these ceremonies ran counter to the quest for national unity. In 1940, the Court ruled, in *Minersville v. Gobitis*, that the need for national unity and security overrode the constitutional rights of Jehovah's Witness children who had been expelled from school for refusing to participate in saluting the flag or participating in the pledge of allegiance.[24] Justice Felix Frankfurter, in his majority opinion, articulated a narrow reading of the free exercise clause that resembled the belief-action test of *Reynolds*. "Conscientious scruples have not, in the course of the long struggle for religious toleration," Frankfurter contended, "relieved the individual from obedience to a general law not aimed at the promotion or restriction of religious beliefs."[25] Much like the belief-action test, Pfeffer found the "general or neutral law principle" to be an inadequate protection for religious liberty as well since it "adds little if any protection to that afforded by other constitutional provisions."[26] Pfeffer found agreement with Justice Harlan Stone who, in his dissent in *Gobitis*, was unconvinced that "inconveniences which may attend some sensible adjustment of school discipline in order that the religious convictions of these children may be spared presents a problem so momentous or pressing as to outweigh the freedom from compulsory violation of religious faith."[27]

The Court would reverse its *Gobitis* decision three years later in *West Virginia State Board of Education v. Barnette*, holding that children could not be expelled from the public schools for refusal to salute the flag.[28] While Justice Jackson's majority opinion relied more on free speech principles than free exercise of religion, the opinion became one of the most famous defenses of First Amendment freedoms. "If there is any fixed star in our constitutional constellation," Jackson famously declared, "it is that no official, high or petty, can prescribe what shall be orthodox in politics, nationalism, religion, or other matters of opinion."[29] Despite such sweeping language, Jackson avoided the issue of the relationship of religious freedom to neutral, generally applicable laws. Pfeffer viewed *Barnette* as "illustrative of the unimportance attached to religious claims during this period." In looking at free exercise cases from *Reynold's* through *Barnette*, Pfeffer observed that the limited protection the narrow reading of the Free Exercise Clause provided. "In every case in which a claim under the free exercise clause was upheld, it was bracketed with a free speech or free press claim"; Pfeffer explained, "conversely, whenever free exercise stood alone it was unsuccessful." "Free exercise did not have a separate but equal existence, or even one that was separate and unequal," he concluded, "it practically had no existence at all."[30]

It was the Jehovah's Witnesses' aggressive proselytization techniques, however, that ultimately forced the Court to recognize the Free Exercise Clause. Their direct evangelism took them door-to-door as well as to street corners handing out tracts, books, and other materials. Their literature often included attacks on Catholics and other religious groups. As a result, public officials in many communities sought to restrict the activities of the Jehovah's Witnesses by passing ordinances directed at these techniques. Jehovah's Witnesses were not apprehensive to use the courts to seek judicial relief, and, as a result, were involved in an unprecedented number of civil liberties cases including the landmark free exercise case of *Cantwell v. Connecticut* in 1940.[31] *Cantwell* involved a Jehovah's Witness and his sons who, on the streets of a predominantly Catholic neighborhood in New Haven, Connecticut, played a recording entitled "Enemies" which attacked the Roman Catholic Church. Complaints were filed, and the Jehovah's Witnesses were arrested for breach of the peace and for failure to obtain a "certificate of approval" for such activities.[32] The Cantwells had refused to seek a permit from a local official because they were not engaging in a commercial activity, but rather fulfilling a religious obligation. In challenging their conviction, the Cantwells argued that putting a local authority in charge of determining whether their activities were "bona fide religious or charitable" was nothing less than censorship as well as a violation of their free exercise rights. The U.S. Supreme Court eventually overturned the Cantwell's conviction and declared the ordinance unconstitutional on free exercise grounds. In doing so, the Court, for the first time, applied the Free Exercise Clause to the states by invalidating a local ordinance that conflicts with religious liberty. Cantwell is also significant because the Court went beyond the belief-action test of *Reynolds* and held that the state must show a "clear and present danger" to the public interest before restricting religious exercise.[33]

Pfeffer viewed the struggles of the Jehovah's Witnesses as foundational in the quest for the free exercise of religion carried out by religious minorities. "America owes a great debt of gratitude to the Witnesses," he once said. "Much of the current law relating to religious freedom resulted from the Witnesses' persistence in asserting their constitutional rights in the teeth of persecution and doggedly appealing adverse lower court verdicts to the Supreme Court. The sincerity, integrity, and self-sacrifice of Jehovah's Witnesses can hardly be questioned."[34]

The rapid growth of new religious movements in the 1960s and 1970s placed a variety of new free exercise issues before the courts during Pfeffer's career. Many of the new religious groups practiced aggressive recruitment of new converts as well as separation from mainstream society. This latter practice on occasion led to the alienation of converts from their families.[35] The widely reported mass suicide of the members of People's Temple in Jonestown, Guyana, in 1978 heightened negative public perception of new and nonmainstream religious groups.[36] The term "cult" was applied to those new religious groups whose practices brought them under increasing public suspicion.

These developments led to political pressure to investigate the practices and potential dangers of "cults." Accusations of brainwashing, violence, and financial abuses motivated lawmakers on both the state and national levels to call for scrutiny as well. Quickly an anti-cult movement developed in the United States. Particular attention was given to groups, such as the Church of Scientology, the Unification Church, and the Hare Krishna movement, all of which experienced public hostility. One phenomenon of the anti-cult movement was the practice of deprogramming. Simply, deprogramming was the abduction of a "cult" member in an attempt to convince the person to leave the cult and return to his or her former faith. Legislative efforts to revise guardianship laws in order to facilitate deprogramming were passed in several states. In light of the accusations of brainwashing by "cults," the deprogramming efforts received substantial publicity during the 1970s and 1980s.[37] Writing in 1984, Pfeffer observed that "the past decade has witnessed what might be called a crusade against newly formed unpopular religions, commonly called cults."[38] Pfeffer, criticized the use of the term "cult," arguing that it was typically used in a derogatory manner and to delegitimize religious movements. According to Pfeffer, "The crux of the matter is that our Constitution does not recognize any distinction between accepted religions and hated 'cults,' and that use or abuse of law to destroy the latter threatens the security of the former and of all persons committed to First Amendment values."[39]

In defending unpopular religions, Pfeffer compared the post-Jamestown hysteria surrounding cults to the Salem anti-witchcraft trials as well as the persecution of religious minorities in American history. Baptists, Quakers, and Catholics were all viewed with the same suspicion at different times during American history,[40] and persecution was fueled, in large measure, by majority religions which sought to eliminate the influence of new religions. Pfeffer argued that this was a truism in religious history: "In reality, every new faith group challenging existing faiths is condemned and fought by the established faiths."[41] Yet new and unpopular religions were at the heart of the story of religious freedom. "The history of the struggle for religious freedom and church-state separation," Pfeffer explained, "is in large measure one against persecution and for equality of treatment on behalf of religions which in their formation days were hated and feared by the general community."[42]

Pfeffer argued that the same principles of the First Amendment's unitary guarantee held true no less for "cults" than they did for more mainstream religions. In addition to a broad free exercise protection, so-called cults were also protected by an Establishment Clause that forbade the state from singling out marginal religions for discriminatory treatment and preferring majority religions. Furthermore, neither the size nor the doctrine of a religious group was constitutionally meaningful. "Theoretically, every faith is automatically legitimated on its profession, and this is so whether it is espoused by one person, one hundred persons, or one hundred million persons."[43] In a secular state barred from having any "cognizance of religion," the nature of the religious claims had no constitutional bearing for Pfeffer as well. "The freedom and independence of churches would be in grave danger," Pfeffer warned, "if the state undertook to define religious heresy or orthodoxy."[44] To drive this point home, Pfeffer frequently utilized the Court's declaration in *Watson v. Jones*: "The law knows no heresy, and is committed to no dogma, the establishment of no sect."[45]

Some observers have feared that such a blanket protection for religious profession might enable fraud or other illegal practices to be perpetuated in the name of religion. Such was the claim made in *United States v. Ballard* where the Court, for the first time, had to weigh the free exercise claims against the argument that leaders of the "I Am" movement had committed mail fraud. Guy, Edna, and Donald Ballard had claimed to be divine messengers and to possess supernatural healing powers. The criminal indictment filed against them contended that they knew their claims were false but established businesses, solicited donations, and sold memberships through the mail to defraud the public. Nonetheless, the U.S. Supreme Court ruled in favor of the Ballards. In Justice William Douglas's majority opinion, he declared that the Constitution barred the courts from passing judgment on the legitimacy of religious beliefs. "The religious view espoused by respondents may seem incredible, if not preposterous, to most people," he declared, "but if those doctrines are subject to trial before a jury charged with finding their truth or falsity, then the same can be done with the religious beliefs of any sect."[46] Nonetheless, the Court did hold that a jury could determine the sincerity of religious beliefs. This, then, would become the key inquiry utilized by the Court in other cases where it sought to distinguish between "faith and fraud." Pfeffer found the sincerity inquiry "imperfect" as it no doubt was used as the "shield of innumerable charlatans." Nonetheless, he concluded that "this may be the necessary price to pay for freedom of religion."[47]

On several occasions, Leo Pfeffer submitted legal briefs on behalf of "cults," defending their constitutional rights. In 1979, for instance, Pfeffer drafted a friend-of-the-court brief, representing several Christian and Jewish organizations, in which he defended the rights of the Worldwide Church of God against the state of California. Founded in the 1930s by Herbert W. Armstrong, the Worldwide Church of God had developed a radio and television ministry from its offices in California. A millenarian group, the Church observed the Sabbath and the Church's founder, Herbert W. Armstrong, was believed to be the appointed apostle of Jesus Christ on earth. The attorney general of California, upon the instigation of several dissident members from the Worldwide Church of God, including the excommunicated son of the founder, filed a lawsuit seeking to compel the Church to submit to an examination, audit, and investigation into its internal financial affairs. Church leaders were accused of using church funds for personal benefit and were forced to disclose all their records and assets. For two months, the Worldwide Church of God was placed in receivership. Claiming that churches were "public trusts," much like other charitable organizations, the attorney general of California argued that the Worldwide Church of God was subject to regulatory intrusion.[48] Essentially, he held that Church funds were no different than any other charitable funds and, as a result, financial affairs of churches were entitled to no special First Amendment protection.

The widespread opposition of the religious community to the state of California's actions was witnessed in the numerous and diverse sponsors of

Pfeffer's amicus brief filed on behalf of the Church.[49] For Pfeffer, the implications for religious liberty in this case were clear:

> The case represents a startling and, we believe, unprecedented situation in the history of church-state relations under a constitution that forbids the establishment and secures the free exercise of religion. The state-authorized actions of the Attorney General are predicated on the assumption that a thriving, completely solvent church with an enviable credit rating, enjoying the full support of the overwhelming majority of its membership, can be taken over and managed by state officials as if it were a failing business corporation unable to meet its debts or pay its workers.[50]

It was clear to Pfeffer that had the Worldwide Church of God been a recognized mainstream religion, such actions by the state would never have been considered.

Pfeffer's free exercise argument was that the California attorney general used a facially neutral law, in this instance, the illegality of corporate fraud, to persecute an unpopular religion. Pfeffer drew parallels between the Worldwide Church of God and the Jehovah's Witnesses who had reached a level of public acceptance "only after a period of trials and tribulations instigated by government officials." Pfeffer concluded: "It need hardly be argued that the Attorney General's actions" Pfeffer argued, "restrict the free exercise of religion."[51] Since the Church was financially solvent and enjoyed the support of a vast majority of its adherents, Pfeffer argued that the state of California showed no interest compelling enough to infringe the rights of the members of the Worldwide Church of God by determining "how and by whom their affairs shall be governed and their voluntary contributions expended."[52]

Pfeffer argued that the actions of the state of California violated the Establishment Clause of the First Amendment as well. California had violated the Lemon Test because the attorney general's actions constituted impermissible state participation in the affairs of a religious organization. The purpose and effect of the state's actions were clearly to inhibit religion, he asserted, and the attempt to determine the legitimacy of religious activities was beyond the scope of the state. "The State claims that it is merely acting to prevent fraud," Pfeffer explained, "but this it may not do in anything touching the profession and practice of religious doctrine as between a church and its congregants."[53] The state's intervention in the affairs of the Worldwide Church further violated the excessive entanglement prong of the *Lemon* test. According to Pfeffer, this was the "most flagrant violation." "The idea of a state-appointed official controlling the functions and operations of a live, ongoing church is frightening."[54] While the U.S. Supreme Court rejected appeals by the Worldwide Church of God, the California legislature ended the struggle by withdrawing the power of the attorney general to investigate religious organizations. Nevertheless, the Church had been subject for two months to a government appointed leader, the firing of church employees, and the expenditure of over $100,000 of church funds.

If groups such as the Worldwide Church of God, which professed to be part of the Christian tradition and who, for more than fifty years, reached millions through its radio and television ministries, faced discriminatory treatment by the state, what then was the status of those new religions whose teachings bear little resemblance to traditional religions? This question motivated Pfeffer to become involved in the defense of the Reverend Sun Myung Moon, leader of the Unification Church. The "Moonies," as his followers were popularly known, were under suspicion for suspected "brainwashing" techniques. Consequently, many of the prominent deprogramming efforts were aimed at converts to the Unification Church. Despite the Church's outspoken opposition to communism and defense of capitalism, the Unification Church found itself embroiled in numerous legal battles over tax exemption and other conflicts with government authorities. In fact, the litigation surrounding the Unification Church caused some scholars at the time to conclude that it had "succeeded the Jehovah's Witnesses as today's most litigated religious movement."[55]

In 1981, Reverend Moon was convicted of tax evasion after a five-year investigation by the IRS. He was accused of filing false tax returns, perjury, and obstruction of justice all based on the fact that the church's bank and stock accounts were held in his name. While the state contended that they were for his personal benefit, Moon argued that he held them as a trustee of the church. Moon's request for a nonjury trial, for fear of public prejudice toward him and his religion, was denied.[56] Upon Moon's appeal to the U.S. Supreme Court, Pfeffer filed a brief of amicus curiae dealing primarily with the denial of a nonjury trial. A number of other religious groups filed briefs protesting the state's intervention in the Unification Church's financial affairs as well as the perceived singling out of a controversial religious figure for prosecution.[57] In his brief, Pfeffer argued that The Free Exercise Clause mandated that a nonjury trial be granted to a defendant seeking to minimize religious prejudice. He also provided evidence that a nonjury trial was necessary due to the negative popular sentiment toward "cults" such as the "Moonies." The use of the term "Moonies" was derisive, Pfeffer argued, and was proof that Moon would unlikely be given a fair jury trial. Pfeffer stated Moon's dilemma clearly: "We submit that . . . imposition of a jury trial upon the leader of a church in a criminal case directly involving his church leadership violates the Free Exercise Clause in respect to him and the church, at least where there is among the general population, a universal fear and hatred of both."[58] As he had done in other briefs, Pfeffer placed Moon in the long history of persecution of nonconventional religions in America. Moon was merely a "recent manifestation of a tragic history of unfair and unconstitutional efforts in America directed against new and unpopular religions, currently called 'cults.'"[59]

Moon's conviction was upheld at the appellate court level, and again the U.S. Supreme Court refused to review the case. Pfeffer was nevertheless joined by a wide coalition of religious and political leaders denouncing the selective prosecution of Moon. It was clear to Pfeffer and others that the tax laws were being utilized to punish a leader of an unpopular religious group.[60] Moreover, Pfeffer believed the case had broader implications for religious liberty:

> We suggest that, if juries are allowed to translate their fear and hatred of 'cults' into guilty verdicts in criminal trials, or into exorbitant damage awards in civil cases, such groups may well find that, in order to survive, they have no choice but to radically alter their sincerely and deeply held religious beliefs and practices. This result, we respectfully submit, would constitute the very antithesis of religious liberty.[61]

Pfeffer's involvement in the Worldwide Church of God and Unification Church cases illustrates his belief that the health of religious freedom in America was evidenced by the constitutional protections enjoyed by marginal religions. These cases also illustrated for Pfeffer why the general or neutral law principle was an inadequate protection for religious freedom. Facially neutral, secular laws in themselves should not be free from constitutional challenge since they could be used to hinder or destroy unpopular religions.

THE SABBATARIANS' DILEMMA

As an observant Jew, Pfeffer was keenly interested in issues involving Sabbatarians. Laws prohibiting commercial activity on Sundays had a long history in the Western world and can be traced back to the requirement in the Ten Commandments to keep the Sabbath holy. Despite the Constitution's ban on laws respecting an establishment of religion, Sabbath laws persisted in American society as well. Restricting most forms of labor on Sundays was justified as an attempt to preserve the Sabbath as it was practiced by the majority of Christians in society. Others argued that there were secular justifications for giving workers a day off each week as well. In tracing the history of these statutes, Pfeffer concluded that they were products of church-state union and that they had invariably been religiously motivated laws.[62] To

Pfeffer, it was obvious that such prohibitions were religiously discriminatory, placed groups such as the Seventh-day Adventists and Jews at an economic disadvantage, and penalized Sabbatarians for adhering to their religious beliefs.[63]

During the first half of the twentieth century, commercial interests pressured state legislatures to make some exceptions to Sunday law statutes. Gradually, some products were allowed to be sold and certain forms of entertainment were no longer prohibited on Sundays. Yet, there seemed to be no clear rationale or consistency in how the exceptions were made. According to Pfeffer, what resulted over the years was a "crazy quilt pattern of inclusions and exclusions." For instance, a New York statute allowed for the sale of milk and eggs on Sunday but not uncooked meat or fish. Tobacco was likewise open for sale but not the pipe to smoke it with. Wrestling and boxing were prohibited, but basketball and football were allowable after 2:00 p.m. Enforcement of these laws lacked "consistency or justice" according to Pfeffer who observed that were more likely to be applied exclusively to small merchants while large offenders were typically ignored. Despite the fact that nonreligious exemptions continued to expand, however, Jewish merchants were largely unsuccessful in their attempts to obtain religious exemptions from Sunday closing laws.[64]

Initially, there was hesitation within the Jewish community to challenge Sunday laws. Many Jews did not observe the Sabbath and others feared that litigation challenging their constitutionality would encourage anti-Jewish sentiment. Jewish leadership had enjoyed some success in gaining legislative exemptions, but by the 1950s, Pfeffer and the American Jewish Congress began challenging the legality of the Sabbath laws altogether. Emboldened by the U.S. Supreme Court's broad separationist interpretation of the Establishment Clause in the *Everson* and *McCollum* decisions in the 1940s, Pfeffer believed, the timing was right to forge ahead with litigation.[65] Consequently, Pfeffer began developing a legal argument that not only claimed Sunday laws contravened the Establishment Clause but also that they created an economic hardship on Sabbatarians seeking to fulfill their free exercise of religion.

In 1951, Pfeffer directed a suit filed by two Jewish butchers challenging the New York Sunday law statute. Sam Friedman and Sam Praska were each fined $10 for selling uncooked meat on Sunday. Finding no relief in the New York state court system, Pfeffer drafted an appeal to the U. S. Supreme Court arguing that Sunday laws violated both religion clauses of the First Amendment. On the one hand, he argued that Sunday laws were essentially religious laws and thus violated the Establishment Clause: "There is hardly a more flagrant use of the engine of government to further the purposes of the Christian religion than the legal recognition of Sunday as holy time."[66] On the other hand, the statute violated the free exercise of religion because those whose religion forbade them from doing business on Saturdays were put at an economic disadvantage.[67] Pfeffer argued that Jewish merchants were being penalized for their religious beliefs and that the inconsistent exemptions as well as the inconsistent enforcement of the statute violated the equal protection of the law as well. Beyond the religious liberty claims, Pfeffer suggested that one's likelihood to get cited for breaking the blue laws depended on whether one provided a financial contribution to a particular political group or police officer. While the U.S. Supreme Court dismissed the appeal, Pfeffer's brief in *Friedman* would lay the groundwork for future challenges to Sunday laws. According to Pfeffer, "Every one of the innumerable challenges to Blue Laws brought in courts all over the country during the ensuing twenty-five years was based on one or more of the claims asserted and rejected in the *Friedman* case."[68]

Pfeffer reiterated these objections ten years later in the landmark "Sunday Law Cases" involving four legal disputes that had made their way to the U.S. Supreme Court. In *McGowan v. Maryland* and *Two Guys from Harrison-Allentown v. McGinley*, two large department stores sought to continue to open their businesses seven days a week. The other two cases, *Gallagher vs. Crown Kosher Super Market* and *Braunfeld v. Brown*, concerned stores owned by Orthodox Jews who did not open for business on Saturdays. In a friend-of-the-court brief in *Gallagher v. Crown Kosher Super Market*,[69] Pfeffer stridently challenged the constitutionality of Massachusetts and Pennsylvania Sunday laws. Again he argued that they violated both the free exercise and no establishment clauses, while also raising an equal protection challenge. Pfeffer challenged the state's contention that the laws were secular welfare laws merely providing workers a day of rest. Instead, he argued that the history of such laws reflected a religious rather than secular orientation. Noting that Sunday sporting events had been allowed on Sunday afternoons and that one of the law's chief protagonists was an organization called the "Lord's Day Alliance," Pfeffer asserted that the religious purpose of the law was transparent. Since the state already had labor laws requiring twenty-four hours off for employees every seven days, Pfeffer concluded that "the legislature's intent to aid religion by closing all roads other than those leading to church seems to us to be incontrovertible."[70]

Pfeffer contended in his brief that Sabbath laws violated the free exercise of religion. Comparing the economic dilemma Sunday laws created for Sabbatarians to religious taxes in colonial America, Pfeffer asserted that "in large measure the history of the free exercise of religion clause of the First Amendment is a history of the struggle to be free of economic sanctions for adherence to one's religion." In essence, Pfeffer held that the Massachusetts and Pennsylvania laws forced Sabbatarians to choose between economic survival and religious observance.[71] Even if the economic sanction was indirect, Pfeffer held, it still violated the free exercise of religion.[72] As in the *Friedman* case, Pfeffer argued that the Sunday statutes were "irrational in nature" due to their "crazy quilt pattern" of exclusions and exemptions. This was exemplified by the fact that it was legal to "sell fish and food stuffs at wholesale, but not at retail, to dig for clams but not to dredge for oysters." As a result, Pfeffer argued that the statutes bore "nor resemblance to reason" and violated the due process and equal protection clauses of the Fourteenth Amendment as well.[73]

Ruling 8-1 in the department store cases and 6-3 in the Jewish merchant cases, the Court upheld all of the Sunday laws in question. The Court explained that the laws no longer had a religious purpose and they served merely to provide a day of rest for American workers. In his majority opinion in *McGowan*, for example, Chief Justice Earl Warren explained: "As presently written and administered, most of them, at least, are of a secular rather than a religious character, and that presently they bear no relationship to the establishment of religion as those words are used in the Constitution"[74] Warren focused most of his majority opinion on the Establishment Clause challenge arguing that the laws served a secular purpose. "The present purpose and effect . . . is to provide a uniform day of rest for all citizens; the fact that this day is Sunday, a day of particular significance for the dominant Christian sects, does not bar the state from achieving its secular goals." To rule otherwise, Warren continued, "would give a constitutional interpretation of hostility to the public welfare." Warren cited the Court's reasoning in *Everson v. Board of Education* (where it upheld the reimbursement of transportation costs for children attending parochial schools) as a similar public welfare statute.

Pfeffer's hopes for a more substantive reading of the Free Exercise Clause were dashed by Chief Justice Warren's majority opinion in *Braunfeld* as well. Warren dispensed with the religious free exercise challenge by claiming the burden on the Sabbatarian merchants to be merely "incidental." Echoing the belief/action test in *Reynolds*, Warren argued that while beliefs enjoy absolute protection, actions are not completely free from legislative restrictions. According to Warren, "If the State regulates conduct by enacting a general law with its power, the purpose and effect of which is to advance the State's secular goals, the statute is valid despite its indirect burden on religious observance unless a state may accomplish its purpose by means which do not impose such a burden."[75] Since the statute in question neither criminalized belief nor forced anyone to embrace a faith, it did not burden free exercise according to Warren. In response to the argument that the state could grant religious exemptions and still achieve its secular goals, Warren contended that exemptions would be difficult to regulate and could cause economic incentives to seek fraudulent exemptions. "Reason and experience teach that to permit the exemption might well undermine the state goal of providing a day that, as best as possible, eliminates the atmosphere of commercial noise and activity."[76]

Justice William O. Douglas was the lone dissenter in all four decisions, although he was joined by Justices Brennan and Stewart in the Jewish merchant cases. In general, Douglas's dissent followed closely the arguments raised in Pfeffer's briefs, including his argument that the Sunday laws to be a violation of both religion clauses. "There is an 'establishment of religion' in the constitutional sense if any practice of any religious group has the sanction of law behind it," he asserted, and "there is an interference with the 'free exercise of religion' if what in conscience one can do or omit doing is required because of the religious scruples of the community."[77] Citing Pfeffer's, *Church, State, and Freedom*, Douglas went on to conclude that "'the sanction imposed by the state for observing a day other than Sunday as holy time is certainly more serious economically than the imposition of a license tax for preaching,' which we struck down in *Murdock v. Commonwealth of Pennsylvania*."[78]

Justice Stewart's dissent is even more significant as his arguments would become the basis for the Court's rationale for granting unemployment compensation benefits to Sabbatarians who had lost their jobs due to conflict between their work and religious obligations. Stewart called the Sunday laws a "cruel choice" for the Orthodox Jew who is compelled "to choose between his religious faith and his economic survival." For Stewart, "the impact of this law upon the appellants grossly violates their constitutional right to the free exercise of their religion."[79]

Thus, in the Sunday Law cases, the Court seemed to have abandoned the clear and present danger test and reverted to a strict neutrality and reasonableness standard. Justice Frankfurter did hint at a compelling interest by suggesting that granting Sabbatarians exemptions might "impede the effective operation of the Sunday statutes" and "produce harmful collateral effects."[80] Nevertheless, his general philosophy was that the courts should not "set aside the judgment of those whose duty it is to legislate only if there is no reasonable basis for it."[81] "The rub of the matter," Pfeffer said reflecting on the Sunday law cases, "was that the plurality in *Braunfeld*, although not as explicitly and frankly as in Justice Frankfurter's concurrence, applied the reasonableness standard and withheld from free exercise the protection of strict judicial scrutiny long according to its first amendment brethren."[82] Pfeffer conceded that the Sunday Law decisions were a serious setback, but later opined that what he could not achieve through the courts was happening nonetheless because of American capitalism. "Sunday Closing Laws have come to an end almost everywhere in the country, not by the bang of a Supreme Court decision, nor even by a whimper from the Lord's Day Alliance or other Christian groups, but by the potency of American capitalism that could not sanction a day in which people were not allowed to spend money." While disappointed that the Court was not persuaded by the Constitutional arguments against Sunday laws, Pfeffer took comfort in the fact that economic pressures had made such laws "for all practical purposes . . . dead letter laws."[83]

Some of the most prominent free exercise conflicts involving Sabbatarians have included the quest for exemptions from Saturday work. Here Pfeffer and the American Jewish Congress were actively involved in defending not only the rights of Jewish employees and other Sabbatarians from work on the Sabbath but also the also the right of Sabbatarians to receive unemployment compensation even when refusing employment that would require work on Saturdays. These cases are illustrative of Pfeffer's broad view of the free exercise of religion and generated debate over whether religious exemptions could be reconciled with the no aid interpretation of the Establishment Clause.

In 1954, Pfeffer defended an Orthodox Jew named Mary Jane Heisler who was denied unemployment benefits because she refused to take a job that required her to work on the Sabbath. Pfeffer argued, on free exercise grounds, that constitutionally she should receive unemployment compensation because the state was forcing her to choose between her faith and her livelihood. However, the lower court in Ohio, in *Heisler v. Board of Review*,[84] rejected the religious liberty contention by claiming that there was no interference with Heisler's right to worship or conscience. Rather, the state was merely declining to compensate her for refusing to work on Saturdays. Moreover, the court found that if Heisler were granted the compensation, then the state would be discriminating against all of those workers not claiming exemptions.[85] While the *Heisler* case did not receive appellate review, it provided Pfeffer the opportunity, much like in *Friedman*, to hone constitutional arguments for future free exercise contests.

Undeterred, Pfeffer continued to advocate a broad free exercise protection for Sabbatarians. In the landmark 1963 case, *Sherbert v. Verner*[86] Pfeffer reiterated the religious liberty claims for Sabbath exemptions before the U.S. Supreme Court in a friend-of-the-court brief. Sherbert was a Seventh-Day Adventist who lost her position at a South Carolina textile plant because of her refusal to work on Saturdays after the plant had changed from a five- to a six-day work week. Sherbert was also denied unemployment compensation benefits by the state after refusing other job offers that would require her to work on Saturdays. In rejecting her request, the state Employment Security Commission determined Sherbert was "without good cause" in rejecting the job offers. After the Court of Common Pleas and the South Carolina Supreme

Court upheld the Commission's decision, Sherbert appealed to the U.S. Supreme Court.[87]

Pfeffer's brief to the Court challenged the South Carolina court's ruling on several grounds. Pfeffer urged that even if the South Carolina unemployment compensation statute's purpose was not to discriminate against Sabbatarians, the effect of the statute forced Sherbert to choose between her employment and her religion. The conflicting interests of the state and the individual had to be weighed, Pfeffer argued, and in this instance, the free exercise rights of Sherbert should prevail. In making this argument, Pfeffer utilized the "clear and present danger" test to determine the weight of the state's interest in this case. According to Pfeffer, restriction on one's religious liberty "is constitutionally permissible only if clearly and immediately necessary for the avoidance of a grave danger to the public welfare, and only if no method not infringing on religious liberty is available to avoid the change."[88] For Pfeffer, allowing Sherbert to receive unemployment benefits did not pose a "clear and present danger" to the integrity of the South Carolina unemployment compensation system for two primary reasons. First, Sherbert was willing to work six days a week and any day except Saturday. Second, there were so few Seventh-Day Adventists and other Sabbatarians in South Carolina that challenges in finding them work would not unduly burden the unemployment compensation administration. In fact, Pfeffer found that in Sherbert's home town, only one other Seventh-Day Adventist was having difficulty finding a workplace exemption.[89]

In his brief, Pfeffer again argued that a Sabbatarian was faced with a choice between economic viability and religious devotion. To Pfeffer, the *Sherbert* case represented an even greater violation of free exercise than the Sunday law cases. For even if unemployment compensation was deemed a privilege as opposed to a right, he argued, "the grant of a privilege may not be conditional upon the forfeiture of a right secured by the First Amendment."[90] Pfeffer's brief reiterated his belief in the interconnectedness of the two religion clauses of the First Amendment. This "direct infringement on freedom of conscience" was a violation of both clauses despite the fact that the statute was secular and facially neutral. In connection with the Sunday law cases, Pfeffer claimed that the unemployment compensation statute violated the Establishment Clause as well. The South Carolina law favored those religions that viewed Sunday as a day of rest since no disqualification of benefits applied to those refusing to work on Sunday. This violated the constitutional prohibition against the preference of one faith over others as well as the equality of all religions mandated by the Establishment Clause. Equally relevant, according to Pfeffer, was the No Religious Test Clause of Article VI. By placing Sabbatarians at a disadvantage, the statute "imposes a religious test for the right to receive unemployment benefits."[91]

Pfeffer was unconvinced by the claim that in allowing benefits, preference would be shown to Sabbatarians in violation of the Establishment Clause. Justice Potter Stewart would make this very argument in his dissenting opinion: "To require South Carolina to so administer its law as to pay public money to the appellant under the circumstances of this case is thus clearly to require the state to violate the Establishment Clause as construed by this court."[92] To Pfeffer, closure on Sundays had already served as an accommodation to a majority of religious adherents in South Carolina. A similar accommodation for observers on Saturday merely guaranteed equal protection under the law.[93]

Justice William Brennan wrote the opinion for the seven-to-two majority finding in favor of Sherbert. Brennan, who had dissented in the Jewish merchant Sunday law cases, ruled that "to condition the availability of benefits upon this appellant's willingness to violate a cardinal principle of her religious faith effectively penalizes the free exercise of her constitutional liberties."[94] As a result, putting Sherbert in such a position violated her free exercise rights to the same extent as a fine for Saturday worship.[95] Like Pfeffer, Brennan dispensed with the Establishment Clause objection: "The extension of unemployment benefits to Sabbatarians in common with Sunday worshipers reflects nothing more than the governmental obligation of neutrality in the face of religious differences and does not represent that involvement of religious with secular institutions which it is the object of the Establishment Clause to forestall."[96] Significantly, Brennan also held that the state must have a "compelling state interest" to restrict the free exercise of religion. This "compelling state interest" broadened the protection of the free exercise of religion and placed the burden on the government to prove that such an interest existed, even for an indirect infringement of religious liberty. Pfeffer had argued for such a test in his brief in which he stated the state must prove a "clear and present danger" before abridging constitutional liberties. Thus, the *Sherbert* decision expanded the protection of the free exercise of religion to an unprecedented level. Pfeffer would seize upon the "compelling state interest test" in his defense of other free exercise claimants.

The progeny of the *Sherbert* case would center on the extent to which accommodations must be granted to Sabbath observers. Leo Pfeffer's track record suggests that he supported widespread exemptions for Sabbatarians even when their employers claimed that such accommodations would create financial hardship. For instance, Pfeffer filed a brief of amicus curiae in the 1977 case of *T.W.A. v. Hardison*[97] arguing for a Sabbath exemption for Hardison who, as a member of the Worldwide Church of God, sought to be exempt from work from Friday sundown to Saturday sundown.[98] *T.W.A. v. Hardison* was one of several cases involving the religious discrimination prohibitions administered by the Equal Opportunity Employment Commission whose authority was granted by the Civil Rights Act of 1964. EEOC regulations held that employers must make reasonable accommodations of employees' religious needs as long as they do not create "undue hardship on the conduct of the employer's business."[99]

While an employee of T.W.A., Hardison had converted to the Worldwide Church of God and sought a position that would not conflict with observance of his Sabbath. At first, he was placed in a night shift position that accommodated his schedule, but then obtained a transfer to a day shift which, because of his low seniority level, made him ineligible for the Sabbath exemption. The labor union was unwilling to violate the seniority provisions and T.W.A. rejected Hardison's offer to work four days a week for four days' pay. Hardison subsequently lost his job for refusing to report to work on Saturday.[100] Hardison sued on the basis of the Civil Rights Act. While the district court found T.W.A. had made reasonable accommodations for Hardison's beliefs, the appellate court reversed and found in favor of Hardison. Attorneys for T.W.A. argued in their brief that the Civil Rights Act religious accommodation provision violated the Establishment Clause. Citing the Lemon Test, T.W.A. contended that the provision had a religious purpose, advanced the interests of Sabbatarians, and preferred Hardison's religious interest over others who observed their Sabbath on other days. Entanglement between church and state would also result as the state would be put in the position of determining the legitimacy of religious accommodation claims.[101]

These contentions were challenged in a brief filed by Pfeffer on behalf of the American Civil Liberties Union. The civil rights regulation did not advance religion, he argued, but rather protected the equal employment opportunity of those "who observe a day other than Sunday as their day of rest."[102] Nor did it violate the Establishment Clause because it was not limited to those who observed Sabbath on Saturday. Pfeffer rejected the excessive entanglement argument as well arguing that the Court has upheld other claims where "judgment as to the sincerity of belief was required." "To determine whether a claim asserted thereunder is made in good faith," Pfeffer concluded, "can hardly be held to entail forbidden excessive entanglement."[103]

On appeal, the U.S. Supreme Court found, over the dissents of William Brennan and Thurgood Marshall, in favor of T.W.A. and the union. It avoided the issue of the EEOC provision's constitutionality and instead ruled on the basis that T.W.A. had made reasonable accommodations for Hardison. The decision hinged on the fact that T.W.A. made a valid effort to find Hardison another position but that the company was not required to violate the union's seniority system in doing so.[104] Moreover, the Court held that the overtime costs the company would have to pay in order to accommodate Hardison would constitute more than a minimal cost. Thus, the undue hardship created by accommodating Hardison absolved T.W.A. from any constitutional obligations.[105] In reflecting on the decision, Pfeffer predicted that the Court would not be able to avoid the constitutional question as EEOC religious accommodation cases would likely increase in the years to come. "The Hardison decision does not give sufficient light to predict with assurance how the Court would respond" to other religious accommodations," Pfeffer reasoned, "although the tenor of the opinion suggests that it would be no more sympathetic to the claims of the employees."[106]

The free exercise rights of Sabbatarians illustrated for Leo Pfeffer the ebb and flow of religion clause jurisprudence. In the early 1960s, he described the Sunday Law decisions as the "nadir" of free exercise, but was heartened, if not emboldened, as a broader reading of the Free Exercise Clause was adopted by the Court in *Sherbert v. Verner*. Historian Naomi Cohen has argued that, after the *Sherbert* decision, "Christianity was no longer synonymous with public religion and when the major battles on schools and Sunday laws had been fought, Jewish organizations expanded their horizons." Utilizing the compelling state interest test, Pfeffer and his counterparts at other Jewish agencies began to broaden their advocacy from mere protection of Jewish beliefs from Christian majoritarian laws and practices to "government accommodation of variant religious practices."[107] A more robust affirmation of religious pluralism was the goal, but, as Cohen queried, would the tool of a more substantive free exercise clause conflict with the broad Establishment Clause utilized in the past to insure Jewish equality? According to Cohen,

> To be sure, government accommodation of variant religious practices blurred the line between the strictures of no establishment and free exercise. Indeed, it contradicted the strict interpretation of establishment which Jews themselves had usually defended. But the new emphasis better suited the reality of a pluralist setting. An exclusively negative focus on minority usages was outdated, a relic of the era when America was, or at least aspired to be, a homogeneous Protestant society.[108]

Pfeffer would certainly take issue with the Cohen's claim that a broad reading of both religion clauses was incompatible. But Cohen's narrative does reflect the trajectory of Pfeffer's jurisprudence. As stated above, it was only after *Sherbert* that Pfeffer more actively pursued rights of new religious movements and other minority faiths. In 1953, Pfeffer wrote to a colleague: "I have placed the religious liberty items before the church-state items. This is in accord with your suggestion, although I differ with you on this point. Religious liberty issues are less critical, less interesting and less thought provoking, and our contribution has been smaller in this area."[109] Yet by the late 1970s, Pfeffer's perspective on free exercise cases seemed to have changed as he was taking a special interest in defending "disfavored" religions from "what might be called a crusade against newly formed unpopular religions, commonly called cults."[110]

Overall, the cases involving Sabbath observance and exemptions reflect the broad extent to which Leo Pfeffer would allow free exercise claims to be granted. He was often willing to go further than the U.S. Supreme Court in granting these exemptions and in doing so affirmed the constitutionality of the religious discrimination prohibitions of the EEOC guidelines. Rather than an unconstitutional establishment of Sabbatarians, Pfeffer found that the mandated protections of these individuals "give a minority employee the equal treatment to which he is entitled in fairness and justice (and, we believe, in the implementation of 'free exercise values'), a law such as this is a necessity."[111]

FREE EXERCISE AND COMPULSORY EDUCATION LAWS

Leo Pfeffer was a staunch defender of public education and strenuously opposed religious exercises in the public schools as well as aid to religious schools. Nonetheless, he recognized the right of parents to choose a private religious education for their children as well as supported free exercise claims of religious minorities seeking free exercise exemptions from compulsory education laws.[112] In the landmark free exercise case, *Wisconsin v. Yoder*, Pfeffer supported the exemption of Amish children from compulsory education laws. The case centered on a Wisconsin law that required all children to attend school until the age of sixteen. The Amish argued that their religious beliefs compelled them to remain separated from the corrupting influences of the world. By attending high school, their children would be exposed to ideas and attitudes contrary to the Amish faith. Moreover, sending their children to high school might invite censure from the rest of the religious community and may threaten their children's salvation.[113]

Attorneys for the state of Wisconsin argued that its compulsory education laws had the overriding purpose of ensuring an educated citizenry as well as an economically viable population so as to not be a "burden on society."[114] Wisconsin also asserted that the state had an interest in protecting children from a community that would hinder their ability to successfully navigate the secular world if they were ever to leave the Amish faith.[115] Both of these contentions, they argued, reflected a compelling state interest that should override the free exercise claims of the Amish.

At issue for Pfeffer was the conflict between the rights of parents in the upbringing of their children and the interest of the state in the welfare of children. When the *Yoder* case reached the U.S. Supreme Court in 1971, Pfeffer addressed, in an *amicus* brief on behalf of the Synagogue Council of America and the American Jewish Congress, two primary arguments for granting the exemption to the Amish. First, Pfeffer sought to dispose of the strict neutrality approach to free exercise claims. Just because the compulsory education law was a neutral and secular statute that did not single out the Amish for religious discrimination, it was not immune from free exercise challenge. "Decisions which have rejected claims of unconstitutional infringement upon the free exercise of religion are justifiable not on the ground that the First Amendment may never require exemptions from general nondiscriminatory welfare laws," Pfeffer argued, "but because of the presence of a paramount, overriding societal need, such as preservation of the monogamous family society (Reynolds) or national defense (Hamilton)."[116] Second, Pfeffer challenged the concern that the integrity of the public school system would be threatened if religious exemptions were allowed. Pfeffer responded that, like *Sherbert*, the number of people seeking religious exemptions would be small and would pose no threat to the public school system. In fact, there would be a smaller potential for fraud in this instance than there would be in *Sherbert*. Moreover, Pfeffer suggested that eight years of schooling was enough to provide for an informed citizenry to participate productively in a democracy.[117]

Much like his briefs in Establishment Clause cases, Pfeffer emphasized the importance of preserving religious pluralism in America as well as the integrity of faith traditions. Providing an exemption was important in preserving the Old Order Amish. Otherwise, increased exposure of Amish children to high school education would lead to "the eventual disappearance of the Amish community culture."[118] Pluralism was a cornerstone of democracy, Pfeffer insisted, and it ensured domestic tranquility.[119]

In his opposition to religious exercises in the public schools, Pfeffer often identified the psychological damage children of religious minorities faced due to the practice of majoritarian religious exercises in the public schools.[120] Similarly, Pfeffer addressed the dilemma Amish children would face between obeying the law and their religious convictions. "We suggest too that in weighing these interests consideration must be given to the psychological hurt suffered by these youths if they are forced by law to engage in a practice which they believe to be against the will of God and inimical to their own salvation."[121] Thus, Pfeffer urged the Court to uphold its ruling in *Sherbert* by requiring the state to show a "compelling state interest" before rejecting the Amish request for an exemption.

In *Wisconsin v. Yoder*,[122] a unanimous U.S. Supreme Court supported the Amish claim for exemption. The Court concluded that the "enforcement of the State's requirement of compulsory formal education after the eighth grade would gravely endanger if not destroy the free exercise of respondent's beliefs."[123] Rejecting Wisconsin's interest in protecting Amish children as well as broader societal interests, the Court stated that "accommodating the religious objections of the Amish by foregoing one, or at most two, additional years of compulsory education will not impair the physical or mental health of the child, nor result in an inability to be self-supporting, or to discharge the duties and responsibilities of citizenship, or in any other way detract from the welfare of society."[124] Neither did the Court find an Establishment Clause conflict by granting an exemption to the Amish. "The Court must not ignore the danger than an exception from a general obligation of citizenship on religious grounds may run afoul of the Establishment Clause," Burger observed, "but that danger cannot be allowed to prevent any exception no matter how vital it may be to the protection of values promoted by the gifts of free exercise."[125]

Pfeffer believed the *Yoder* decision to have special significance. Until *Sherbert*, the U.S. Supreme Court had not been particularly supportive of free exercise claims challenging generally applicable, secular laws. Usually success only came when the free exercise claims were coupled with free speech contentions. When free exercise stood alone, it usually failed.[126] This led Pfeffer to conclude that prior to *Sherbert* "realistically, free exercise did not have a separate but equal existence, or even one that was separate and unequal, it practically had no existence at all."[127] With the *Sherbert* decision and its requirement of a "compelling state interest," the Free Exercise Clause had achieved an equal status with other First Amendment freedoms. However, *Yoder* had raised free exercise to a new level of significance. Not only did the Court uphold the broader protection of free exercise begun in *Sherbert* but also seemed to go out of its way to elevate free exercise to become, in Pfeffer's words, "the favored child of the First Amendment."[128]

CONSCIENTIOUS OBJECTION AND THE CHALLENGE OF DEFINING RELIGION

The clash of conflicting interests between the state and individual conscience has been no more clearly illustrated than in the issue of conscientious objection to war. While one of the paramount interests of the state is national security, there has been a long history of pacifism among some religious traditions. Typically, however, the nation's security has been viewed as superior to pacifist claims. As a result, the U.S. Supreme Court has often accepted the restriction of individual liberties when the nation's security is threatened. Citing the legal adage "the Constitution is not a suicide pact," Leo Pfeffer noted that often "individual liberties secured by the Constitution must yield when the nation's safety is in peril."[129]

If national security is of primary importance, then the exemption from combat due to religious scruples is not deemed a constitutional right. Rather, conscientious objectors' status has been determined to be a legislative grant. Thus, the crux of the constitutional debate over conscientious objection in American history has centered on how the conscientious objection exemptions in military draft laws have been interpreted and applied. Beyond the First Amendment questions, equal protection issues arise since some clergy, avowed pacifists of "peace churches," have long been granted exemptions. How would, then, individual pacifists or members of less recognized pacifist traditions be treated by the legislative and judicial branches became an important and increasingly litigated question in the twentieth century.

An on-going problem in this area has been determining who fits the conscientious objector profile. During the American Revolution, pacifist religious groups, such as Quakers and Mennonites, suffered fines and imprisonment for their refusal to be involved in combat. While some states attempted to provide exemptions from military duty to members of recognized pacifist religions, the record was inconsistent and the loyalty of the members of these groups often called into question. During the Civil War, conscientious objectors in the North were able to substitute combat service by either paying for a replacement or serving in a noncombat duty. This exemption was provided for by the Federal Conscription Act of 1864 so long as the objector was a member of a religious group whose articles of faith prohibited the bearing of arms.[130] Similar exemption rules were adopted in the South.

The next universal military conscription was passed in 1917 during World War I. Again, conscientious objection became an issue as opposition was raised to the limiting of the exemption to ordained ministers and members of "well-recognized" religious sects or organizations. A new Selective Service Act passed during World War II expanded the exemption to include those who by "religious training and belief" were opposed to war in any form.[131] In 1948, however, Congress sought to clarify the Selective Service Act to exclude nonreligious based objections and amended the law to state that "religious training and belief in this connection means an individual's belief in a relation to a Supreme Being involving duties superior to those arising from any human relation, but does not include essentially political, sociological, or philosophical views or a merely personal moral code."[132]

Prior to Pfeffer's involvement in conscientious objector cases, the U.S. Supreme Court had addressed the issue on a number of occasions. Many of these cases did not concern draft laws, but rather oaths required of aliens seeking naturalization. In 1929, for instance, the Court upheld the denial of naturalization of a Hungarian woman who refused to take an oath affirming that she would take up arms to defend the country.[133] Naturalization was also denied to a Yale professor who sought the right to determine on a case-by-case basis whether as war was just or not.[134] In 1946, however, the U.S. Supreme Court determined that Congress had not intended to make combat oaths a requirement for naturalization.[135] If nothing else, what the naturalization cases illustrate is that the Court continued to recognize that exemptions from military service were a legislative grant rather than a Constitutional right.[136]

In the 1960s, conscientious objection gained renewed attention, particularly due to the controversy surrounding the United States' military action in Vietnam. The opposition to the War by many young Americans, many of whom burned their draft cards as a sign of protest, led to concern over the ability to determine the sincerity and legitimacy in granting conscientious objector status. Draft boards were inundated with applications for conscientious objector status, many of whom based their claims on nonconventional religious beliefs. This was exacerbated by the religious experimentation among the American populous during the 1960s.[137] American religious life witnessed an ever expanding religious pluralism which included nontraditional indigenous religious movements as well as increasing numbers of adherents to nontheistic faiths.

It was in this context that the conscientious objector case *U.S. v. Seeger* arose.[138] *Seeger* was one of three similar conscientious objection cases the U.S. Supreme Court decided with one opinion in 1965. Prosecuted in New York for his refusal to submit to induction in the U.S. military, Daniel Seeger claimed conscientious objector status after having used student status to avoid the draft for previous years. Subsequently, he claimed that he was opposed to war in any form for "religious" reasons, but declined to affirm that his belief was based on a "Supreme Being." Citing Plato, Aristotle, and Spinoza, Seeger explained that he believed in "devotion to goodness and virtue for their own sakes, and a religious faith in a purely ethical creed."[139] Although his belief was understood to be sincere and based on individual training, Seeger was convicted in the district court primarily on the basis that his belief was not in relation to a Supreme Being as required by the Universal Military Training and Service Act. The district court's decision was reversed by the appellate court which held that the Act was unconstitutional insofar as it required a theistic belief.[140]

The *Seeger* case provided Leo Pfeffer the opportunity to raise several constitutional objections to the exemption requirements of the Selective Service Act. In his brief of amicus curiae, Pfeffer identified the basic issue of the case to be "whether Congress may, consistently with the First Amendment, limit the exemption from military service of conscientious objectors to those who believe in the existence of a Supreme Being."[141] In defense of Seeger, Pfeffer challenged the military draft law as inconsistent with the First Amendment. While the focus of Pfeffer's brief was on Seeger's free exercise rights, Pfeffer argued that the Selective Service Act violated the Establishment Clause as well. Primarily, the law preferred theistic religions over nontheistic ones because of its requirement of a belief in a Supreme Being. The *Torcaso v. Watkins* religious oath case was especially relevant here according to Pfeffer. The Court had ruled in *Torcaso* that the state cannot aid "those religions based on a belief in the existence of God as against those religions founded on different beliefs."[142] This Pfeffer reiterated in his *Seeger* brief: "Religion and belief in God, as was pointed out in *Torcaso*, are not synonymous. There are ancient, well-recognized religions that are not theistic, religions such as Buddhism, Taoism, and Confucianism."[143] Again, the concepts of equality and separation of church and state informed Pfeffer's understanding of the Religion Clauses. Consequently, in violating the Establishment Clause, the Act led to the restriction of Seeger's free exercise rights as well.

The other major argument appearing in Pfeffer's brief was that military officials were being put in the position of making theological judgments. While recognizing that the draft boards will inevitably have to determine whether a motivation for exemption is religious and is sincerely held, the constitutional prohibition clearly arises when the state distinguishes between religions.[144] According to Pfeffer:

> In order to protect conscientious professors in the free exercise of religion it may well be necessary to determine whether that which they are exercising is indeed religion. To this extent, inquiry into what is more properly the domain of theology and philosophy may be unavoidable. But beyond that, we submit, the Constitution does not permit civil agencies to go. They may neither define God nor equate religion with belief in a constitutionally undefinable God.[145]

The Court held in Seeger's favor, but did not find the use of the term Supreme Being in the draft act's language unconstitutional. Instead, it determined Seeger's beliefs to be consistent with belief in relation to a Supreme Being. Use of the term Supreme Being, the Court explained, was intended to be interpreted much more broadly than traditional conceptions of God. It further held that "religious belief" was one "which is sincere and meaningful and occupies a place in the life of its possessor parallel to that filled by the orthodox belief in God of one who clearly qualifies for the exemption."[146] While Seeger's description of his religious beliefs seems difficult to reconcile with belief in a Supreme Being, the Court's generous interpretation of "religious belief" covered his nontheistic convictions. Pfeffer believed this was demanded by the Establishment Clause to avoid any preference for a particular religious belief. According to Pfeffer, "Ever since the *Everson* decision in 1947, it had been the law of the land that under the Establishment Clause government could not prefer some religions over others."[147]

Advocates of strict neutrality would argue that Pfeffer's approach created a constitutional dilemma. By seeking broad exemptions from neutral laws while advocating for neutrality between religion and non-religion, Pfeffer and like advocates had pushed the Court into a constitutional corner. Pfeffer instead viewed this approach as a way of maximizing religious freedom without justices becoming the arbiters of what constituted legitimate theological convictions. Nonetheless, this would seem to raise a constitutional objection to any exemption from military service based on religious belief. Recognizing this, Pfeffer concluded that the court's broad interpretation of religious belief and focus on sincerity was done, in part, to avoid such a situation. "What this meant is that depth and sincerity can be substituted for dogma and creedal affiliation," Pfeffer explained. "The decision assumed the importance of being earnest, but not necessarily of being religious, at least as that word would be understood by the man in the street."[148] Thus, while Pfeffer understood exemptions from military service for reasons of conscience not to be a right, but a legislative grant, he held that if the exemptions were to be granted, the state may not discriminate between different types of religious belief or nonreligious belief.

Some have argued that determining sincerity would seem to be just as problematic as engaging in theological inquiry.[149] While the sincerity test is an imperfect solution, Pfeffer believed the Court needed to have some criteria for determining disingenuous conscientious objection claims. As one scholar has explained, some intrusiveness into at least the sincerity of an individual or group is unavoidable "if the Court is to be protected from fraudulent or sham claims under the free exercise clause."[150]

FREE EXERCISE AND ABORTION RIGHTS

As with other free exercise conflicts, Leo Pfeffer viewed laws that restricted abortion rights as implicating both religion clauses. According to Pfeffer, any "categorical imperative (related to abortion) binding upon all the particular theology of one or more religions is literally a law respecting an establishment of that religion and prohibiting the free exercise of other religions which do not embrace that theology."[151] The American Jewish Congress had historically affirmed abortion rights, but, as the debate over abortion became more contentious, the AJC became more reticent to engage this issue due to concerns about community relations. As a result, the AJC chose to pull out of formally supporting a 1980 amicus curiae brief authored by Pfeffer challenging the constitutionality of the Hyde Amendment. The Hyde Amendment, passed by Congress in 1976, prohibited Medicaid funds to be used to finance abortions except for cases of rape and incest. The controversial amendment would be challenged as a violation of both the Due Process Clause of the Fifth Amendment and the religion clauses of the First Amendment in *Harris v. McRae* (1980).[152]

The Religious Coalition for Abortions Rights, a national organization representing eighteen religious bodies, invited Pfeffer to draft an amicus curiae brief challenging the Hyde Amendment. Pfeffer did so with the hopes raising both the Establishment and Free Exercise Clause contentions largely ignored by the Court in *Roe v. Wade*. Three key arguments shaped Pfeffer's constitutional objection to the Hyde Amendment. First, he argued that it preferred religions that opposed abortion over those that did not. Second, it violated the purpose and effect provisions of the Lemon Test by possessing a clearly religious purpose and advancing some religions while inhibiting others. "The conclusion is inescapable," Pfeffer declared, "that a primary effect of the exclusion of abortion procedures from Medicaid coverage is to advance the religious doctrine of those who hold abortion to violate God's law."[153] Third, it violated the freedom of conscience of those that sought abortions by imposing "the prohibitions of those religions that deem abortions sinful upon persons whose religious beliefs do not exclude abortion procedures."[154]

Even though the Federal District Court found that the "funding restrictions of the Hyde Amendment" impinged upon the Free Exercise Clause when abortion is resorted to "in conformity to religious belief and teaching," the U.S. Supreme Court was less sympathetic with the religious liberty arguments. Writing for a five-to-four majority, Justice Potter Stewart declared that the Due Process Clause did not require the government to subsidize abortions and found the First Amendment arguments against the Hyde Amendment unpersuasive as well. The fact that the Hyde Amendment's funding restrictions were consistent with the teachings of the Roman Catholic Church was "coincidental" according to Stewart, who retorted that "just because the Judaeo-Christian religions oppose stealing does not mean that a State or the Federal Government may not, consistent with the Establishment Clause, enact laws prohibiting larceny." Stewart likewise dismissed the free exercise claim because none of the appellees "alleged, much less proved, that she sought an abortion under compulsion of religious belief."[155]

Pfeffer was convinced that historically, theological convictions were at the root of opposition to abortion. He did recognize that "a law religious in origin may through changes in the course of time lose its religious purpose and become secularized."[156] Yet in tracing the historical development of the Catholic Church's teaching on abortion, he believed the opposite had taken place. As the Church's teaching on abortion had become more conservative, laws had become more restrictive. Pfeffer was no more persuaded that framing the abortion debate in terms of general morality, rather than theology, changed the constitutional issues at hand: "Framing the legal debate on abortion in terms of morality in effect brands as immoral or at best indifferent to moral values the many respected clergymen who do not deem it immoral."[157] Pfeffer was not persuaded by Stewart's abortion/stealing analogy as well. Unlike laws punishing theft which are of ancient origin and across various cultures and religions, "it doesn't just happen that restrictions on abortion coincide with the tenets of some religions," Pfeffer responded. "If they didn't coincide, it is hardly likely that the statute would have been enacted."[158]

For a variety of reasons, the religious arguments for abortion rights have been marginalized in subsequent reproductive rights cases. Most cases continue to hinge on due process and equal protection claims. Moreover, evangelical Protestants have increasingly embraced the more absolutist pro-life position and have formed alliances with pro-life Catholics. And while progressive Protestants still often support abortion rights, most pro-choice groups avoid religious liberty arguments knowing that they will get little traction in the courts. Pro-life advocates argue that the debate over abortion is less theologically laden than in the past and, with the advances in medicine and changes to fetal viability, the arguments against abortion have become more secularized. Nonetheless, there remain pro-choice advocates that argue fetal personhood remains a theological question and one that Congress and the courts should no longer avoid.[159]

While Pfeffer had little success convincing the Court to view abortion as a religious liberty issue, he did witness the Court embrace a broad reading of the Free Exercise Clause for much of his career. The high point of this was the 1973 *Wisconsin v. Yoder* decision that he argued represented the "supremacy of free exercise." Nonetheless, the broad reading of free exercise the Court seemed to embrace did not guarantee that free exercise claimants always prevailed. At times, the state's interest was deemed compelling. As one scholar has explained, religious claimants "lost as many as they won, particularly when their religious exercise touched on fundamental issues of public policy or criminal law."[160]

As Pfeffer's career was coming to a close, the Court, in a series of cases culminating in the 1990 *Oregon v. Smith* decision, increasingly upheld restrictions on free exercise claims if the law or regulation in question was neutral. In *Goldman v. Weinberger*, for instance the Court denied a Rabbi and military psychologist an exemption from military dress codes so that he could wear his yarmulke while on duty in a military clinic. The majority concluded that the need for military discipline and uniformity outweighed Weinberger's religious claim.[161] Similarly, in *Bowen v. Roy*, the Court upheld the requirement that participants in federal welfare programs provide society security numbers. Stephen Roy refused to obtain a social security number for his daughter fearing that, based upon his Native American beliefs, such a practice would "rob the spirit" of his daughter. An eight member majority of the U.S. Supreme Court sided with the government concluding that "the Free Exercise Clause simply cannot be understood to require the Government to conduct its own internal affairs in ways that comport with the religious beliefs of particular citizens."[162]

Following this trend, the Court, in *O'Lone v. Estate of Shabazz*, held that the free exercise rights of Muslim prisoners was not violated when a prison deprived them of their ability to attend Friday worship. Significantly, the Court declared that as long as the prison regulations were "reasonably related to a legitimate penological objective," they were constitutional.[163] And in *Lyng v. Northwest Indian Ceremony Protective Association*, the Court upheld the Forest Service's plan to build a paved roadway "through property that had a long history of being used by Native Americans for religious rituals." Writing for a five-to-three majority, Justice Sandra Day O'Connor argued that the government's actions did not literally "prohibit" the Native American's free exercise of religion. The adverse impact on the Indian's practice was "incidental" she argued. "However much one might wish it were otherwise, government simply could not operate if it were required to satisfy every citizen's religious needs and desires," O'Connor concluded.[164]

The trend toward a narrower reading and application of the Free Exercise Clause culminated in the hotly contested *Oregon v. Smith* decision in 1990. In *Smith*, a Native American was denied unemployment compensation after losing his job as a drug counselor for ingesting peyote. Since peyote was an illegal drug in Oregon at the time, Smith was disqualified for benefits due to the criminal nature of his actions. Arguing that he had ingested peyote as a sacramental practice, Smith filed suit arguing that his free exercise rights had been violated.

In yet another five-to-four decision, Justice Antonin Scalia wrote the majority opinion ruling against Smith's claims, and, in doing so, undermining the compelling state interest test introduced in *Sherbert v. Verner*. Scalia declared, for a plurality of the Court, that laws need only to be neutral and generally applicable to prevail over religious claims even if they create a burden on religious practices. Relief from such burdens should be sought in the legislative branch as opposed to the courts, according to Scalia. He believed that it was unrealistic, in both a religious cosmopolitan nation and one with extensive laws and regulations, to presume laws unconstitutional if they conflicted with religious behaviors and practices. Citing *Reynolds*, Scalia argued that each person otherwise would become "a law unto himself." Taking a more restrictive reading of the Free Exercise Clause, Scalia concluded that the compelling state interest test should only apply in those instances in which a law targets a religion or religious practices.[165]

Scalia's rejection of the compelling state interest test brought staunch opposition, including from Justice O'Connor who, in her concurring opinion, argued that without the compelling state interest test, "the fate of minority religions would indeed be left up to the political process, which is precisely what the Bill of Rights was intended to prevent."[166] Nonetheless, in finding with the majority, she concluded that Oregon's need to combat drug abuse and violence constituted a compelling state interest.

In one of his last published writings, Leo Pfeffer criticized the U.S. Supreme Court's decision in *Oregon v. Smith* for reversing nearly thirty years of free exercise jurisprudence.[167] The decision deeply troubled Pfeffer who saw it as a return to the neutrality and reasonableness standards of earlier years that provided little free exercise protection of religious minorities. Pfeffer was not alone in his criticism as a scholarly debate over the scope of free exercise, particularly over the constitutionality of judicially granted religious exemptions from generally applicable laws, ensued. Most critics of the Court's decision in *Smith* held a substantive view of the Free Exercise Clause claiming that the constitutionally religious exemptions should be the presumption short of an overriding state interest.[168] Other scholars agreed, at least in principle, with Justice Scalia's claim that the Free Exercise Clause did not mandate religious exemptions.[169] Many of these argued that a broad reading of the Free Exercise Clause that mandated exemptions was irreconcilable with a broad reading of the Establishment Clause that required neutrality between religion and irreligion. Some commentators specifically identified the strict separationist position advocated by Pfeffer as having exacerbated the tension between the two clauses.[170]

Widespread opposition to the *Oregon v. Smith* decision, especially the sweeping nature of Scalia's majority opinion, led Congress to pass, overwhelmingly, the Religious Freedom Restoration Act in 1993. R.F.R.A.'s attempt to restore the compelling state interest test to free exercise jurisprudence was struck down by the Court in *Boerne v. Flores*,[171] at least in terms of its applicability to the states. Nineteen states passed their own Religious Freedom Restoration Acts (RFRA) and Congress responded by passing the Religious Land Use and Institutionalized Persons Act (RLUIPA) in 2000. This law prohibited federal land use or regulations and federally funded prisons from imposing a substantial burden on free exercise rights unless it was to further a compelling governmental interest. RLUIPA was subsequently upheld in *Cutter v. Wilkinson* against an Establishment Clause challenge in 2005.[172]

Despite passage of the RFRA and RLUIPA, the debate over the appropriate interpretation of the Free Exercise Clause remains. Central to this dispute is whether a broad reading of free exercise invariably creates a constitutional conflict with no establishment. In the "clash of conflicting interests" as Pfeffer described the conflicts between religious free exercise and state interests, some commentators have suggested that the strict neutrality approach creates the least constitutional conflict. This view argues that the better course of wisdom is for religious claimants to seek exemptions from the legislative branch, not judges. The virtue of this approach is that it avoids the problem of judges making determinations about the legitimacy or sincerity of religious claims.

Other commentators have argued that the strict neutrality approach would be "subject to the same ambiguities of formal neutrality under the Equal Protection Clause." There is a fine line between a neutral and a discriminatory law according to these commentators. "Laws that appear quite neutral to a majority may seriously burden a religious minority," one scholar has suggested. As a result, a more substantive reading of the Free Exercise Clause that recognized the special constitutional status of religion and better protects the rights and equality of religious minorities is necessitated.[173] Similarly, John Witte has argued for a multi-principled approach to free exercise, including equality, freedom of conscience, and separation of church and state. These, he fears, are diminished in the neutrality approach that would prove to be an inadequate protection for religious liberty. A more substantive reading of free exercise that would include exemptions and exclusions were both "countenanced and created" by the Free Exercise Clause. While he would take issue with Pfeffer's strict separationist approach to the Establishment Clause, Witte would likely agree with the claim that the founders religion was special and deserved protection.

In many ways, the contemporary debates over free exercise echo the competing views advanced by Pfeffer and constitutional scholar Philip Kurland nearly fifty years earlier. While Kurland affirmed the unitary nature of the religion clauses in his *Religion and the Law: Of Church and State and the Supreme Court*, he argued that the symbiotic relationship between the religion clauses was preserved through strict neutrality. According to Kurland: "The freedom and separation clauses should be read as a single precept: that government cannot utilize religion as a standard for action or inaction because these clauses, read together as they should be, prohibit classification in terms of religion in either to confer a benefit or impose a burden."[174]

In a review of Kurland's book, Pfeffer argued that Kurland's neutrality approach would have grave consequences for free exercise of religion. While "many, perhaps most of the decisions (if not opinions) of the Supreme Court under the religion clause of the First Amendment are consistent with the religion-blind thesis," Pfeffer argued, "the practical consequence of the adopting of his proposition" would include prohibiting not only "judicial discretion but also legislative" in granting exemptions to religious claimants. Conscientious objection, ministerial exemptions, some tax exemptions, Sabbatarian exemptions, government paid chaplains, and references to God in official documents would all be "outlawed" under Kurland's interpretation. "It is hardly an overstatement to suggest that faithful and consistent application of Professor Kurland's doctrine would effect a revolutionary change in our society," Pfeffer concluded, "and that is the organized religious bodies . . . that would suffer the most from the change," Pfeffer concluded.[175]

SUMMARY

Leo Pfeffer championed an expansive view of the free exercise of religion out of a commitment to religious freedom and equality. He utilized his broad reading of the Free Exercise Clause to defend the freedom of nonconventional religions, conscientious objectors, Sabbatarians, and challenged religiously based prohibitions on abortion rights. In this "clash of conflicting interests" between the state and the individual's conscience, Pfeffer consistently held that the state must show a compelling interest before restricting the free exercise of religion. His briefs in support of the Worldwide Church of God and the Rev. Sun Myung Moon against claims of corporate fraud and tax evasion illustrated his contention that neutral, secular laws had often been used to discriminate against nonconventional religions.

In cases involving Sabbatarians, Pfeffer believed that enforcement of Sunday laws violated not only the free exercise of religion of Sabbatarians but also the Establishment Clause by preferring religions that observed Sunday as the holy day. Similarly, Pfeffer urged that free exercise exemptions be granted to Sabbatarians in the workplace who were put in the position of choosing between their religion and their livelihoods.

Pfeffer's broad interpretation of the Free Exercise Clause also led him to argue that Amish children should be exempt from compulsory education laws and that freedom of religion protected conscientious objectors. He asserted that the military, in granting conscientious objector status to those opposed to participation in war as a matter of conscience, could not limit its exemptions to those whose beliefs were based on more conventional forms of religious belief.

The breadth and continuity of Leo Pfeffer's understanding of religious freedom and the separation of church and state is revealed as well in his advocacy for abortion rights. While less successful in this area of advocacy, Pfeffer's arguments illustrate the challenge of identifying when laws are rooted in theology or have been sufficiently secularized not to offend both the liberty of conscience and the separation of church and state.

According to Pfeffer, the holding of an expansive view of the Free Exercise Clause did not conflict with an equally absolutist view of the Establishment Clause. In light of the unitary guarantee, Pfeffer argued that the two clauses worked in tandem for the goal of religious liberty. His legal briefs in free exercise cases again reveal his belief in the unitary nature of the First Amendment's religion clauses—that a violation of one clause often was also a violation of the other. Pfeffer's free exercise advocacy further illustrated his concern for the freedom and integrity of religious faith. In pursuing exemptions from generally applicable laws, Pfeffer sought not only the removal of barriers to freely exercise faith but also to provide all religions a seat at the table of American culture.

NOTES

1. Pfeffer, *Church, State, and Freedom*, 609.
2. Ibid.
3. Pfeffer, *Religion, State and the Burger Court*, 233.
4. Pfeffer, *Church, State, and Freedom*, 611–18.
5. Michael A. Paulsen, "Religion, Equality, and the Constitution: An Equal Protection Approach to Establishment Clause Adjudication," *Notre Dame Law Review* 61 (1986): 31; Choper, "A Century of Religious Freedom," *California Law Review* 88 (2000): 1711, citing *Walz v. Tax Commission* 397 U.S. 664 (1970) at 668–69.
6. Pfeffer, "Amici in Church-State Litigation," 94; "The Current State of the Law in the United States and the Separationist Agenda," *The Annals of the American Academy of Political and Social Science* 446 (November 1979): 1.
7. 310 U.S. 296 (1940).
8. 406 U.S. 2015 (1972).
9. See *Sherbert v. Verner*, 374 U.S. 398 (1963).
10. The conventional thesis that the courts have been more solicitous of individual rights than legislatures has been challenged in recent years by some scholars. See Louis Fisher, *Religious Liberty in America: Political Safeguards* (Lawrence: University Press of Kansas, 2000). Fisher may be correct that legislatures have granted religious exemptions, but the fact remains that most of the foundational free exercise cases have involved religious minorities seeking relief from general laws and regulations.
11. Ronald B. Flowers, Melissa Rogers, and Steven K. Green, *Religious Freedom and the Supreme Court* (Waco, Tex.: Baylor University Press, 2008), 96.
12. Pfeffer, "The Legitimation," 14–15.
13. Pfeffer, "Religious Freedom," 137.
14. Fowler et al., *Religious Freedom and the Supreme Court*, 98; see also Sarah Barringer Gordon, *The Mormon Question: Polygamy and Constitutional Conflict in Nineteenth Century America* (Chapel Hill, NC: University of North Carolina Press, 2002).
15. *Reynolds v. United States*, 98 U.S. 145 (1878).
16. Ibid., at 166.
17. *Davis v. Beason*, 133 U.S. 333 (1890).
18. Ibid., at 342.
19. *Church of Latter-Day Saints v. United States*, 136 U.S. 1 (1890).
20. Pfeffer, "The Legitimation," 16.

21. Pfeffer, *God, Caesar, and the Constitution*, 31.

22. John Witte, Jr. and Joel A. Nichols, *Religion and the American Constitutional Experiment*, 4th ed. (New York: Oxford University Press, 2016), 123.

23. Refusal to salute the flag or receive blood transfusions was based on the biblical prohibition of not worshipping graven images or eating blood. Some important literature on the Jehovah's Witnesses includes David R. Manwaring, *Render Unto Caesar: The Flag Salute Controversy* (Chicago: University of Chicago Press, 1962) and Merlin Owen Newton, *Armed With the Constitution: Jehovah's Witnesses in Alabama and the U.S. Supreme Court, 1939–1946* (Tuscaloosa, AL: University of Alabama Press, 2002).

24. *Minersville v. Gobitis*, 310 U.S. 586 (1940).

25. Ibid., at 594–95.

26. Leo Pfeffer, "The Supremacy of Free Exercise," *Georgetown Law Journal* 61 (May 1963): 1122–23.

27. Ibid.; 310 U.S. 586 at 607.

28. *West Virginia State Board of Education v. Barnette*, 319 U.S. 624 (1942). The Court's reversal has been explained on changes in the Court's makeup. Pfeffer suggested that the explanation lies in the widespread persecution Jehovah's Witnesses faced after the *Gobitis* decision as well as the perception during the War that the Japanese American community represented a greater threat to American security than Jehovah's Witness children; see Pfeffer, *Legitimation*, 18–19.

29. 319 U.S. 624 at 642; Frankfurter reiterated his neutrality approach to free exercise in a dissenting opinion in *Barnette*. Pfeffer concluded that Frankfurter believed political speech to enjoy special protection and was worthy of strict scrutiny, but, otherwise, exemptions from neutral, generally applicable laws should be granted by the legislative branch. Pfeffer, *Church, State, and Freedom*, 618.

30. Pfeffer, "The Supremacy of Free Exercise," 1130.

31. *Cantwell v. Connecticut*, 310 U.S. 296 (1940).

32. Ibid., at 300–08.

33. The Jehovah's Witnesses were not always victorious. In *Cox v. New Hampshire*, 312 U.S. 569 (1941), the Court upheld as a reasonable police regulation the requirement that Jehovah's Witnesses obtain a permit before staging a parade in public streets. Likewise, in *Prince v. Massachusetts*, 321 U.S. 158 (1949), a child labor law was upheld in a conviction of a Jehovah's Witness mother who had her nine-year-old child help distribute literature on a public street corner at night.

34. Pfeffer, *Religion, State and the Burger Court*, 204–05.

35. James E. Wood, Jr., "New Religions and the First Amendment: 'The Law Knows No Heresy'," in *Religion and the State: Essays in Honor of Leo Pfeffer*, ed. James E. Wood, Jr. (Waco, TX: Baylor University Press, 1985), 200.

36. Ibid. For further scholarship on "cults," deprogramming, and the First Amendment, see David Bromley and Thomas Robbins, "The Role of Government in Regulating New and Nonconventional Religions," in *The Role of Government in Monitoring and Regulating Religion in Public Life*, eds. James E. Wood, Jr. and Derek Davis (Waco, TX: J.M. Dawson Institute of Church-State Studies, Baylor University, 1993); David G. Bromley, ed. *The Brainwashing-Deprogramming Controversy* (New

York: The Edwin Mellen Press, 1983); and Thomas Robbins, William C. Shepherd, and James McBride, eds. *Cults, Culture, and the Law: Perspectives on New Religious Movements* (Chico, CA: Scholars Press, 1985).

37. Ibid., 203–05; Pfeffer, *Church, State and the Burger Court*, 211–13.

38. Ibid., 201.

39. Leo Pfeffer, "Countering Cults and the Constitution," *New York Times* 8 (October 1980): A26.

40. Pfeffer, *Religion, State and the Burger Court*, 202–05.

41. Leo Pfeffer, "Equal Protection for Unpopular Sects," New York University Review of Law and Social Change 9 (1979–80): 10.

42. Leo Pfeffer, "Brief of Amicus Curiae," *Moon v. United States*, 466 U.S. 971 (1984): 3.

43. Pfeffer, "The Legitimation," 14.

44. Ibid.

45. *Watson v. Jones*, 13 Wall. 679 (1872).

46. *United States v. Ballard*, 322 U.S. 78 (1944).

47. Pfeffer, *Religion, State, and the Burger Court*, 206–07.

48. *Worldwide Church of God v. State of California*, 446 U.S. 987 (1980) at 988; Pfeffer, *Religion, State and the Burger Court*, 228–30. For an analysis of the case, see Sharon L. Worthing, "The State Takes Over a Church," *Annals of the American Academy of Political and Social Science* 446 (November 1979): 136–48.

49. Sponsors included The National Association of Evangelicals, the National Council of Churches, the Synagogue Council of America, the Baptist Joint Committee on Public Affairs, the Evangelical Lutheran Church, and the United Methodist Church.

50. Brief as Amici Curiae Supporting Petitioner at 11–12, *Worldwide Church of God v. State of California*, 446 U.S. 987 (1980) (No. 79-1348).

51. Ibid., at 26–27.

52. Ibid., at 22.

53. Ibid., at 17.

54. Ibid., at 20.

55. Robert T. Miller and Ronald B. Flowers, *Toward Benevolent Neutrality*, 253. See, for example, *The Holy Spirit Association for the Unification of World Christianity v. The Tax Commission of the City of New York*, 435 N.E. 2d 662 (1982).

56. Miller and Flowers, *Toward Benevolent Neutrality*, 253.

57. A diverse group of religious and civil liberties organizations filed briefs in defense of Moon, including, the National Council of Churches of Christ, the Presbyterian Church, U.S.A., the American Baptist Churches, the National Association of Evangelicals, the Christian Legal Society, the National Conference of Black Mayors, the Church of Jesus Christ of Latter-Day Saints, and the Institute for the Study of American Religions.

58. Ibid., 9.

59. Brief as Amici Curiae Supporting Petitioner at 2, *Moon v. U.S.*, 466 U.S. 971 (1984) (No. 83-1242) (hereinafter Moon Brief.)

60. Tax exemption has been an especially active area of free exercise litigation. See, for example, *United States v. Lee*, 455 U.S. 252 (1982); *Jimmy Swaggart v. Board of Equalization of California*, 493 U.S. 378 (1990); and *Missouri Church of Scientology v. State Tax Commission*, 439 U.S. 803 (1978).

61. Moon Brief at 15.

62. Pfeffer, *Church, State, and Freedom*, 270–73; "Sunday Law and Sabbath Observance," *Congress Weekly* (February 13, 1950): 9–11; for a history of Sunday laws see Justice Felix Frankfurter's concurring opinion in *McGowan v. Maryland*, 366 U.S. 420 (1961) at 470–514.

63. Pfeffer, *Church, State, and Freedom*, 279.

64. Pfeffer, "An Autobiographical Sketch," 489–90; *Church, State, and Freedom*, 273–78. The "crazy-quilt pattern" of exemptions was one of Pfeffer's central challenges to the inequality of Sunday laws: "The crazy-quilt pattern of the exemptions and exceptions of the Sunday law is arbitrary and discriminates unconstitutionally against small retailers"; Pfeffer, "Sunday Law," 11.

65. Cohen, *Jews in Christian America*, 217.

66. Pfeffer, "Sunday Law," 9.

67. See Brief for Appellants, *Friedman v. New York*, 341 U.S. 907 (1951); Naomi Cohen has noted that Pfeffer's brief emphasized the Establishment clause challenge to Sunday laws while the American Jewish Congress *amicus curiae* brief emphasized the free exercise right to exemptions from Sunday regulations.

68. Quoted in Cohen, *Jews in Christian America*, 219.

69. *Gallagher v. Crown Kosher Super Market*, 366 U.S. 617 (1961).

70. Brief for Synagogue Counsel of America and National Community Relations Advisory Counsel as Amici Curiae Supporting Appellees at 5–12, *Gallagher v. Crown Kosher Super Market*, 366 U.S. 617 (1961) (Nos. 11, 67).

71. Ibid., at 14.

72. Ibid., at 15.

73. Leo Pfeffer, "The U.S. Supreme Court Decisions in the Sunday Law Cases," *CLSA Reports* (June 8, 1961): 6–7.

74. *McGowan v. Maryland*, 366 U.S. 420 (1961) at 444.

75. 366 U.S. 420 at 607.

76. Ibid., at 608; Interestingly, the Court's only Jewish member, Felix Frankfurter, made a similar argument in his concurring opinion.

77. 366 U.S. 420 at 576.

78. Ibid., at 578.

79. Ibid., at 616.

80. Ibid., at 520.

81. Quoted in Pfeffer, "The Supremacy of Free Exercise," 1128.

82. Ibid., at 1129.

83. Pfeffer, "An Autobiographical Sketch," 491.

84. *Heisler v. Board of Review*, 156 Ohio St. 395 (1951).

85. See Brief for Appellant, *Heisler v. Board of Review*, 156 Ohio St. 395 (1951). The appeal was eventually dismissed.

86. *Sherbert v. Verner*, 374 U.S. 398 (1963).

87. Ibid., at 399–401.

88. Leo Pfeffer, Brief for Synagogue Counsel of America and National Community Relations Advisory Counsel as Amici Curiae Supporting Appellant at 6, *Sherbert v. Verner*, 374 U.S. 398 (1963) (No. 526).

89. Ibid., at 8–14.

90. Ibid., at 8.

91. Ibid., at 17.

92. *Sherbert* v. *Verner*, 374 U.S. 398 at 415.

93. Ibid.

94. 374 U.S. 398 at 406.

95. Ibid., at 404.

96. Ibid., at 409.

97. *TransWorld Air Lines v. Hardison*, 432 U.S. 63 (1977).

98. See Brief for the American Civil Liberties Union of Amicus Curiae Supporting the Appellees, *TransWorld Airlines v. Hardison*, 432 U.S. 63 (1977) (No. 75-1126) (hereinafter *TWA* Brief); see also Leo Pfeffer, "Worker's Sabbath: Religious Belief and Employment," *The Civil Liberties Review* (November/December 1977): 52–56.

99. See also *Dewey v. Reynolds Metals Company*, 429 F.2d 324 (1970) and *Parker Seal Company v. Cummins*, 429 U.S. 65 (1976).

100. 432 U.S. 63 at 66–70.

101. Pfeffer, "Worker's Sabbath," 52–56.

102. *TWA* Brief, 12.

103. See Ibid., at 19 and Pfeffer, "Fair Employment for Sabbath Observers," *Congress Monthly* 44 (May 1977): 10.

104. Ibid., at 78.

105. Ibid., at 84–85.

106. Pfeffer, "Worker's Sabbath," 55.

107. Cohen, *Jews in Christian America*, 245.

108. Ibid.

109. Leo Pfeffer letter to Dr. Petegorsky, 2 June 1953. Leo Pfeffer Papers, Syracuse University Folder 5: General Files: Church-State Relations 1955.

110. Pfeffer, *Religion, State, and the Burger Court*, 201.

111. TWA Brief at 18–19.

112. See *Pierce v. Society of Sisters*, 268 U.S. 510 (1925).

113. *Wisconsin v. Yoder*, 406 U.S. 205 (1972) at 209–10; For an extended historical and constitutional analysis of this case, see Shawn Francis Peters, *The Yoder Case: Religious Freedom, Education, and Parental Rights* (Lawrence: University of Kansas Press, 2003).

114. Pfeffer, *God, Caesar, and the Constitution*, 136.

115. Ibid.

116. Brief for Synagogue Counsel of America and its Constituents as Amici Curiae Supporting Respondents at 7, *Wisconsin v. Yoder*, 406 U.S. 205 (1972) (No. 70-110). In *Reynolds v. U.S.* 98 U.S. 145 (1898) the Court upheld an anti-polygamy statute against Mormon defendants. In *Hamilton v. Regents of the University of*

California 293 U.S. 245 (1934) the Court upheld the right of the university to expel pacifists who refused to enroll in military training courses.

117. Ibid., at 10–14.

118. Ibid., at 18.

119. Ibid., at 16.

120. See, for instance, Brief for Synagogue Council for America, et al. as Amici Curiae Supporting Appellants, *McCollum v. Board of Education*, 333 U.S. 203 (1948) (No. 90).

121. Ibid., at 23.

122. *Wisconsin* v. *Yoder*, 406 U.S. 205 (1973).

123. Ibid., at 219.

124. Ibid., at 224.

125. Ibid., at 220–21.

126. See the "Sunday Law Cases," above, as well as *Heisler v. Board of Review*, 343 U.S. 939 (1952); *Friedman v. New York*, 341 U.S. 907 (1951); *In re Summers*, 325 U.S. 561 (1945); *Minersville v. Gobitis*, 310 U.S. 586 (1940); *Hamilton v. Board of Regents*, 293 U.S. 245 (1934); and *Reynolds v. U.S.*, 98 U.S. 145 (1898).

127. Pfeffer, "The Supremacy of Free Exercise," 1130.

128. Ibid., 27.

129. Pfeffer, *Church, State, and Freedom*, 618.

130. Miller and Flowers, *Toward Benevolent Neutrality*, 642; see also John A. Rohr, *Prophets Without Honor: Public Policy and the Selective Conscientious Objector* (Nashville: Abingdon Press, 1971), 17–24; Stokes, *Church and State*, 2: 293–306.

131. Stokes and Pfeffer, *Church and State in the United States*, 474–75.

132. Pfeffer, "The Deity," 135.

133. *U.S. v. Schwimmer*, 279 U.S. 644 (1929); see also Ronald B. Flowers, *To Defend the Constitution: Religion, Conscientious Objection, Naturalization, and the Supreme Court* (Lanham, MD: Scarecrow Press, 2002).

134. *U.S. v. Macintosh*, 283 U.S. 605 (1931).

135. *Girouard v. U.S.*, 328 U.S. 61 (1946); In the meantime, the Court upheld in 1934 the suspension of two men at the University of California at Los Angeles for their refusal to participate in a required R.O.T.C. course. Similarly, in *In re Summers*, the Court upheld a refusal of the state of Illinois to admit a conscientious objector to the bar.

136. *U.S. v. Macintosh*, 283 U.S. 605 (1931) at 623.

137. See Ronald B. Flowers, *Religion in Strange Times: The 1960s and 1970s* (Macon, GA: Mercer University Press, 1984); Ahlstrom, *A Religious History*, 1037–54.

138. *U.S. v. Seeger*, 380 U.S. 163 (1965).

139. Ibid., at 166.

140. Ibid., at 167.

141. Brief for the American Jewish Congress of Amicus Curiae Supporting the Appellee at 2, *U.S. v. Seeger*, 380 U.S. 163 (1965) (No. 50) (hereinafter Seeger Brief).

142. Ibid., at 5–6; *Torcaso* v *Watkins*, 367 U.S. 488 (1961) at 495.

143. Seeger Brief at 5–6.
144. Ibid., at 12–15.
145. Ibid., at 15.
146. 380 U.S. 163 at 165–66.
147. Pfeffer, *Religion, State, and the Burger Court*, 152.
148. Pfeffer, "The Deity," 137.
149. See, for example, John T. Noonan, "How Sincere Do You Have To Be To Be Religious?" *University of Illinois Law Review* (1988): 713.
150. Witte, *Religion and the American Constitutional Experiment*, 120.
151. Leo Pfeffer, Pamphlet entitled *Abortion and Religious Freedom* (Washington, DC: Religious Coalition for Abortion Rights, 1976), 3; originally published as "Abortion and Religious Freedom," *Congress Monthly* 43 (June 1976): 9.
152. *Harris v. McRae*, 448 U.S. 297 (1980).
153. Brief for American Ethical Union et al. as Amici Curiae Supporting Appellee at 20, *Harris v. McRae*, 448 U.S. 297 (1980) (No. 79-1268).
154. Ibid., at 3.
155. *Harris v. McRae*, 448 U.S. 297 at 317–20.
156. Pfeffer, *Abortion and Religious Freedom*, 6.
157. Ibid., 9.
158. Pfeffer, *Religion, State, and the Burger Court*, 243.
159. Stephanie Russell Kraft, "The Right to Abortion and Religious Freedom," *The Atlantic*, March 3, 2016; see also Peter S. Wenz, *Abortion Rights as Religious Freedom* (Philadelphia, PA: Temple University Press, 1992).
160. Witte, *Religion and the American Constitutional Experiment*, 136.
161. *Goldman v. Weinberger*, 575 U.S. 503 (1986).
162. *Bowen v. Roy*, 476 U.S. 693 (1986) at 699.
163. *O'Lone v. Estate of Shabazz*, 482 U.S. 342 (1987) at 351.
164. *Lyng v. Northwest Indian Ceremony Protective Association*, 485 U.S. 439 (1988) at 452.
165. 494 U.S. 872 at 885.
166. Ibid., at 891–907.
167. *Oregon v. Smith* 493 U.S. 378 (1990); see Leo Pfeffer, "Forward" to Derek H. Davis *Original Intent: Chief Justice Rehnquist and the Course of American Church-State Relations* (Buffalo, NY: Prometheus Books, 1991), xiii–xiv.
168. Michael W. McConnell has spelled out the historical argument for this position in "The Origins and Historical Understanding of Free Exercise of Religion," *Harvard Law Review* 103 (1990): 1409–73; see also Douglas Laycock, "The Remnants of Free Exercise," *The Supreme Court Review* (1990): 1–68.
169. See Philip A. Hamburger, "A Constitutional Right of Religious Exemption: An Historical Perspective," *George Washington Law Review* 60 (1992): 915–48; Gerard v. Bradley, "Beguiled: Free Exercise Exemptions and the Siren Song of Liberalism," *Hofstra Law Review* 20 (1991): 245–319; and Ellis West, "The Case Against the Right to Religion-Based Exemptions," *Notre Dame Journal of Law, Ethics, and Public Policy* 4 (1990): 567–90.

170. Paulsen, "Religion, Equality, and the Constitution," 31; Choper, "A Century of Religious Freedom,", citing *Walz v. Tax Commission* 397 U.S. 664 (1970) at 668–69.

171. *Boerne v. Flores*, 521 U.S. 507 (1997).

172. *Cutter v. Wilkinson*, 544 U.S. 709 (2005).

173. Bette Novit Evans, "Constitutional Language and Judicial Interpretations of the Free Exercise Clause," in *The Oxford Handbook of Church and State in the United States*, ed. Derek H. Davis (New York: Oxford University Press, 2010), 166; see also, Bette Novit Evans, *Interpreting the Free Exercise of Religion: The Constitution and American Pluralism* (Chapel Hill: University of North Carolina Press, 1997).

174. Kurland, *Religion and the Law*.

175. Leo Pfeffer, "Religion-Blind Government," *Stanford Law Review* 15 (March 1963): 389–406.

Chapter 5

The "Pfefferian Inversion" Reconsidered

Leo Pfeffer and the Role of Religion in Public Life

In 1984, Richard John Neuhaus's book, *The Naked Public Square*[1] initiated a proliferation of publications addressing the role of religion in public life.[2] Many of these echoed Neuhaus's concern that a strict adherence to the separation of church and state, particularly by the U.S. Supreme Court, has marginalized religious voices to the detriment of American culture. Consequently, the strict separationist position is now widely understood to mean that religion is divisive and dangerous due to its absolutist claims and, as a result, should be kept out of public life.[3]

This stands in contrast to the separationist writings of Leo Pfeffer. In fact, it was Neuhaus who identified Pfeffer as the chief protagonist of the separationist position in an article entitled "The Pfefferian Inversion."[4] According to Neuhaus, "Leo Pfeffer, now rich in years and honors, has done more than anyone else to shape the law regarding religion and the state in America." "But for him," Neuhaus contended, "religion is an exclusively private thing: what he is against is religion in public."[5] Neuhaus concluded that the separation of church and state had consequently become the separation of religion from government and, "as the government has become ever more expansive, the separation of religion from public life."[6]

Pfeffer's commitment to a high wall of separation was not *intended* to marginalize religion from the public square, but rather to create a level playing field among the various religious participants in public debate. Pfeffer envisioned a robust public sphere where all religious (and nonreligious) voices competed actively to shape American culture and law. To be sure, the public versus private distinction that Pfeffer advocated was at times ambiguous. Nevertheless, his interpretation of the religion clauses of the First Amendment, his religious identity, his defense of the free exercise rights of religious minorities, his desire to end tax exemption for churches and other religious institutions to free them to participate in public debate, his work with a Jewish defense organization, and his concern for the integrity of both church and state illustrate his belief in the legitimacy of religious voices in public life.

Even if it was not Pfeffer's intent to create a "naked public square," others have argued that his absolutism with regard to the separation of church and state had that *effect*. Pfeffer was unquestionably vigilant in challenging support, recognition, or sponsorship of religion by the state and challenged, in particular, both religious exercises at public schools as well as public aid to religious institutions. The fervency with which Pfeffer and other separationists opposed any state support or accommodation of religion has led Neuhaus and other commentators to conclude that there is a direct connection between separation and secularization. These claims notwithstanding, there is much evidence to suggest that religion remains a vital element in American culture and continues to exert significant influence on American public life.

THE "PFEFFERIAN INVERSION"

Richard John Neuhaus viewed the Pfeffer-influenced Supreme Court's separationist decisions as having misread the purpose of the First Amendment's religion clauses. According to Neuhaus, "free exercise is the purpose of the religion clauses; nonestablishment is a means to that end. But today the party of 'strict separationism' treats nonestablishment as an end in itself."[7] This "Pfefferian Inversion," as Neuhaus called it, has resulted in the marginalization of religion in public life or, in his oft-cited phrase, a "naked public square." In holding up a high wall of separation by ruling against religious symbols in public institutions as well as various forms of aid to parochial schools, Neuhaus asserted that the "the Supreme Court has ruled religion a private matter. The problem is that as the government increasingly absorbs all public space, religion gets squeezed into an ever tighter corner of privacy."[8]

Interestingly, Neuhaus's critique of Leo Pfeffer's church-state jurisprudence begins with a declaration of his belief in the unity of the two religion clauses as well. His key contention is that the clauses work together toward the goal of religious liberty. However, while he referred to them in the singular, he subordinated the Establishment Clause to the Free Exercise Clause. Neuhaus viewed the Establishment Clause as merely a means to the end of protecting free exercise of religion. "Both historically and logically," Neuhaus asserted, "there is no reason for nonestablishment other than to protect religious freedom."[9]

Neuhaus's religious liberty argument has a long history in church-state law and commentary. During the debates over the 1952 *Zorach v. Clausen* released-time religious education decision, Wilber Katz argued that the separation principle in the first amendment must be read to be limited by the principle of religious liberty. According to Katz, "the limits of the separation doctrine are to be found by reference to the constitutional principle of religious liberty, not vice versa."[10] Since Katz's essay, Neuhaus's view of the religion clauses has enjoyed a significant amount of support in the scholarly community.[11] Michael McConnell has similarly argued that "only an interpretation of the Religion Clauses based on religious liberty—an interpretation grounded in the political theory underlying the Constitution—satisfactorily distinguishes permissible accommodations from impermissible establishments."[12]

Despite Pfeffer's declared belief in the unitary nature of the religion clauses, Neuhaus argued that Pfeffer inverted them by giving "practical priority" to the Establishment Clause. This "inversion" Neuhaus contended has led to a long line of confusing and inconsistent court decisions that have contributed to the marginalization of religion in the public sphere. Neuhaus was certainly not alone in making this criticism as other commentators have argued that the Court's past Establishment Clause decisions have been "unprincipled," "ad hoc," and "meandering."[13] Neuhaus's invective was not leveled at the separationist metaphor *per se*. Rather, it was the strict separationist position that sought to "preclude the significant impingement of religion on our public life" that he deplored. In fact, Neuhaus criticized not just separationists but also some accommodationists such as the late Chief Justice William Rehnquist for unwittingly accepting the Pfefferian Inversian by calling for a balancing of the two religion clauses. "Their argument too assumes that the First Amendment contains an 'establishment clause' that must be balanced against a 'free exercise clause," Neuhaus contended. Religious liberty is inevitably restricted, Neuhaus argued, by giving the Establishment Clause a distinct and separate value, instead of merely working in the service of free exercise. Neuhaus called it a "delicious irony" that the Pfefferian Inversion of no establishment had led to the violation of religious freedom.[14]

The Pfefferian Inversion, according to Neuhaus, is rooted in a misunderstanding of the purposes of the religion clauses as well. For Neuhaus, the purpose of the Establishment Clause was to keep the state out of the church, not the church out of the state. Since the Establishment Clause serves exclusively as a check on government, churches are free to advocate for whatever policies it might want—even to the point of seeking to become an established church. As Neuhaus explained it: As wrongheaded as it might be, religions are perfectly free to agitate to have themselves established, for that too is part of religious freedom. What is prohibited by the First Amendment is the free exercise of government power in giving in to such agitation. And the only reason the government is not free to establish a religion is that it would violate religious freedom."[15] The problem with the Pfefferian Inversion is that it viewed the Establishment Clause as a check on religion as well. Consequently, the Establishment Clause had been used as a tool by committed secularists to privatize religion. "To create or preserve the naked public square," Neuhaus concluded, "religion is to be tolerated only when it is hermetically sealed off in the private sphere of life."[16]

The consequences of a privatized religion strike at the very health of democracy for Neuhaus. He saw the removal of religiously based moral values on public life as opposed to "the very idea of democratic governance." According to Neuhaus, "In our society, the vast majority of the people profess to believe that morality is derived from religion, and their moral judgement cannot be excluded because of its source." Neuhaus believed that his view of the religion clauses would create a "genuine pluralism" in which all perspectives can be brought into public debate. This may include perspectives that may be "abhorrent, dangerous, or plain silly."[17] Without "genuine pluralism," then, the public square will be controlled by "cultural elites" who do not share the values of the majority of Americans.[18]

In his two-volume work entitled *The Supreme Court and Religion in American Life*, historian James Hitchcock also argues that the Establishment Clause is no longer understood to protect religious liberty. Rather, Hitchcock contends that "it places restrictions on it by excluding religion from public education and from the formation of public policy."[19] Hitchcock also shares Neuhaus's broader concerns of a purely privatized religion for democracy. Much like Neuhaus, Hitchcock argues that "absent either an overtly religious foundation for politics or an accepted theory of natural law, the state in practice cannot help but treat rights as conferred by itself." Hitchcock concludes that "the test that now faces the liberal polity is whether its embrace of secularization has gone so far that citizens must now abandon the claim that they have been endowed by their Creator with certain unalienable rights."[20] Neuhaus's connection between secularization and strict separation has been echoed by other scholars as well. Political scientist Frank Guliuzza, for instance, argues a "strong linkage" between secularization and separation. In fact, secularists have seized upon separation as an important tool for their ultimate goal of a completely secularized society, he claims.[21]

Much of the scholarship that has followed *The Naked Public Square* has endeavored to address the proper role of religion in a modern, pluralistic, liberal democracy. Scholars such as Ronald Theimann contend that some of the inherent assumptions in modern political liberalism, such as government neutrality, have laid the groundwork for the marginalization of religion from the public square.[22] Modern political liberal theorists such as John Rawls and

Bruce Ackerman, he argues, are strong supporters of the separation of church and state because they believe that fundamental democratic values such as freedom, equality, and toleration are threatened when religion and religiously based arguments are utilized in the public arena. For Thiemann, neutrality and separation do not account for the fluid relationship between religion and politics. Consequently, "the notion of neutrality, a fundamental concept in philosophy, bedevils every attempt of the Court to develop a consistent and coherent framework for interpretation of the First Amendment religion clauses."[23] Thiemann does not call for the jettisoning of liberal political thought but seeks a revised liberalism less committed to the problematic concepts of government neutrality, government secularity, and strict distinctions between the public and the private.[24]

Similar concerns have been raised by a number of Jewish commentators as well. They have questioned the overwhelming commitment of American Jews to political liberalism, in general, and the separation of church and state, in particular.[25] According to Alan Mittleman, the Jewish adherence to separation in the short run provided protection for Jews in a Christian majority state,[26] but in the long run lacked a constructive element that contributed to the common good. "Separationism neglects the task of recovering a free and democratic public life," Mittleman asserted, "sustained by the practical reasoning, public virtue, and dedication to the common good of the moral and spiritual communities."[27] Others have argued that the Jewish community's overwhelming support for the separation of church and state has blinded them to the potential societal problems that result from "the exclusion of religiously grounded values." They contend that such a religiously vacuous state created the anti-Jewish public philosophies of Nazi Germany and Soviet Russia.[28] Jonathan Sarna has suggested that "history also teaches Jews to oppose secularization as a force leading to assimilation, social decay, and sometimes to the persecution of all religions, Jews included."[29]

According to Noah Pickus, neoconservative Jewish commentators, such as Murray Friedman, argue that Jewish commitment to political liberalism, the separation of church and state, and secularism has handicapped Jews from bringing the unique values of their religious tradition to bear on social and political issues. He contends that Jewish leaders and organizations have become indistinct from organizations like the American Civil Liberties Union in how they approach issues such as abortion. Articulating their position as merely one of choice, the Jewish community has failed to bring the full Jewish ethical and theological tradition to bear on such complex social issues. Consequently, Friedman believes that the wall of separation has led Jews to support not only a secular state but also a secular "public life."[30] Nathan Glazer has further warned that while the separation of church and state provided protection for Jews in a Christian majority state, its ultimate achievement will be the inability of Judaism to preserve its own integrity in modern society unless Jews are willing to change their understanding of the role of religion in American public life.[31]

Building upon these critiques, Alan Mittleman has sought a "postseparationist public philosophy" for Jews. In doing so, he argues that "separationism is essentially a negative strategy," in that it provides no "positive philosophy of religion in public life." Rather Mittleman suggests that Jews recover a positive view of the role of religion in public life that fosters civic virtue and the common good.[32]

CREEDS IN COMPETITION

In reading Pfeffer's critics, one gets the impression that, as a separationist, he was a committed secularist who saw no public role for religion in society. Indeed, he has been characterized as a secularist by some scholars.[33] However, a more complete observation of Pfeffer's writings reveals that he did not believe that elimination of religion from public life was either desirable or possible. In his 1958 work, *Creeds in Competition*, Pfeffer devoted attention to the on-going dialogue and debate among religions and other social forces seeking to shape American culture according to their own scale of values or vision of the common good.[34] Pfeffer viewed "cultural competition" to be "consistent with the American spirit and American competition."[35] Thus, Pfeffer envisioned a robust public sphere in which all religions actively participated. Conflict and competition were not to be diminished as long as the rules of fair play were adhered to.[36] Plus, Pfeffer optimistically viewed this competition as essential to societal progress and genuine pluralism.[37]

Pfeffer believed that the "rules of fair play" were essential to protect Americans' ability to make "free and informed" choices. These included condemning any use of force in religious conflict or the suppression of any sect or its activities. Governmental involvement or influence should be strictly avoided as should any "manifestations of religiosity" on the part of the state. Conversely, the church should not use "ecclesiastical sanctions" to influence governmental actions. "Verbal blows" or appeals to "passions or prejudice" likewise thwarted free competition as did questioning the motives of one's cultural competitors. Here Pfeffer criticized Protestants who claimed that the Catholic Church sought "the attainment of power and the exercise of power for its own sake." He similarly chided Catholics for claiming that opposition to aid to Catholic schools was motivated solely by "anti-Catholic bigotry and prejudice." Avoiding chauvinism that claimed certain ideas were more "American" than others was essential to fair competition. For Pfeffer, "fair competition required that every proposal be adjudged on its own merits." Pfeffer concluded by arguing that economic boycotts should not be engaged in if they were designed to influence the opinion of those outside of the religious tradition. It is one thing for members of a particular religious tradition to avoid certain literature or movies, it is another for them to boycott a bookstore or theater altogether. "This is unfair competition," Pfeffer concluded, "because it prejudices free enlightened choice by the use of economic force to restrict expression."[38] Pfeffer expressed unbridled optimism that not only change, but also change for the better, will result from cultural competition if these rules of fair play were followed.[39]

LEO PFEFFER'S RELIGIOUS IDENTITY

Pfeffer's perspective on the role of religion in public life was also rooted in his experience as an American Jew. Political liberalism and separation of church and state were naturally embraced by the Jewish community as protections in a Christian majority state. Chapter 1 discussed how Pfeffer's views on church and state were shaped existentially as well. In particular, his childhood exposure to a released time religious education program led to his parents withdrawing him from the public schools and enrolling him in an Orthodox religious school. Particularly noteworthy was Pfeffer's objections that the program divided "school children according to their religious belief" and that these divisions were "particularly harmful to children of minority faiths."[40]

It is important to reiterate that Pfeffer's commitment to political liberalism and the separation of church and state was not the product of the marginalization of religious commitment in his own life. A diminishing religious commitment among many upwardly mobile Jews reinforced for some observers the connections between separation and secularization. And, as previously noted, many who worked for the Jewish defense agencies, like the AJC, were seemingly "indifferent if not hostile to religion." Pfeffer, however, attended a Conservative synagogue and remained an observant and pietistic Jew. If anything, Pfeffer's commitment to the separation of church and state was rooted in his concern for maintaining the integrity of religion. He was an avid student of the Bible and expressed concern about competition from "common denominator" faith like civil religion "where everybody considers religion a good thing but few take it very seriously."[41] Pfeffer drew from the prophetic and social justice tradition in ways that informed his civil rights and liberties activism. All of these illustrate the existential importance of religion to Pfeffer personally and at least suggests that he believed faith had a profound influence on the shaping of public life and attitudes.[42]

THE TRIUMPH OF SECULAR HUMANISM?

Like many American Jews, Pfeffer was naturally drawn to political liberalism, particularly its commitment to individual liberty and equality. Consequently, Pfeffer drew from this tradition and championed the Enlightenment's influence on the framers of the First Amendment. Citing especially Thomas Jefferson and James Madison, Pfeffer argued that their vision of a limited state, one that was secular or neutral toward religion, was the intent of the framers and the best approach to securing true religious liberty. Pfeffer's influential separationist historical narrative was not limited to the political liberalism of deists, however. Rather, Pfeffer likewise emphasized the advocacy of orthodox and revivalist Christian traditions which also championed the separation of church and state. Thus, it wasn't just a Jeffersonian anti-clerical fear of religious influence on the state, but also a commitment of evangelical faiths like Baptists to religious liberty, that brought about the First Amendment. This led Pfeffer to argue frequently that "the principle of strict separation is based on friendliness to religion rather than on enmity."[43]

Nonetheless, some commentators have argued that the separationist's advocacy of a secular state contradicts the theological underpinnings of religious freedom articulated by the nation's founders. "Those who believe that the separation of church and state mandates the removal of religion from the public sphere," Ronald Thiemann contends, "must deal with the fact that Madison's argument securing those basic first amendment rights is overtly theological."[44] These theological bases of religious freedom are something that Neuhaus would argue "secular elites" are embarrassed by and "are seeking to expunge from public debate."[45]

Despite his articulation of the theological and philosophical rationales for the separation of church and state, Pfeffer did frequently make statements such as "Religion was a private matter, a matter which lies solely between man and his God, a matter not within the scope or cognizance of political society."[46] And Pfeffer's tireless efforts at challenging any form of aid or accommodation of religion might suggest he sought to create a public sphere that was cleansed of religion. Understandably, Pfeffer's use of the term "private" when discussing religion can lead to confusion. Yet "private" to Pfeffer did not mean elimination from any public role, but rather freedom from governmental help, hindrance, or accommodation. According to Pfeffer:

> The explanation of the Supreme Court's decisions on the subject dealt with here lies principally in one sociohistoric fact: that, notwithstanding occasional visits by a charismatic Pope or periodic religious revivals by Protestants, the American people are committed to a culture that can best be described as secular humanism, at least where government is involved. Put somewhat simplistically,

> this means that religion is a private matter, not for government either to inhibit or advance. So long as the American people remain committed to this concept, that commitment will be reflected in Supreme Court decisions.[47]

Finding its origins in the deism of American founders such as Jefferson and Paine, "secular humanism" reflects deism's emphases on human goodness, anti-authoritarianism, secularism, egalitarianism, voluntarism, and libertarianism. Its influence, Pfeffer concluded, is best witnessed in the fact that the Declaration of Independence and Bill of Rights "breathe its spirit."[48] Pfeffer viewed secular humanism as a "cultural force" that had joined forces with liberal Protestantism and Judaism to shape American political culture.[49] Pfeffer did believe the Protestant-Humanist alliance, however, was in cultural competition with the Catholic Church that desires "a close and co-operative relation between religion and the state" that is "diametrically opposed to the concept of complete separation espoused by Protestant dissent and secular humanism."[50] Consequently, many of the major cultural and legal battles over religion in schools, aid to parochial schools, public morality, and censorship were frequently products of the competing claims of the Protestant-Humanist alliance and the Catholic Church.[51]

Writing nearly twenty years after the publication of *Creeds in Competition*, Pfeffer argued that most of the interreligious conflicts rooted in doctrinal differences earlier in the century had diminished. Rather, secular humanism, with its liberalizing and secularizing tendencies had triumphed. Post Vatican II American Catholicism, for example, had led to the dogmas of "one true church" and "papal infallibility . . . seem today to be as remote as the practice of exorcism."[52] Catholic opposition to the school prayer and Bible reading decisions seemed to have lessened as had its "campaign against obscenity." While aid to parochial schools and abortion remain highly contested issues, Pfeffer anticipated a "denouement" in these areas as well. Thus, for Pfeffer, a "spirit of secular humanism" had permeated "American cultural and political life."[53]

Pfeffer's seeming advocacy of the values of secular humanism reveals his commitment to political liberalism. Moreover, his confidence that secularization of American institutions and life would continue unabated gives credence to those that claimed Pfeffer and his fellow separationists sought not just a secular state, but a secular society.[54] While there certainly appears to be a celebratory tone regarding the "triumph of secular humanism," Pfeffer did not argue that contrary voices should be banned from bringing arguments to bear upon public deliberations. He fully recognized the historically important role religion and religious groups have played in social reform movements such as the abolition of slavery—if not the adoption of the First Amendment itself.[55] Moreover, Pfeffer chided Protestants and others who condemned and criticized the political activity of the Catholic Church. Pfeffer saw no problem with the Catholic Church engaging in electioneering and advocating certain positions on legislation. While Pfeffer did argue that "the most serious challenge to American cultural patterns and values fixed by a Protestant Humanist alliance comes from Roman Catholicism," he went on to argue that the resulting cultural competition may lead to changes in the "traditional American way of life."[56] Striking an idealistic tone, Pfeffer concluded that competition produced positive results. Even challenges to the Protestant–Humanist alliance were "desirable and worthwhile; for American society is dynamic, not static, and competition among religious cultures is creative, not destructive."[57]

Ironically, Pfeffer's declaration of the triumph of secular humanism was written on the eve of the emergence of the Religious Right as a powerful force in American politics. In many ways, this marked a new alliance between conservative Evangelicals and Catholics on a number of social issues that supplanted the Protestant-Humanist alliance in political influence. Moreover, rather than denouement, abortion remains a key area of cultural competition with its constitutional legitimacy ever so tenuous under the current U.S. Supreme Court. One wonders if Pfeffer would still be as optimistic today that cultural competitions are inevitably "desirable and worthwhile" and "will justify the American experiment."[58]

Despite Pfeffer's affirmation of cultural competition, the question remains as to whether his broad or strict separationist reading of the Establishment Clause, as one detractor put it, forced "believers into conformity with the spirit of liberal democracy."[59] To the extent that liberal democracy assumed a free marketplace of ideas this is true. Yet Pfeffer, while committed to advancing the values of liberal democracy, did not view the Establishment Clause as prohibiting illiberal or absolutist religious claims from public debate. Rather, Pfeffer viewed the Establishment Clause as prohibiting the government from privileging one position over another. Pfeffer recognized that "differences among the religious faiths are founded upon basic differences of ideology and principle and the good way of life."[60] Yet genuine pluralism, for Pfeffer, was only achievable in the free marketplace of ideas. And the free marketplace of ideas was only possible in a secular state. Rather than handicapping democracy, as Neuhaus argued, a strong Establishment Clause and secular state fostered true pluralism that aided democracy.

Clearly, Pfeffer's understanding of cultural competition is rooted in the modern liberal assumptions that truth was discernable and progress inevitable as long as rational principles of engagement and understanding of the social order are adhered to. To a large extent, Hitchcock is right in drawing connections between separation and a seeming liberal hegemony. Yet one is hard pressed to construct a better arrangement for a religiously pluralistic nation such as the United States. Hitchcock's own advocacy of a return to the original understanding of the nation as a "Christian Republic" seems particularly untenable. Furthermore, as Kathleen Sullivan has argued, "even if the culture of liberal democracy is a belief system comparable to a religious faith, it simply does not follow that it is the equivalent of a religion for political and constitutional purposes." For Sullivan, liberal democracy becoming a totalitarian orthodoxy is limited by its own values such as free speech. In other words, freedom of conscience and expression keep "anyone from being forced to accept the culture of liberal democracy."[61]

Thus, for Pfeffer, the First Amendment created a level playing field for all religions. In religiously pluralistic America, making religion a private enterprise was the only way to ensure that all faiths were equal participants.[62] What was uniquely American about this competition, Pfeffer believed, was that it had been largely peaceful and facilitated religious pluralism—seen as indispensable to a democratic society. Moreover, free and uncoerced competition enabled the religious communities to contribute to public morality and laws through persuasion, not codification of a particular creed.[63]

FREE EXERCISE AS CULTURAL COMPETITION

To that end, Pfeffer was actively involved in protecting the free exercise rights of religious minorities. His broad reading of the Free Exercise Clause, discussed in the previous chapter, led him to defend the free exercise rights of nonconventional religions, conscientious objectors, and Sabbatarians. In the "clash of conflicting interests" between the state and the individual's conscience, Pfeffer consistently held that the state must show a compelling interest before restricting the free exercise of religion.[64]

Pfeffer's free exercise jurisprudence is difficult to reconcile with the "Pfefferian Inversion" thesis. If Pfeffer viewed the Free Exercise Clause to be subordinate to the Establishment Clause, as Neuhaus claims, then it would seem to follow that he would be unwilling to support religiously based exemptions from neutral, generally applicable, laws. Rather, Pfeffer frequently argued that the state must show a "compelling interest" before denying a religious exemption from secular laws. Otherwise, the free exercise rights, particularly of religious minorities, had little protection.[65]

Would not Pfeffer's expansive view of the Free Exercise Clause conflict with an equally absolutist view of the Establishment Clause? This query was advanced by Justice Potter Stewart in his dissenting opinion in *Sherbert v. Verner* where the Court ruled that South Carolina must pay unemployment compensation benefits to a Seventh-Day Adventist that had lost her job after her employer moved to a six-day work week. "To require South Carolina to so administer its law as to pay public money to the appellant under the circumstances of this case," Stewart asserted, "is thus clearly to require the state to violate the Establishment Clause as construed by this court."[66] To Pfeffer, closure of businesses on Sunday had already served as an accommodation to a majority of religious adherents in South Carolina. A similar accommodation for observers on Saturday did not raise any serious constitutional problems. In his majority opinion, Justice William Brennan likewise dispensed with the apparent dilemma: "The extension of unemployment benefits to Sabbatarians in common with Sunday worshipers reflects nothing more than the governmental obligation of neutrality in the face of religious differences and does not represent that involvement of religious with secular institutions which it is the object of the Establishment Clause to forestall."[67]

Pfeffer's belief in the public advocacy of religious bodies led him to question the longstanding practice of tax exemptions for churches and other religious bodies. Unpersuaded by Dean Kelley's influential argument that religious bodies have a free exercise right to tax exemption,[68] Pfeffer broke with many of his separationist allies by asserting that tax exemption had disabled religious bodies from influencing legislation. Moreover, he believed tax exemption made it possible for government to compel religious bodies to change doctrine or for the state to become excessively entangled in church affairs.[69] Pfeffer's Establishment Clause opposition to tax exemption in *Walz v. Tax Commission*[70] revealed not only the extent of his views of the separation of church and state[71] but also his concern for the right of religious bodies to be uninhibited from advocating in the public square.

PLURALISM AND PERSUASION

While religious bodies have the right to speak out on moral or political issues, Pfeffer believed the state must provide a secular justification for its legislation. In *Harris v. McRae*,[72] Pfeffer challenged the right of federal or state governments to deny Medicaid benefits for abortions where the paramount purpose of the denial was based on the fact that a particular religious group believes abortion to be a sin. According to Pfeffer, "Today's opposition to abortion, including the effort to enact a constitutional amendment nullifying *Roe v. Wade* and the instant restriction on government financing of the procedure for the economically disadvantaged, reflect religious rather than secular values."[73] Thus, Pfeffer believed religious groups and individuals have every right to speak out on moral or political issues and use their powers of persuasion to change society and eventually laws. Legislation, however, was barred by the First Amendment from reflecting a narrowly sectarian interest or religious doctrine. "In resorting to Congress and state legislatures," Pfeffer concluded, "the churches are calling upon government to do by compulsion that which they have themselves been unable to achieve by persuasion."[74]

It would be a mischaracterization of Pfeffer's position, then, to say that he did not believe religious arguments should be brought into public debate. One might ask, however, how religious arguments are to then be translated into secular public policies. While Pfeffer did not provide an extended commentary on this transition, one might conclude that he would agree with some modern political theorists that religious convictions, while inevitably a part of public debate and discussion, must ultimately be translated into secular justifications before becoming law. As Robert Audi has argued, "I think that sound ethics itself dictates, that out of respect for others as free and dignified individuals, we should always have and be sufficiently motivated by adequate secular reasons for our positions on those matters of law or public policy in which our decisions might significantly restrict human freedom."[75]

On several occasions, Pfeffer attempted to clarify his position by arguing that "the objective of competition is not to capture the state, but to convince the community." The goal was to persuade the ultimate political power of a democracy—the people. What was not allowed under the Constitution was "commanding the state (as in theocracies) nor by partnership with it (as in nations where church and state are united)." As long as the religious groups' values are translated into "communal values" then they are fair game for legislative sanction.[76]

Pfeffer's belief that legislation should have a secular rationale was reflected clearly in his opposition to public school sponsored religious exercises. In *Abington v. Schempp*, Pfeffer challenged the claim that public school prayer and Bible reading were non-sectarian and voluntary. Arguing that religious activities were outside the competence and jurisdiction of the state and its instrumentalities,"[77] Pfeffer reiterated his belief that the Establishment Clause required government to use only secular means and seek secular ends. According to Pfeffer, "Invalidation of the regulations here challenged would place the responsibility for religious exercises where it properly belongs—the home, the church, the synagogue and on the individual conscience."[78]

One might contend, however, that the requirement of secularity of purpose could marginalize or even mask religious motivations. As Phillip Hammond has argued, "This simply isn't so. The public square does not rule out religious words and motives; it simply does not accord them authority until they are translated." Hammond recognizes that the separation of church and state has led to the marginalization of religious arguments to the extent that they must be based upon "empirical, rational, or logical grounds." Nevertheless, "such privatization is not *required*, however, nor is the public square *off limits* to religious persons using religious language." In affirmation of Pfeffer's

Creeds in Competition thesis, Hammond concludes that "religions, then, are not being unfairly treated but simply being asked to play by the uniform rules."[79]

Pfeffer's arguments for a secular state were embraced by the Court, whose decisions on the prayer and Bible reading cases "essentially redefined religious pluralism."[80] The decisions marked the end of a dominant Protestant-Catholic ethos in America, and the beginning of an era of religious pluralism. Pfeffer concluded that, as a result, "all creeds are equal participants in American society."[81] It was separation and neutrality, rather than accommodation, then, that fostered pluralism according to Pfeffer.

A "NAKED PUBLIC SQUARE"?

While it is clear that Pfeffer's intent was not to create a "naked public square," do Neuhaus and other critics have a legitimate claim that the Pfeffer-inspired separationist decisions of the U.S. Supreme Court have led to greater secularization of public life? Typically, critics point to the Court's Establishment Clause decisions in the area of aid to religious institutions as illustrative of the inherent hostility of the separationist position to religion in public life. "In education, social services, and other dimensions of public life," Neuhaus contended, "it is claimed that, for the sake of the nonestablishment of religion, Americans must surrender the free exercise of religion." For example, Neuhaus believed that denying state benefits to parents wanting to provide their children a religious education "is religious freedom penalized in the name of a First Amendment designed to protect religious freedom."[82]

Frank Guliuzza likewise argued that the separationist decisions denying parochial schools publicly supported remedial education teachers and funding was an "extreme" application of the "separationist doctrine" that generated "disastrous results." He also identified the separationist challenge to allowing student-led religious clubs on public school campuses fostered "the perception that the establishment clause erects a wall of separation can cut deeply into the rights of those who, though required by law to attend school, wish to exercise their religious beliefs in ways that, perhaps unlike prayer or Bible reading, do not foster coercion or oppression."[83]

In contrast, Pfeffer contended that the quest for religious liberty in the United States was inextricably connected to the struggles "against compulsory taxation for religious purposes." Providing taxpayer aid to religious institutions, even on a nondiscriminatory basis, was the constitutional violation, not denial of government aid to religious institutions, according to

Pfeffer.[84] Moreover, funneling aid to religious institutions, whether directly or indirectly, by subordinating the Establishment Clause to the Free Exercise Clause ran counter to the philosophical and historical roots undergirding the First Amendment. For Pfeffer, the Establishment Clause had little meaning under such a reading of the First Amendment.

Other critics have argued that Pfeffer's absolutism with regard to the separation of church and state leads to the diminishment of individual free exercise of religion. David Dalin, for instance, claims that the U.S. Supreme Court's decision in *Goldman v. Weinberger*[85] "is but one more recent and especially troubling example of what the Pfefferian ideal of strict separationism has wrought."[86] In *Goldman*, a divided Court denied Sachma Goldman's free exercise claim that he should be exempted from an Air Force regulation prohibiting the wearing of headgear while indoors because of his religious obligation to wear a yarmulke. Dalin concludes that the Court denied Goldman his religious freedom because to allow him an exemption would breach "the wall of separation between church and state."

Dalin's choice of the *Goldman* case to illustrate the problems of the separationist position is highly problematic. First, the majority opinion was written by the Court's most vocal critic of the no-aid separationist position—William Rehnquist. Second, two of the most separationist justices on the Court, William Brennan and Thurgood Marshall, dissented and would have upheld Goldman's claim. Third, the thrust of the majority and concurring opinions' assertion was that the Air Force regulation was an "objective, completely neutral standard" and that the First Amendment does not require the military to accommodate such practices in the face of its view that to do so would detract from the uniformity sought by the dress regulations. Contrary to Dalin's claim, one searches Rehnquist's majority opinion in vain to find the rationale that allowing an exemption would violate the Establishment Clause. Rather, Rehnquist bases his opinion primarily upon the paramount importance of military discipline and uniformity. Ironically, the *Goldman* decision presages a trend of a plurality of accommodationist justices on the U.S. Supreme Court to not uphold free exercise exemptions from neutral and generally applicable laws.[87] Finally, even a cursory reading of Pfeffer's free exercise jurisprudence would suggest that he most likely would have supported Goldman's free exercise claim.[88]

Toward the end of his career, Pfeffer regularly faced the argument that the separationist interpretation of the Establishment Clause produced inconsistent decisions. There seemed to be no clear pattern of when aid would be upheld or struck down by the Court, leading critics to claim that the separationist position was an Establishment Clause theory. Pfeffer responded that it was not the separationist interpretation, but rather the Court's inconsistent application of the Establishment Clause that was to blame. Indeed, Pfeffer once argued, if the Court had agreed with him in every case, it would have been "fully consistent." Yet Pfeffer's claim does beg the question: What if the Court had ruled in his favor in all of those cases? Would his separationist position lead to the elimination of all religious symbols and traditions in public life? Would "In God We Trust" be removed from coins and "under God" be ruled unconstitutional in The Pledge of Allegiance? Or, as a number of commentators have suggested, would the no-aid and separationist positions, taken to their logical extremes, prohibit police and fire protection for churches and other religious institutions?

Theoretically, Pfeffer did view religious references such as court oaths that included "So help me God" and coins that declared "In God We Trust" as violations of at least the spirit of the First Amendment. However, he believed such symbols and utterances to be largely ceremonial. More importantly, he believed that as a practical matter they were too difficult to challenge: "These various ceremonial references are too trivial to provoke legal action except by rare extremists, and these have no way of effectively challenging the references."[89] Of greater concern to Pfeffer was the fact that these vestiges of American religious heritage were used to justify more serious violations of the religion clauses. In particular, Pfeffer cited the Court's use of such examples for upholding the New York released-time religious education program in *Zorach v. Clausen*. Pfeffer concluded that utilizing instances of "ceremonial deism" to justify greater cooperation between church and state was problematic for three reasons. First, it is not clear that those who initiated such practices would have approved of their use in justifying released-time programs or other practices that raise church-state conflicts. Second, "these references to God that are used to justify concrete practices are themselves assumed to be constitutional only because they have not been adjudged unconstitutional." In other words, just because they are too trivial to be challenged in court does not make them consistent with the Constitution. Finally, Pfeffer found the Constitution's silence on religion problematic for those that would seek to use religious references as a justification for certain practices. According to Pfeffer: "Citing references to God in court oaths, legends on coins, Presidential proclamations, and the like would appear to be relying on secondary evidence where the primary evidence does not sustain the contention sought to be proved."[90]

Police and fire protection given to churches were little more than the government fulfilling its responsibility of promoting the general welfare of the citizens. Yet Pfeffer did believe that churches had the responsibility of helping compensate for these governmental services. His opposition to tax exemption for church properties was rooted not only in the premise that churches should pay their fair share of governmental services but also that tax exemption essentially amounted to an indirect subsidy from the state to the religious institution.[91]

Beyond the debate over the application of the Establishment Clause, Neuhaus's *The Naked Public Square* is difficult to reconcile with the continued religious vitality in American society.[92] To be sure, the past decade has seen dramatic changes in American religion. A rapidly growing percentage of Americans, particularly young adults, are leaving traditional religion behind.[93] Both post-denominational and post-Christian trends have been witnessed, leading some to declare the death of white, Christian America.[94] It is important to note, however, that these trends have taken place during a period of time when the U.S. Supreme Court has moved in a decidedly accommodationist direction. To lay secularization at the feet of separation, then, is misplaced. Moreover, religion in America "has enjoyed continuous vitality" compared to many developed democracies.[95] Evangelical Protestants remain a powerful voting block and continue to play an influential role in the Republican Party. Churches and other faith-based organizations can exert powerful pressure on politicians as well. Pfeffer frequently identified this religious vitality as the best evidence of the beneficial effect on religion that the separation of church and state has had in America. Interestingly, during the period of the U.S. Supreme Court's most separationist decisions, the percentage of Americans claiming belief in god as well as membership in communities of faith remained among the highest in the industrialized world.[96] Rather than creating a hostile environment for religion, a high wall of separation insured its independence from the state and enabled to thrive on its own.[97] The integrity and authenticity of religion was better guaranteed by a high wall of separation as well. As one scholar recently argued: "The bar on government promotion of faith assists religious communities in retaining control of their messages, thus helping to ensure their authenticity."[98]

Moreover, the separation of church and state has not limited the church's active role in politics. As James E. Wood, Jr. declared: "the courts have never denied the right of the churches to participate actively in public life." Wood likewise argues that the separation of church and state was never understood to exclude religion from public life. Rather, the United States has a long tradition of religious groups actively engaged in the political process seeking to influence politics and the legislative process.[99] And as Melissa Rogers has argued more recently in her book *Faith and American Public Life*: "While the Constitution *prohibits* government-backed religion, it *protects* the rights of religious individuals and organizations to promote their faith."[100] Indeed, Pfeffer commits a chapter of his magnum opus, *Church, State, and Freedom*, to the topic of "church intervention in state affairs." Here Pfeffer chronicles, among a number of issues, the active role of churches in politics throughout the course of American history. From slavery battles to other "social gospel" initiatives, Pfeffer recounts the active role of "churchmen," denominations, and religious interest groups in American political life—even the active role of churches in the push for religious freedom and separation of church and state.[101] While he recognized that church-state conflicts have and will arise when religious institutions participate in the political activism, he concludes that

> the church is not necessarily wrong in entering politics. . . . There is nothing in our laws which does or indeed constitutionally can prevent ministers from using their Sunday sermons to urge their parishioners to vote against a bingo referendum or to urge the President not to send an ambassador to the Vatican. Nor is there anything in the laws which can constitutionally prevent priests from denying the sacraments to citizens who vote for Communist candidates, or even to legislators who vote in favor of birth control legislation.[102]

Ultimately, for Pfeffer, the issue of religious engagement with politics depended upon "what one conceives the church's responsibility to the kingdom of this world."[103] Here Pfeffer is raising a crucial point about the important prophetic role the church has, and can play, in American society. For Pfeffer and other separationists, the problem with viewing the state as having a role in aiding and accommodating religion is that it threatens to make the church a "handmaiden of the state." "The pattern of the religious public square," James E. Wood, Jr. argues, "has generally served to symbolize, if not give credence to, an alliance between religion and the state at the risk of profaning religion and sanctifying the state."[104]

In his article, "Blasphemy on the Potomac," Pfeffer warned of the deleterious effects on the church when it acquired too cozy a relationship with the state. "Religious influence is a pearl of great price," Pfeffer warned, "and the rulers of the state are frequently willing to pay that price." Richard John Neuhaus is certainly right that the long arm of the state seems to extend further all of the time. Yet, for Pfeffer, this was reason to be ever more vigilant in maintaining the independence of the church from the state. "Secular rulers have much to offer the church," he suggested, "and it is hardly to be expected that they will not seek and expect something in return, and that something is that the church allow itself to be used as an instrument of secular policy."[105] A strong Establishment Clause, or separation of church and state, frees the church from "any institutional dependence or subservience to the state that might modify or mute its prophetic voice."[106] In truth, both Neuhaus and Pfeffer would agree that the church plays an important "intermediary voice" in politics and can be an important check upon the totalitarian tendencies of government. The crucial difference between them lies in whether the church can play such a role if it becomes dependent upon the government for its funding and recognition.

SUMMARY

In his 1984 book, *The Naked Public Square*, Richard Neuhaus's argued that the Pfeffer-inspired U.S. Supreme Court's Establishment Clause decisions had marginalized religion in American public life. Neuhaus's contention was based on a misunderstanding of Pfeffer's view of the role of religion in public life. Pfeffer instead sought to ensure a fair and equitable system for religious and nonreligious interests to compete in the shaping of America's culture and laws. The separation of church and state was instrumental in creating a level playing field for the various "creeds in competition."

Rather than being hostile to religion, the wall of separation allowed religion to flourish. American religion's growth, vitality and pluralism were evidence for Pfeffer that the broad reading of both religion clauses of the First Amendment was beneficial to religion. Ultimately, Pfeffer was committed to preserving the integrity of both church and state. This he believed would be best achieved in a secular state. "Complete separation of church and state," he often asserted, "is best for church and best for state, and secures freedom for both."

NOTES

1. Richard John Neuhaus, *The Naked Public Square: Religion and Democracy in America* (Grand Rapids, Mich.: William B. Eerdmans Publishing Company, 1984).

2. See Robert Audi and Nicholas Wolterstorff, *Religion in the Public Square: The Place of Religious Convictions in Political Debate* (Lanham, Md.: Rowman and Littlefield Publishers, Inc., 1997); Stephen L. Carter, *The Culture of Disbelief: How American Law and Politics Trivializes Religious Devotion* (New York: Basic Books, 1993); Hugh Heclo and Wilfred McClay, eds. *Religion Returns to the Public Square: Faith and Policy in America* (Baltimore, Md.: Johns Hopkins University Press, 2003); Frank Guliuzza III, *Over the Wall: Protecting Religious Expression in the Public Square* (Albany, N.Y.: State University of New York Press, 2000); William H. Swatos, Jr. and James K. Wellman, Jr., eds. *The Power of Religious Publics: Staking Claims in American Society* (Westport, Conn.: Praeger, 1999); Ronald F. Thiemann, *Religion in Public Life: A Dilemma for Democracy* (Washington, DC: Georgetown University Press, 1996).

3. Michael Corbett, Julia Corbett-Heymeyer, and J. Matthew Wilson, *Politics and Religion in the United States*, 2nd ed. (New York: Routledge, 2014), 306.

4. See Neuhaus, "The Pfefferian Inversion," 44; see also, "Genuine Pluralism," 69–98; and Neuhaus, "Contending for the Future," 115–29.

5. Neuhaus, "The Pfefferian Inversion," 44.

6. Neuhaus, "Genuine Pluralism," 79.

7. Ibid., 74.

8. Neuhaus, "The Pfefferian Inversion," 44.

9. Neuhaus, "Genuine Pluralism," 73–74; see also Neuhaus, "A New Order of Religious Freedom," *George Washington Law Review* 60 (March 1992): 627.

10. Wilber Katz, "Freedom of Religion and State Neutrality," *University of Chicago Law Review* 20 (1953): 428.

11. See, for example, Thomas McCoy and Gary Kurtz, "A Unifying Theory for the Religion Clauses of the First Amendment," *Vanderbilt Law Review* 39 (1986): 249–74 and "The Williamsburg Charter," reprinted in *The Journal of Law and Religion* 8 (1990): 5–22.

12. Michael W. McConnell, "Accommodation of Religion," 3.

13. See Thiemann, *Religion in Public Life*, 44. For a litany of these inconsistencies in the Court's aid to religious schools decisions, see Jesse Choper, "The Religion Clauses of the First Amendment: Reconciling the Conflict," *University of Pittsburgh Law Review* 41 (Summer 1980): 680.

14. Neuhaus, "Genuine Pluralism," 75–76.

15. Ibid., 76–77.

16. Ibid.

17. Ibid.

18. Neuhaus, "A New Order of Religious Freedom," 623.

19. James Hitchcock, *The Supreme Court and Religion in American Life: Volume II: From "Higher Law" to "Sectarian Scruples"* (Princeton, N.J.: Princeton University Press, 2004), 157.

20. Ibid., 163.

21. Guliuzza, III, *Over the Wall*, 52–56.

22. Thiemann, *Religion in Public Life*, 60.

23. Ibid., 60–62.

24. Ibid., 108.

25. See Milton Himmelfarb, "Jewish Perceptions of the New Assertiveness of Religion in American Life," in *Jews in Unsecular America*, ed. Richard John Neuhaus (Grand Rapids, MI: William B. Eerdmans Publishing Company, 1987), 1–7; and David Dalin, ed. *American Jews and the Separationist Faith: The New Debate on Religion in Public Life* (Washington, DC: Ethics and Public Policy Center, 1993).

26. See Cohen, *Jews in Christian America* and Borden, *Jews, Turks, and Infidels*.

27. Alan Mittleman, "Toward a Postseparationist Public Philosophy: A Jewish Contribution," *This World* 25 (1989): 98.

28. Pickus, "'Before I Built A Wall'," 29.

29. Jonathan D. Sarna, "Christian America or Secular America? The Church-State Dilemma of American Jews," in *Jews in Unsecular America*, ed. Richard John Neuhaus (Grand Rapids, Mich.: William B. Eerdmans Publishing Company, 1987), 18–19.

30. Ibid., 32.
31. Ibid.
32. Mittleman, "Toward a Postseparationist Public Philosophy," 98–102.
33. See, for example, Guliuzza, *Over the Wall*, p. 170.
34. Pfeffer, *Creeds in Competition*. These same themes are repeated in *God, Caesar, and the Constitution: The Court as Referee of Church-State Confrontation* (Boston, MA: Beacon Press, 1975), 2–41; "Issues that Divide," *The Journal of Social Issues* 12 (1956): 21–39; and "Issues that Divide: The Triumph of Secular Humanism," *Journal of Church and State* 19 (Spring 1977): 203–16.
35. Pfeffer, *Creeds in Competition*, 15.
36. Ibid., 160.
37. Ibid., 159.
38. Ibid., 160–65.
39. Ibid., 168.
40. Ibid., 2–4.
41. Leo Pfeffer, "Commentary on 'Civil Religion in America' by Robert N. Bellah," in *The Religious Situation: 1968*, ed. Donald R. Cutler (Boston: Beacon Press, 1968), 361–64.
42. See Chapter 2.
43. Ibid., 165.
44. Thiemann, *Religion in Public Life*, 74.
45. Neuhaus, "A New Order of Religious Freedom," 623.
46. Pfeffer, "No Law Respecting an Establishment of Religion," *Buffalo Law Review* 2 (Spring 1953): 238–39.
47. Leo Pfeffer, "The Future of the Bill of Rights: Church-State Relations," in *The Future of Our Liberties*, ed. Stephen C. Halpern (Westview, Conn.: Greenwood Press, 1982), 126–27.
48. Pfeffer, *Creeds in Competition*, 30.
49. Ibid., 29.
50. Ibid., 154.
51. Ibid., 167.
52. Pfeffer, "Issues that Divide," 204.
53. Ibid., 214–16.
54. "American secular humanism is manifesting its potency in altering long-held doctrine and practice and narrowing the differences that divide Protestants, Catholics, and Jews." Pfeffer, "Issues that Divide," 216; see also, "Review: Secularization: A Case Study," *Texas Law Review* (August 1972): 1288–91.
55. Pfeffer, *Creeds in Competition*, 134.
56. Ibid., 164–68.
57. Ibid.
58. Ibid.
59. Hitchcock, *The Supreme Court and Religion*, 152.
60. Pfeffer, *Creeds in Competition*, 158.
61. Kathleen Sullivan, "Religion and Liberal Democracy," *University of Chicago Law Review* 59 (1992): 200–01.

62. Pfeffer, *God, Caesar, and the Constitution*, 28–38.

63. Pfeffer, *Creeds in Competition*, 17–18.

64. See Chapter 4.

65. Prior to the 1963 *Sherbert v. Verner* decision and its requirement of a compelling state interest, Pfeffer contended, "free exercise did not have a separate but equal existence (with other First Amendment freedoms), or even one that was separate and unequal, it practically had no existence at all." Pfeffer, "The Supremacy of Free Exercise," 1130.

66. *Sherbert v. Verner*, 374 U.S. 398 at 413–15.

67. 374 U.S. 398 at 409.

68. Dean M. Kelley, *Why Churches Should Not Pay Taxes* (New York: Harper and Row, 1977).

69. See Leo Pfeffer, "The Special Constitutional Status of Religion," in *Taxation and the Free Exercise of Religion*, ed. John W. Baker (Washington, DC: Baptist Joint Committee on Public Affairs, 1978), 7–10; and Leo Pfeffer, "Brief of Amicus Curiae," *Walz* v. *Tax Commission*, 397 U.S. 644 (1970).

70. *Walz v. Tax Commission*, 397 U.S. 644 (1970).

71. Many of Pfeffer's separationist allies broke with him on the issue of tax exemption. Groups such as the National Council of Churches and Americans United for Separation of Church and State filed briefs in *Walz* in favor of tax exemption. Pfeffer was even unable to gain support of his own organization, the American Jewish Congress, to take the unpopular decision of challenging the constitutionality of tax exemption. Pfeffer's opposing brief was eventually sponsored by the American Civil Liberties Union.

72. *Harris v. McRae*, 448 U.S. 297 (1980).

73. Brief for American Ethical Union et al. as Amici Curiae Supporting Appellee at 6, *Harris v. McRae*, 448 U.S. 297 (1980) (No. 79-1268); see also, Pfeffer, "Abortion and Religious Freedom,"; statement originally submitted to Subcommittee on Civil and Constitutional Rights, U.S. House Committee on the Judiciary, 24 March 1976, and reprinted as a pamphlet, *Abortion and Religious Freedom*, by the Religious Coalition for Abortion Rights.

74. Ibid., 13; see also Pfeffer, *God, Caesar, and the Constitution*, 112–13. As noted in Chapter 4, anti-abortion contemporary debates over abortion are less theologically oriented and, with the advances in medicine and changes to fetal viability, the arguments against abortion have become more secularized. Nonetheless, there remain pro-choice advocates that argue fetal personhood remains a theological question and one that Congress and the courts should no longer avoid. See Kraft, "The Right to Abortion."

75. Robert Audi, "The Place of Religious Argument in a Free and Democratic Society," in *Law and Religion: A Critical Anthology*, ed. Stephen M. Feldman (New York: New York University Press, 2000), 85; see also Robert Audi, *Democratic Authority and the Separation of Church and State* (New York: Oxford University Press, 2011).

76. Pfeffer, *Creeds in Competition*, 18.

77. Brief for Synagogue Counsel of America and National Community Relations Advisory Counsel as Amici Curiae Supporting Petitioners at 16–17, *Abington v. Schempp*, 374 U.S. 203 (1963) (Nos. 142 & 149).

78. Ibid., at 21.

79. Phillip Hammond, "Can Religion Be Religious in Public?" in *The Power of Religious Publics: Staking Claims in American Society*, eds. by William H. Swatos, Jr. and James K. Wellman, Jr. (Westport, Conn.: Praeger, 1999), 19, 30–31.

80. Ivers, *To Build A Wall*, 113.

81. Pfeffer, "From Religious Monism to Pluralism,": 7; "A Momentous Year," 36.

82. Neuhuas, "A New Order of Religious Freedom," 629.

83. Frank Guliuzza, "The Supreme Court, the Establishment Clause, and Incoherence," in *Religion, Public Life, and the American Polity*, ed. Luis E. Lugo (Knoxville: The University of Tennessee Press, 1994), 135. Guliuzza is referring to *Grand Rapids v. Ball*, 473 U.S. 373 (1985) and *Aguilar v. Felton*, 473 U.S. 402 (1985) where the U.S. Supreme Court struck down programs in which public school teachers were assigned to provide remedial education in nonpublic schools. These decisions were overturned by the more accommodationist Rehnquist Court in *Agostini v. Felton* (1997).

84. Pfeffer, "Federal Funds for Parochial Schools," 310–12.

85. *Goldman v. Weinberger*, 475 U.S. 503 (1986).

86. Dalin, "Leo Pfeffer and the Separationist Faith," 140.

87. Culminating in the controversial *Oregon v. Smith* (1990) peyote case where Justice Antonin Scalia declares that that compelling state interest test was a "luxury . . . we can no longer afford."

88. Pfeffer did not participate in or provide much commentary on the *Goldman* case as it occurred at the end of his career.

89. Pfeffer, *Church, State, and Freedom*, 240.

90. Ibid.; In addressing whether a cross on a county seal should be challenged as a violation of the separation of church and state, Pfeffer once corresponded: "Here de minimus would certainly be an adequate defense if a court wanted to decide against you. This I think is the weakest of all the cases and I am inclined to question to the wisdom of an all out campaign on this issue." Leo Pfeffer to I.H. Prinsmetal, June 3, 1958, Box 16, Leo Pfeffer Papers, George Arendts Research Library, Syracuse University.

91. Brief for Synagogue Counsel of America and its Constituents as Amici Curiae Supporting Appellee, *Walz v. Tax Commission*, 397 U.S. 664 (1970) (No. 135).

92. "Americans are Far More Religious than Adults in Other Nations," Pew Research Center, Washington, DC (July 31, 2018).

93. Pew Research Center, "America's Changing Religious Landscape," (May 12, 2015): 1–4.

94. See Robert P. Jones, *The End of White Christian America* (New York: Simon and Shuster, 2016).

95. Allen Hertzke, Laura Olson, and Kevin Den Dulk, and Robert Booth Fowler, *Religion and Politics in America*, 6th ed. (New York: Routledge, 2019), 49.

96. According to Robert Wuthnow, church attendance hit an all-time high in the late 1950s with nearly 50 percent of Americans claiming they attended worship

in any given week. After a slump in the 1960s, these figures stabilized during the 1970s and 1980s to around 40 percent. Church membership, under 10 percent at the country's founding, grew to over 60 percent during the mid-twentieth century; see Robert Wuthnow, *The Restructuring of American Religion* (Princeton, NJ: Princeton University Press, 1988), 164–65. "Some 95 percent of Americans profess a belief in god or a universal spirit, with over 60 percent claiming never to doubt God's existence. More than six in ten say that religion is 'very important' in their everyday lives and that 'religion can answer all or most of today's problems.' Ninety percent associate with one of the many religious traditions present in the United States. While there is a small but growing segment of secular Americans, the vast majority of Americans continue to make religious faith an important part of their lives." Hertzke et al., *Religion and Politics*, 49; see also Jonathan Evans, "U.S. Adults are More Religious than Western Europeans," *Pew Research Center*, Washington, DC (September 5, 2018), https://www.pewresearch.org/fact-tank/2018/09/05/u-s-adults-are-more-religious-than-western-europeans/.

97. Pfeffer, *Church, State, and Freedom*, 166.

98. Melissa Rogers, *Faith in American Public Life* (Waco, TX: Baylor University Press, 2019).

99. James E. Wood, Jr., "Public Religion Vis-à-Vis the Prophetic Role of Religion," in *The Power of Religious Publics: Staking Claims in American Society*, ed. William H. Swatos, Jr. and James K. Wellman, Jr. (Westport, CT: Praeger, 1999), 44.

100. Rogers, *Faith in American Public Life*, 3.

101. "It is quite significant that the principle of separation of church and state as established in the state legislatures and in the Constitutional Convention of the Federal Government were in large measure the outcome of the activities of church-related bodies." Letter, Leo Pfeffer to Dean M. Kelley, February 7, 1968, Syracuse University Special Collections, Box 13, Leo Pfeffer Papers.

102. Pfeffer, *Church, State, and Freedom*, 222.

103. Ibid., 221.

104. Wood, "Public Religion," 42.

105. Leo Pfeffer, "Blasphemy on the Potomac," *The Christian Register* 134 (March 1955): 11.

106. Wood, "Public Religion," 47.

Conclusion

This book has examined the sources of Leo Pfeffer's interpretation of the religion clauses of the First Amendment, his influence on the development of church-state law, and his understanding of the role of religion in public life. Pfeffer believed that a high wall of separation between church and state as well as broad free exercise protections maximized religious freedom, fostered religious equality, and guaranteed both the autonomy and authenticity of religious faith. Rather than expressing hostility toward religion, the separation of church and state leveled the playing field for participants from differing religious as well as nonreligious perspectives to compete actively to shape American politics and culture. Pfeffer's First Amendment views were shaped by his historical context, his experiences as a practicing Jew in mid-twentieth-century America, and his understanding of the historical development of religious liberty in the United States. For more than forty years, Pfeffer championed his absolutist First Amendment views in numerous religious liberty cases as well as in his many publications.

Leo Pfeffer had a profound impact on the judicial interpretation of church and state. The sheer number of First Amendment cases in which he was involved provides some indication of his influence. Pfeffer filed over 120 briefs in church-state cases in the form of both amicus curiae and as counsel for a party in a case. Often, when Pfeffer's name was not officially attached to the brief, he was working behind the scenes directing the strategy of litigation and, on some occasions, drafting the brief. Moreover, Pfeffer presented the oral arguments before the U.S. Supreme Court in a number of landmark cases.

Pfeffer's influence on the Court can be found in landmark First Amendment decisions. In *McCollum v. Board of Education*,[1] Justice Felix Frankfurter adopted Pfeffer's social scientific evidence of the effect school-sponsored religious education programs had on children of minority faiths. In several cases involving state aid to religious higher education, the Court adopted Pfeffer's profile of religiously affiliated colleges in determining whether an institution was "pervasively sectarian." In *Epperson v. Arkansas*,[2] Pfeffer filed the only brief arguing against the constitutionality of an anti-evolution statute based on Establishment Clause grounds. The Court's majority opinion followed Pfeffer's arguments closely when ruling the statute unconstitutional. Even when the Court did not cite Pfeffer explicitly, its reasoning often followed Pfeffer's arguments closely. When the Court, for example, introduced the purpose and effect tests of what would become the *Lemon* test in *Abington v. Schempp*,[3] it echoed what Pfeffer had been arguing in his legal briefs; namely, that the government's ends must be secular and, in achieving them, its means must be secular as well.

The fact that Pfeffer has frequently been identified, by both friend and foe, as the leading advocate of the broad interpretation of the First Amendment further attests to his influence. As early as the 1960s, Leo Pfeffer was singled out by the Catholic journal, *Commonweal*, as the leading actor in the strict separationist legal agenda. In 1976, Frank Sorauf dedicated a significant portion of his study on American church-state relations to Pfeffer's unparalleled involvement in church-state cases.[4] In the 1980s, Pfeffer remained the most prominent and influential advocate of the separationist agenda. Critics of the Court's separationist decisions, such as Robert Cord and Richard John Neuhaus, specifically identified Pfeffer as the leading shaper of court opinion. Gregg Ivers has noted that when Pfeffer retired from active legal involvement in the church-state arena in the 1980s, "for the first time in over thirty years both the organized Jewish and separationist communities were left without a central figure to coordinate their involvement in the litigation process."[5]

Pfeffer's legacy appears to be undermined, however, by the accommodationist shift of the Court over the past thirty years. The no-aid or "strict separationist" approach has been increasingly criticized for being inflexible and limited as a jurisprudential guide. While the Court continues to have difficulty reconciling school sponsored religious exercises in the public schools with the Establishment Clause, a majority of justices have found greater sympathy with public aid to religious institutions as long as the aid is distributed on an equal or evenhanded basis. Consequently, the Court has overruled a number of Pfeffer-influenced school aid decisions and have upheld, among other things, the provision of instructional equipment, remedial and diagnostic support, and tuition vouchers to religious schools. These have been justified on the basis of a neutrality or equal treatment approach that allows public benefits to "religious students and their parents the same general benefits afforded to others."[6]

The accommodationist drift began in the mid-1980s with several cases that laid the groundwork for a dramatic change in how the Court would rule on aid cases. In the 1986 *Witters v. Washington Department of Services for the Blind* case, the Court ruled that a visually impaired person could not be denied a state vocational rehabilitation grant because he was studying theology at a Bible college. Utilizing the equal treatment, private choice approach, the Court held that "any aid provided under Washington's program that ultimately flows to religious institutions does so only as a result of the genuinely independent and private choices of individuals."[7] Such an approach, if applied to other forms of aid, would make irrelevant questions of the pervasively sectarian nature of the school, the diverting of funds to religious purposes, or other issues that might give rise to the excessive entanglement of church and state.

In the 1993 *Zobrest v. Catalina Foothills School District*, the Court upheld a state providing an interpreter to a deaf student attending a Roman Catholic high school. Opponents of this provision argued that the taxpayer-funded interpreter would be conveying religious teachings to the student in violation of the Establishment Clause. A five-member majority of the Court upheld the provision on several grounds. First, the Individuals with Disabilities Education Act's provision of an interpreter did not provide a financial incentive for parents to send their children to private religious schools. Second, the majority led by Chief Justice Rehnquist argued that the interpreter was not creating or elaborating upon religious content, but rather merely dictating content provided by the parochial school teachers. Third, the Court, echoing the child-benefit theory of *Everson* and *Allen*, concluded that the hearing impaired student was the recipient of the aid, not the religious school. Citing the *Mueller* and *Witters* decisions, Rhenquist argued that "the service in this case is part of a general government program that distributes benefits neutrally to any child qualifying as disabled under the IDEA, without regard to the sectarian-nonsectarian, or public-nonpublic nature of the school the child attends. By according parents freedom to select a school of their choice, the statute ensures that a government-paid interpreter will be present in a sectarian school only as a result of individual parents' private decisions."[8] The fact that a state employee was on the religious school campus, an issue that raised constitutional objections in *Meek v. Pittenger* and *Grand Rapids v. Ball*, was not controlling. "An interpreter, unlike a teacher or guidance counselor," Rehnquist explained, "neither adds to nor subtracts from the sectarian school's environment but merely interprets whatever material is presented to the class as a whole. There is no absolute bar to the placing of a public employee in a sectarian school."[9]

Justice Blackmun's dissent challenged the equal treatment theory's consistency with past Establishment Clause criteria as well as Rehnquist's attempt to distinguish *Zobrest* from earlier school aid decisions. "Until now, the Court never has authorized a public employee to participate directly in religious indoctrination," Blackmun argued. Noting the pervasively sectarian nature of the school, Blackmun also contended that the interpreter would inevitably be facilitating religious indoctrination. Blackmun also took the issue with general welfare or neutral principles approach of the majority. Citing prior aid cases, he argued that "even a general welfare program may have specific applications that are constitutionally forbidden under the Establishment Clause." Providing an interpreter was not an equivalent neutral aid to the loan of secular textbooks. By upholding this form of aid, Blackmun concluded, the Court was straying from "the course set by nearly five decades of Establishment Clause jurisprudence."[10]

Utilizing *Witters* and *Zobrest*, the Court, in subsequent cases, upheld even direct aid at the elementary and secondary level. In the 1997 *Agostini v. Felton* case, the Court took the rare step of explicitly overturning its previous decisions in *Aguilar v. Felton* and *Grand Rapids v. Ball*. In upholding the provision of part-time public education teachers and other instructional aid to parochial schools, the Court concluded that, in light of *Zobrest*, "we have departed from the rule in *Ball* that all government aid that directly aids the educational function of religious schools is invalid."[11]

The pervasively sectarian test, as well as the Lemon Test, faced their most significant attack in the 2000 *Mitchell v. Helms* decision. Here the Court upheld a federally-funded aid program in which state and local agencies purchased educational materials and equipment for public and private elementary and secondary schools. The plurality opinion emphasized the "neutrality-of-aid" doctrine in addressing whether governmental aid to religious schools necessarily leads to religious indoctrination attributable to the state. At the same time, the plurality attacked the pervasively sectarian test and called for its abandonment by the Court. Since the "religious nature of the recipient should not matter to the constitutional analysis," the pervasively sectarian test led to the "offensive . . . trolling through a person's or institution's religious beliefs." The Court concluded that "nothing in the Establishment Clause requires the exclusion of pervasively sectarian schools from otherwise permissible aid programs . . . This doctrine, born of bigotry, should be buried now."[12] In doing so, the majority gutted the Court's opinion in *Meek v. Pittenger*, particularly its holding that the provision of instructional equipment was a form of direct aid that "substantially advanced" religion.

Justices O'Connor and Breyer concurred in the holding of the Court but were not willing to accept that neutrality alone was sufficient to satisfy Establishment Clause concerns in aid cases. Rather, neutrality or equal treatment was one of the several factors that the Court should consider, as was the ability to divert funds to religious purposes. While O'Connor avoided calling for the burial of the pervasively sectarian test, she too admitted that its presumption of religious inculcation or indoctrination in religious schools was problematic. Instead, O'Connor said the emphasis should be on whether aid has been diverted to religious purposes leading to the unconstitutional advancement of religion.[13]

In his dissenting opinion, Justice David Souter found the majority's failure to "recognize the divertibility of funds to the service of religious objectives" particularly troubling. "What is more important," Souter concluded, was the plurality's espousal of "a new conception of neutrality . . . that would eliminate enquiry into a law's effects."[14] Thus, for Souter, not only was the excessive entanglement inquiry largely ignored under the neutrality inquiry, but the key question of whether aid advances religion might likewise be avoided. The plurality opinion, as a result, generated a lot of speculation over whether the Lemon Test had met its demise.

While *Mitchell* involved direct aid, it was limited to instructional equipment like computers and other technology. In 2002, the Court addressed the constitutionality of school vouchers that eligible students could use to pay tuition at private, including religious, schools. While an indirect form of aid, this taxpayer funded program had a more deleterious effect on the no-aid principles of *Everson* that Pfeffer had worked so hard to uphold. In many ways, the *Zelman v. Simmons-Harris* voucher case laid bare the distinctions between the separationist and the accommodationist interpretations of the Establishment Clause. *Zelman* involved a Cleveland, Ohio program that provided low-income parents of students in struggling Cleveland public schools vouchers that provided tuition assistance to attend a participating public and private schools of their choice. Participating schools could not discriminate based upon religion in admissions and voucher checks were made payable to parents who signed them over to the chosen school. About 82% of the participating schools were religious and 96% of the participants chose religious schools.[15]

In a five-to-four decision, the Court upheld the Cleveland voucher program. Writing for the majority, Chief Justice William Rehnquist argued the neutrality of choice argument based upon the *Mueller*, *Witters*, and *Zobrest* decisions. Noting that the Court's jurisprudence regarding "direct aid programs had 'changed significantly' over the past two decades," Rehnquist contended that neutral aid programs offered to "a broad class of individuals" have been upheld. Any "incidental advancement" of religion in such a program, he argued, "is reasonably attributable to the individual recipient, not to the government."[16]

Justice David Souter provided a full-throated dissent arguing that the Court's decision was irreconcilable with *Everson*. "How can a Court consistently leave *Everson* on the books and approve the Ohio vouchers," he queried. "The answer is that it cannot. It is only by ignoring *Everson* that the majority can claim to rest on traditional law in its invocation of neutral aid provisions and private choice to sanction the Ohio law." To Souter, the voucher program was particularly egregious in its constitutional infirmities because the aid would fund all aspects of the pervasively sectarian institution's mission, not just textbooks or equipment. "The money will thus pay for eligible students' instruction not only in secular subjects but in religion as well."[17] As a result "every objective underlying the prohibition of religious establishment is betrayed by this scheme."[18] In furthering his argument, Souter revived Pfeffer's religious divisiveness contention, suggesting that "religious teaching at taxpayer expense simply cannot be cordoned from taxpayer politics, and every major religion currently espouses social positions that provoke intense opposition."[19]

Mitchell, *Zelman*, and other more recent accommodationist decisions undermined a number of Pfeffer-era decisions that had ruled unconstitutional most direct and indirect form of aid to religious elementary and secondary schools. The influence of free speech principles that increasingly informed Establishment Clause decisions facilitated the equal treatment approach to aid cases as well. Free speech or "equal access" arguments were used to determine that public elementary and secondary schools as well as public universities could not engage in content discrimination by restricting access to facilities or student activities funds to religious groups if their funds were available to other organizations.[20] Equal access has provided further constitutional leverage to accommodationists seeking aid to religious institutions. By arguing that denial of funds constituted religious discrimination that violated freedom of speech and free exercise principles, accommodationists could avoid Establishment Clause objections to aid (even aid used for explicitly religious purposes) as long as it was distributed on a neutral or evenhanded basis.

The neutrality theory, then, threatened to sound the death knell for the pervasively sectarian test as well as the more modest restrictions on aid to religious higher education. Yet, religious schools may find their state constitutions more prohibitive of funds than the current U.S. Supreme Court's permissive interpretation of the Establishment Clause. In the 2004 *Locke v. Davey* decision, the Court denied a challenge by Joshua Davey who was told he could not use his publicly funded "Promise Scholarship" to study pastoral ministry at a church of God-related Northwest College in Washington. The no-aid to religion provision of the Washington state constitution was upheld by Chief Justice Rehnquist in his majority decision. Rejecting Davey's claim that his free exercise rights were violated, Rehnquist argued that the case involved a "play in the joints" between the two religion clauses in that it "concerns a state action that is permitted by the Establishment Clause but not required by the Free Exercise Clause." Affirming the Court's previous decisions upholding indirect aid to religious institutions, particularly when the "link between government funds and religious training is broken by the private choice of recipients," Rehnquist conceded that Washington could allow scholarship funds to go to the study of theology. However, he concluded that the Free Exercise Clause did not require the state to do so in light of its own constitutional prohibitions.[21]

A number of factors explain the shift in the Court's approach to Establishment Clause issues since Pfeffer's departure from active litigation in the mid-1980s. The most obvious were the changes in the Court's personnel. Ronald Reagan, elected president in 1980, appointed four conservative members to the U.S. Supreme Court each of whom, to varying degrees, was sympathetic to an accommodationist reading of the Establishment Clause in aid cases. With few exceptions, partisan appointments to the Court have continued to shape the Court's outcomes in religious liberty cases with Republican presidents appointing nine of the last thirteen justices to serve on the Court.

Recently, scholars have challenged the argument that changing court personnel best explains the Court's accommodationist direction. They argue that church-state separation "has always been an indeterminate legal principle" in light of the fact that justices during the separationist era of the Court were at times divided over not only its application but also its broader purposes. No longer defined by the Protestant-Catholic debates of the 1940s and 1950s, separation, by the 1960s, was running headlong into an increasingly pluralistic culture and a growing sympathy toward church-state cooperation. This was hastened with the advent of the Great Society programs, including the massive funding of education through the Elementary and Secondary Education Act. Steadily a pro-aid coalition was forming among justices, politicians, and the public who perceived the strictures of the separationist position increasingly unrealistic, if not hostile to religion. Consequently, these scholars argue that the nondiscrimination or equal treatment principle enjoyed more widespread appeal.[22]

To be sure, shifting majorities emerged even among separationist justices as the Court did not always apply the Establishment Clause as consistently as Pfeffer would have liked. Indeed, even in the Court's earliest landmark church-state case, *Everson v. Board of Education*, the Court was narrowly divided 5–4 on whether transportation reimbursements to parents of parochial school students violated the Establishment Clause despite the fact that there was broad consensus on the no-aid interpretation of the First Amendment among the justices. Justices are certainly influenced by the changing social and political contexts and are often limited by the facts of the cases they decide. These scholars provide compelling evidence that the no-aid separationist principle was losing traction as early as the 1960s. Nonetheless, it was not until a growing number of accommodationist members joined the Court that the assault on the wall of separation and the Lemon Test prevailed. In fact, virtually all of the major aid decisions during the Rehnquist and Roberts Courts have been narrowly divided along ideological lines.

As discussed in chapter 2, a new wave of scholarship has argued that the separation of church and state was the product of late-nineteenth-century nativism aimed at a growing Catholic Church and parochial school system. This historical evidence led Justice Clarence Thomas to conclude that state constitutional amendments barring aid to religious schools were "born of bigotry" rather than principle. Thus, the no-aid interpretation of the Establishment Clause was rooted not in the desire to protect religious liberty, but rather anti-Catholic animus. The argument that the strict separationist approach to aid was little more than thinly veiled anti-Catholicism has been utilized to engender greater support for the equal treatment reading of the Establishment Clause.

There is no doubt that anti-Catholic sentiments drove some of the Protestant support for separationism and explains in part why the principle was easily abandoned by some Protestants in more recent years. Yet, the separationist arguments championed by Pfeffer existed prior to the nativist movements of the late nineteenth century and have endured long past the mid-twentieth-century Protestant-Catholic intramural battles. To dismiss no-aid separationism as nothing more than anti-Catholicism also ignores Pfeffer's oft repeated claim that the separation of church and state protected religion. It was the integrity of the parochial school that was at stake by opening them up for tax dollars. This was key to understanding Pfeffer's insistence on separation and is echoed later by dissenting justices challenging the new accommodationist trend. As Justice Souter argued in *Zelman*, vouchers violated not only the freedom of conscience of the taxpayer, but also would lead to the corruption of religion. Noting that the Ohio voucher plan barred religious discrimination in admissions and had the potential of prohibiting schools from "choosing a member of its own clergy to serve as a teacher or principle," Souter warned of the "growing regulation of religious practice in the school."[23] Pfeffer did find himself frequently at odds with Catholics who advocated the accommodationist perspective. Often they were his loudest critics. While he identified the Catholic Church as the biggest challenge to the "cultural patterns and values fixed by a Protestant Humanist alliance," he saw this cultural competition as positive and he defended the right of the Catholic Church to engage the public square. As a whole, Pfeffer's conflicts with the Catholic Church were born out of his commitment to principle rather than bigotry.

Despite the accommodationist shift, the basic principles for which Pfeffer argued remain central to the debates over the meaning of the Establishment Clause. Even though the primary effect and excessive entanglement prongs of the Lemon Test have been curtailed, the essential principle that the government is prohibited from directly funding or endorsing religious teachings at religious institutions has not been overturned. The Court remains divided on church-state issues with a number of justices who still advocate, at least in principle, the separationist perspective. In the recent *Trinity Lutheran v. Comer* decision, where the Court upheld a state grant given directly to a church to resurface its playground on free exercise grounds, Justice Sonya Sotomayor declared in her dissent: "History shows that the Religion Clauses separate the public treasury from religious coffers as one measure to secure the kind of freedom of conscience that benefits both religion and government. If this separation means anything, it means that the government cannot, or at the very least need not, tax its citizens and turn that money over to houses of worship. The Court today blinds itself to the outcome this history requires and leads us instead to a place where separation of church and state is a constitutional slogan, not a constitutional commitment."[24] While the *Trinity Lutheran* decision further erodes Establishment Clause restrictions, Sotomayor's words echo the key no-aid principles for which Pfeffer long advocated.

The enduring principles of the separationist position are also found in the different trajectory the Court has taken in cases involving religious exercises in the public schools. Unlike the aid cases, the U.S. Supreme Court justices have had a harder time justifying public school sponsored religious exercises, including formal prayers at graduation exercises and football games to be consistent with the Establishment Clause principles. The election of Ronald Reagan in 1980 not only raised the specter of more accommodationist justices being appointed to the Court, but also the reintroduction of public school prayer as a source of political division and constitutional adjudication. Critical of the Court's school prayer decision, the Religious Right had become a powerful force in Republican politics. Championing a platform of traditional family values, these religious conservatives identified the *Engel v. Vitale* decision as a touchstone event that precipitated a steep moral decline in the nation. Republicans such as Reagan sought to make allies with these family values crusaders by advocating for a return of "voluntary" school prayer to the public schools. This position found its way into the 1980 Republican Party Platform. At the same time, Republicans such as North Carolina senator, Jesse Helms, and Reagan's attorney general, Edwin Meese, supported bills that would strip the Supreme Court's jurisdiction over several controversial issues, including school prayer. By 1982, Reagan sought to consummate his relationship with these religious conservatives by introducing a school prayer amendment. What ensued was a renewed and intense debate over the proper role of religion in public life. This time the divisions were not so much between than across denominational lines. Conservatives were pitted against progressives as opposed to the Catholic-Protestant divisions of years past.[25]

Despite these efforts, the Court has struck down school-sponsored religious exercises in the public schools, particularly if there was evidence of endorsement by the state or coercion to participate. Even an Alabama "moment of silence" statute was struck down by the Court in 1984 because its legislative intent revealed a purpose to "retain prayer in the public schools."[26] In the 1992 *Lee v. Weisman* decision, the Court invalidated clergy led prayers at public school graduation exercises as a violation of the Establishment Clause. "The controlling precedents as they relate to prayer and religious exercises in primary and secondary schools compel the holding here," the Court declared. "It is beyond dispute that, at a minimum, the Constitution guarantees that the government may not coerce anyone to support or participate in religion or its exercise."[27] The *Lee v. Weisman* decision provided the legal basis for the Court to strike down student-led and initiated prayers at public high school football games. The Court determined that public school football prayers could "not properly be characterized as 'private' speech," since they were delivered "on school property, at school-sponsored events, over the school's public address system, by a speaker representing the student body, under the supervision of school faculty, and pursuant to a school policy that explicitly and implicitly encourages public prayer." For Justice John Paul Stevens, this represented an impermissible "school sponsorship of a religious message."[28] While in these cases the Court focused less on the Lemon Test's provisions than on questions of government endorsement and coercion, both cases reflected the concerns of school sponsorship, coercion, and student impressionability that can be traced back to Pfeffer's brief in *McCollum v. Board of Education*.

As First Amendment scholar John Witte has noted, "separationist norms" have largely carried the day when it comes to religious exercises in the public schools. "The establishment clause cases on the place of religion in the public schools—from *McCollum* (1948) to *Santa Fe* (2000)—," Witte has explained, "is among the Court's most consistent application of the First Amendment religion clauses." There have been a minority of justices who believe organized religious activities can occur on public schools on an equal or nonpreferential basis, but most justices, some of whom are accommodationists on public aid to religious institutions, find such practices difficult to fashion in a way that will "protect against religious coercion or endorsement by government."[29]

The broad reading of the Free Exercise Clause that Pfeffer advocated has generated significant legal and scholarly debate as well, especially after the Court undermined the compelling state interest test in *Oregon v. Smith*. Subsequently, however, both federal and state legislatures have passed laws protecting the free exercise rights of individuals and religious bodies from discriminatory laws as well as generally applicable laws that happen to conflict with their free exercise rights. Religious claimants have successfully challenged neutral and generally applicable laws by appealing to the Religious Freedom Restoration Act and the Religious Land Use and Institutionalized Persons Act.[30] Nonetheless, a battle continues to be waged over the appropriateness of religious exemptions from laws that seek to promote the general welfare as well as protect against discrimination based upon gender or sexual orientation. Here Pfeffer's broad reading of the free exercise clause is both ironic and instructive. On the one hand, it's hard to imagine that Pfeffer could have foreseen the exemptions he championed for religious minorities from neutral laws and regulations would be used to insulate large for-profit corporations like Hobby Lobby from providing certain health care benefits to their employees based upon the owners' religious convictions.[31] It is also difficult to conceive of Pfeffer being sympathetic with religious freedom claims being used by for-profit business owners to discriminate against customers based upon their sexual orientation.[32] Of course, this is purely speculative. Nevertheless, both of these recent cases represent what Pfeffer called the "clash of conflicting interests" that characterized many free exercise disputes. Pfeffer recognized that, inevitably, justices would have to weigh the merits of competing constitutional claims. On the other hand, religious minorities seeking freedom from burdensome neutral laws should not have to rely upon statutory exemptions that are a product of a majoritarian political process. This does not mean that legislatures have not been solicitous at times of religious claimants, but fundamental religious freedoms should not have to rely upon legislative grants.

Leo Pfeffer's approach to the role of religion in public life remains instructive. A high wall of separation ensures the autonomy and voluntary nature of religious belief and better contributes to the crucial prophetic role churches and religious institutions play in society. And a robust free exercise clause better protects religious minorities from both intended and unintended discriminatory treatment. The current Supreme Court has adopted weak protections for both free exercise and no establishment. The neutral, generally applicable approach to free exercise in *Oregon v. Smith* still stands despite widespread opposition. And the equal treatment approach to the Establishment Clause has carried the day in cases involving government aid to religious institutions. Informed by free speech principles, these approaches to free exercise and no establishment have diminished the special protections and status of religion guaranteed by the religion clauses of the First Amendment.

Any perceived secularization of American society or marginalization of religious voices would be difficult to pin on the separation of church and state. Rather than being hostile to religion, the courts' commitment to the separation of church and state paid dividends. Religious pluralism and vitality flourished during the Court's most separationist era and, for Pfeffer, justified the broad interpretation of the First Amendment. Religion remains robust in the United States. Nonetheless, there has been a dramatic decline in adherence to traditional expressions of religious faith. It is difficult not to point out that this trend has coincided with the U.S. Supreme Court's move in a more accommodationist direction.

To be sure, the broad separation that Pfeffer advocated may seem antiquated in an era of abundant public-private partnerships, but at what cost? The wall of separation Pfeffer so strenuously advocated was to protect churches from the long-arm of the state. Indeed, churches and other religious institutions run the risk of compromising their beliefs in the competition for public funds and may find them to be, in Pfeffer's words, a "pearl of great price." As taxpayer funds and grants become more available to churches and other pervasively sectarian institutions, challenges to their ability to hire and proselytize according to their religious beliefs will grow. In short, the equal treatment approach poses a greater threat to the integrity of religious institutions than does the wall of separation.

A host of other questions arise in light of the accommodationist direction of the Court. Will all religious groups and institutions be treated equally in this scheme, or will better resourced, more mainstream, religious groups be more likely to enjoy the lion's share of the funding? Does this approach treat groups whose theology prohibits cooperation with the government in an equitable fashion? Will support for this view wane or conflict arise as less mainstream or more controversial religions seek funding? Does equal treatment undermine the argument for exemptions from neutral health care and civil rights regulations? If not, should taxpayers be required to support beliefs and discriminatory practices they find, in the words of Thomas Jefferson, "sinful and tyrannical"?

The U.S. Supreme Court and religious liberty advocates would do well to revisit Pfeffer's arguments for a broad reading of both religion clauses. In recent years, the United States has witnessed an increase in attacks on religious minorities and hate speech is no longer relegated to the margins of social media. Muslims, Jews, and other religious and ethnic groups have been targets of violence and other hate crimes. Immigration and foreign policies have unfairly, if not unconstitutionally, targeted religious groups. While these outbreaks of religious discrimination are the product of a number of factors, they do provide a compelling reason to reconsider how best to guarantee religious liberty for all Americans. Pfeffer's belief that the religion clauses provided a unitary guarantee of religious liberty is worth preserving. While a high wall of separation and broad protections for the free exercise of religion may create tensions between the religion clauses, they better ensure the equality, authenticity, and vitality of religious faith in the United States.

NOTES

1. *McCollum v. Board of Education*, 333 U.S. 203 (1948).
2. *Epperson v. Arkansas*, 393 U.S. 97 (1968).
3. *Abington v. Schempp*, 374 U.S. 203 (1963).
4. See Sorauf, *The Wall of Separation.*
5. Ivers, *To Build a Wall*, 193.
6. Witte, Jr. and Nichols, *Religion and the Constitutional Experiment*, 196.
7. *Witters v. Washington Department of Services for the Blind*, 474 U.S. 481 (1986) at 487.
8. *Zobrest v. Catalina Foothills School District*, 509 U.S. 1 (1993) at 2.
9. Ibid., at 8–14.
10. Ibid., at 18–24.
11. *Agostini v. Felton*, 521 U.S. 203 (1997) at 225.
12. *Mitchell v. Helms*, 530 U.S. 793 (2000) at 810–819.
13. Ibid., at 840–41.
14. Ibid., at 869.
15. 536 U.S. 639 (2002) at 539–553.
16. Ibid., at 652.
17. Ibid., at 687–688.
18. Ibid., at 711.
19. Ibid., at 716.
20. See, for example, *Widmar v. Vincent*, 454 US 263 (1981); *Board of Education of the Westside Community Schools v. Mergens* 496 U.S. 226 (1990), and *Rosenberger v. Rector*, 515 U.S. 819 (1995).
21. *Locke v. Davey*, 540 U.S. 712 (2004) at 712–715.
22. Green, *The Third Disestablishment*, 353–354; see also Douglas Laycock, "Why the Supreme Court Changed its Mind about Government Aid to Religious Institutions: It's a Lot More than Just Republican Appointments," *Brigham Young University Law Review* (2008): 275–294.
23. *Zellman v. Simmons-Harris*, 536 U.S. 639 (2002) at 715.
24. *Trinity Lutheran Church of Columbia, Inc. v. Comer*, 137 S. Ct. 2012 (2017) at 2028.
25. See Emma Long, "Yet Another Threat to Religious Freedom?: Continuity and Change in the Church-State Debate," *Journal of Church and State* 60 (Winter 2018): 1–21.
26. See *Wallace v. Jaffree*, 472 U.S. 38 (1985).
27. Ibid., at 577.
28. *Santa Fe School District v. Doe*, 530 U.S. 290 (2000) at 309–10.
29. Witte, Jr. and Nichols, *Religion and the American Constitutional Experiment*, 179.
30. See, for example, *Gonzales v. O Centro Espirita Beneficente Uniao Do Vegetal,* 546 U.S. 418 (2006) where the Court ruled that RFRA demanded the state provide a compelling state interest to justify enforcing drug laws against a church

that used *hoasca* for sacramental purposes; and *Holt v. Hobbs*, 574 U.S. 352 (2015), where a Muslim prisoner successfully challenged a prison regulation that prohibited inmates from growing beards. Under RLUIPA, the Court upheld the right of the prisoner to seek an accommodation for his religious beliefs.

31. *Burwell v. Hobby Lobby Stores*, 573 US 682 (2014).

32. *Masterpiece Cakeshop, Ltd. v. Colorado Civil Rights Commission*, 138 S. Ct. 1719 (2018).

Bibliography

Abraham, Henry J. and Barbara A. Perry. *Freedom and the Court: Civil Rights and Liberties in the United States*. 6th ed. New York: Oxford University Press, 1994.

Ahlstrom, Sydney A. *A Religious History of the American People*. New Haven: Yale University Press, 1972.

Antieau, Chester James, Arthur T. Downey, and Edward C. Roberts. *Freedom from Federal Establishment: Formation and Early History of the First Amendment Religion Clauses*. Milwaukee, WI: The Bruce Publishing Company, 1964.

Audi, Robert. *Democratic Authority and the Separation of Church and State*. New York: Oxford University Press, 2011.

Audi, Robert, and Daand Nicholas Wolterstorff. *Religion in the Public Square: The Place of Religious Convictions in Political Debate*. Lanham, MD: Rowman and Littlefield Publishers, Inc., 1997.

Auerbach, Jerold S. "Liberalism and the Hebrew Prophets." *Commentary* 84 (August 1987): 58–60.

———. *Rabbis and Lawyers: The Journey from Torah to Constitution*. Bloomington: Indiana University Press, 1990.

Bailyn, Bernard. *The Ideological Origins of the American Revolution*. Cambridge, MA: Harvard University Press, 1967.

Ballmer, Randall. "The Real Origins of the Religious Right." *Politico Magazine* (May 27, 2014).

Barry, John M. *Roger Williams and the Creation of the American Soul: Church, State, and the Birth of Liberty*. New York: Viking Press, 2012.

Beaver, R. Pierce. "American Missionary Efforts to Influence Government Indian Policy." *Journal of Church and State* 5 (1963): 77–94.

———. "Church, State, and the Indians: Indian Missions in the New Nation." *Journal of Church and State* 4 (1962): 11–30.

Bellah, Robert N. "Civil Religion in America." *Daedalus* 96 (Winter 1967): 1–21.

Berg, Thomas. "Anti-Catholicism and Modern Church-State Relations." *Cumberland Law Review* 33 (Summer 2002): 121–72.

Blum, Virgil C. *Freedom in Education: Federal Aid for All Children*. Garden City, NY: Doubleday, 1965.

———. "Review of *Church, State, and Freedom* by Leo Pfeffer." *The Georgetown Law Journal* 43 (1954–55): 147.

Boles, Donald E. *The Bible, Religion, and the Public Schools*. Ames, IA: Iowa State University Press, 1961; 1964.

———. *The Two Swords: Commentaries and Cases in Religion and Education*. Ames, IA: Iowa State University Press, 1967.

Bonomi, Patricia U. *Under the Cope of Heaven: Religion, Society, and Politics in Colonial America*. New York: Oxford University Press, 1986.

Borden, Morton. *Jews, Turks, and Infidels*. Chapel Hill: The University of North Carolina Press, 1984.

Bowlby, David Dean. *The Garden and the Wilderness: Church and State in America to 1789*. Lanham, MD: Lexington Books, 2012.

Bradley, Gerard V. "Beguiled: Free Exercise Exemptions and the Siren Song of Liberalism." *Hofstra Law Review* 20 (1991): 245–319.

———. *Church-State Relationships in America*. Westport, CT: Greenwood Press, 1987.

Brauer, Matthew J., Barbara Forrest, and Steve G. Gey. "Is It Science Yet?: Intelligent Design, Creationism, and the Constitution." *Washington University Law Quarterly* 83 (2005): 1–149.

Bromley, David G., ed. *The Brainwashing-Deprogramming Controversy*. New York: The Edwin Mellen Press, 1983.

Buetow, Harold A. *Of Singular Benefit: The Story of Catholic Education in the United States*. New York: Macmillan Co., 1970.

Butts, R. Freeman. *The American Tradition in Religion and Education*. Boston, MA: Beacon Press, 1950.

Carter, Stephen L. *The Culture of Disbelief: How American Law and Politics Trivializes Religious Devotion*. New York: Basic Books, 1993.

Choper, Jesse H. "A Century of Religious Freedom." *California Law Review* 88 (2000): 1711–1741.

———. "The Religion Clauses of the First Amendment: Reconciling the Conflict." *University of Pittsburgh Law Review* 41 (Summer 1980): 673–701.

———. *Securing Religious Liberty: Principles for Judicial Interpretation of the Religion Clauses*. Chicago: University of Chicago Press, 1995.

Cobb, Sanford H. *The Rise of Religious Liberty in America: A History*. New York: Macmillan Co., 1902.

Cogley, John, ed. *Religion in America: Original Essays on Religion in a Free Society*. New York: Meridian Books, 1958.

Cohen, Naomi. *Jews in Christian America: The Pursuit of Religious Equality*. New York: Oxford University Press, 1992.

Corbett, Michael and Julia Mitchell Corbett. *Politics and Religion in the United States*. New York: Garland Publishing, Inc., 1999.

Cord, Robert L. *Separation of Church and State: Historical Fact and Current Fiction*. New York: Lambeth Press, 1982.

Corwin, E. S. "The Supreme Court as National School Board." *Law and Contemporary Problems* 14 (Winter 1949): 3–22.

Creed, J. Bradley. "John Leland: American Prophet of Religious Individualism." Ph.D. diss., Southwestern Baptist Theological Seminary, 1981.

Curry, Thomas J. *The First Freedoms: Church and State in America to the Passage of the First Amendment*. New York: Oxford University Press, 1985.

Dalin, David G., ed. *American Jews and the Separationist Faith: The New Debate on Religion in Public Life*. Washington, DC: Ethics and Public Policy Center, 1993.

———. "Leo Pfeffer and the Separationist Faith." *This World* 24 (1988): 136–40.

Davis, Derek. *Original Intent: Chief Justice Rehnquist and the Course of American Church-State Relations*. Buffalo, NY: Prometheus Books, 1991.

———, ed. *The Oxford Handbook of Church and State in the United States*. New York: Oxford University Press, 2010.

———. *Religion and the Continental Congress, 1774–1789: Contributions to Original Intent.* New York: Oxford University Press, 2000.

———. "Resolving Not to Resolve the Tension between the Establishment and Free Exercise Clauses." *Journal of Church and State* 38 (Spring 1996): 245–60.

Dierenfield, Bruce J. *The Battle Over School Prayer: How Engel v. Vitale Changed America*. Lawrence: University Press of Kansas, 2007.

Dierenfield, Richard B. *Religion in American Public Schools.* Washington, DC: Public Affairs Press, 1962.

Diner, Hasia R. *The Jews of the United States, 1654–2000*. Berkeley: University of California Press, 2004.

Douglas, William O. *The Bible and the Schools*. Boston, MA: Little, Brown, 1966.

Drakeman, Donald. *Church, State, and Original Intent.* New York: Cambridge University Press, 2009.

Dreisbach, Daniel L. *Real Threat and Mere Shadow: Religious Liberty and the First Amendment.* Westchester, IL: Crossway Books, 1987.

———. *Thomas Jefferson and the Wall of Separation between Church and State.* New York: New York University Press, 2003.

Eastland, Terry, ed. *Religious Liberty in the Supreme Court: The Cases That Define the Debate over Church and State*. Grand Rapids, MI: William B. Eerdmans Publishing Company, 1993.

"Editorial: To Our Jewish Friends." *America* 107 (September 1, 1962): 665–66.

Esbeck, Carl H. "Myths, Miscues, and Misconceptions: No-Aid Separationism and the Establishment Clause." *Notre Dame Journal of Law, Ethics, and Public Policy* 13 (1999): 285–319.

Esbeck, Carl H. and Jonathan J. Den Hartog, eds. *Disestablishment and Religious Dissent: Church-State Relations in the New American States, 1774–1833.* Columbia: University of Missouri Press, 2019.

Evans, Bette Novit. *Interpreting the Free Exercise of Religion: The Constitution and American Pluralism.* Chapel Hill: University of North Carolina Press, 1997.

Feldman, Noah. *Divided By God: America's Church-State Problem–And What We Should Do About It.* New York: Farrar, Straus, and Giroux, 2006.

———, ed. *Law and Religion: A Critical Anthology.* New York: New York University Press, 2000.

Fellman, David. "How High the Wall of Separation? Pfeffer on Religion and the State." *American Bar Foundation Research Journal* 1 (1986): 123–37.

Fessenden, Tracy. "The Nineteenth-Century Bible Wars the Separation of Church and State." *Church History* 75 (December 2005): 784–811.

Fichter, Joseph H. *Parochial Schools: A Sociological Study.* Notre Dame, IN: University of Notre Dame Press, 1958.

Fisher, Louis. *Religious Liberty in America: Political Safeguards.* Lawrence: University Press of Kansas, 2000.

Flowers, Ronald B., Melissa Rogers, and Steven K. Green. *Religious Freedom and the Supreme Court.* Waco, TX: Baylor University Press, 2008.

Flowers, Ronald B. *Religion in Strange Times: The 1960s and 1970s.* Macon, GA: Mercer University Press, 1984.

———. *To Defend the Constitution: Religion, Conscientious Objection, Naturalization, and the Supreme Court.* Lanham, MD: Scarecrow Press, 2002.

Formicola, Jo Renee and Hubert Morken, eds. *Everson Revisited: Religion, Education, and Law at the Crossroads.* Lanham, MD: Rowman & Littlefield Publishers, 1997.

Fowler, Robert, Allen Hertzke, Laura Olson, and Kevin Den Dulk. *Religion and Politics in America.* 3rd ed. Boulder, CO: Westview Press, 2004.

Friedman, Murray. *The Utopian Delimma: American Judaism and Public Policy.* Washington, DC: Ethics and Public Policy Center, 1985.

Frommer, Morris. "The American Jewish Congress: A History." Ph.D. diss., Ohio State University, 1978.

Fuchs, Lawrence H. *The Political Behavior of American Jews.* Westport, CT: Greenwood Press, 1980.

Gaustad, Edwin S. "The Backus-Leland Tradition." *Foundations* 2 (1959): 131–52.

Gaustad, Edwin S. and Leigh E. Schmidt. *The Religious History of America.* Rev. ed. New York: HarperSanFrancisco, 2002.

Glazer, Nathan. *American Judaism.* Chicago: University of Chicago Press, 1957.

Goodman, Lenn Evan. "Equality and Human Rights: The Lockean and the Judaic Views." *Judaism* 25 (Summer 1976): 357–62.

Gordon, Sarah Barringer. *The Mormon Question: Polygamy and Constitutional Conflict in Nineteenth Century America.* Chapel Hill: University of North Carolina Press, 2002.

Gordis, Robert. *The Root and the Branch: Judaism and the Free Society.* Chicago: University of Chicago Press, 1962.

Green, Steven K. "'Bad History': The Lure of History in Establishment Clause Adjudication." *Notre Dame Law Review* 81 (2016): 1717–54.

———. "'Blaming Blaine': Understanding the Blaine Amendment and the 'No-Funding' Principle." *First Amendment Law Review* 2 (Winter 2003): 107–52.

Greenawalt, Kent. *When Free Exercise and No Establishment Conflict.* Cambridge, MA: Harvard University Press, 2017.

Greene, L. F., ed. *The Writings of John Leland.* New York: Arno Press, 1969.

Griswold, Erwin N. "Absolute is in the Dark." *Utah Law Review* 8 (1963): 167–85.

Guliuzza III, Frank. *Over the Wall: Protecting Religious Expression in the Public Square.* Albany: State University of New York Press, 2000.

———. "The Supreme Court, the Establishment Clause, and Incoherence." In *Religion, Public Life, and the American Polity*, ed. Luis E. Lugo. Knoxville: The University of Tennessee Press, 1994, 115–44.

Hamburger, Philip. "A Constitutional Right of Religious Exemption: An Historical Perspective." *George Washington Law Review* 60 (1992): 915–48.

———. *Separation of Church and State.* Cambridge, MA: Harvard University Press, 2002.

Handlin, Oscar. *Adventure in Freedom: Three Hundred Years of Jewish Life in America.* New York: McGraw-Hill Book Company, Inc., 1954.

Handy, Robert T. *A Christian America: Protestant Hopes and Historical Realities.* 2nd ed. New York: Oxford University Press, 1984.

Healey, Robert M. *Jefferson on Religion and Public Education.* New Haven, CT: Yale University Press, 1962.

Henderson, Jennifer Jacobs. "The Jehovah's Witnesses and Their Plan to Expand First Amendment Freedoms." *Journal of Church and State* 46 (Autumn 2004): 811–32.

Herberg, Will. *Protestant-Catholic-Jew: An Essay in American Religious Sociology.* Garden City, NY: Doubleday and Co., 1955.

Hertzberg, Arthur. *The French Enlightenment and the Jews.* New York: Columbia University Press, 1968.

Hitchcock, James. *The Supreme Court and Religion in American Life: Volume II: From "Higher Law" to "Sectarian Scruples."* Princeton, NJ: Princeton University Press, 2004.

Holcomb, J. David. "Religion and Higher Education." In *Church-State Issues in America Today: Religion, Family, and Education* Vol. 2, Ann W. Duncan and Steven L. Jones, eds. Westport, CT: Greenwood, 2008.

———. "Religion in Public Life: The 'Pfefferian Inversion' Reconsidered." *Journal of Law and Religion* 25 (2009–10): 57–95.

Howe, Mark DeWolfe. *The Garden and the Wilderness: Religion and Government in American Constitutional History.* Chicago: University of Chicago Press, 1965.

Hudson, Winthrop S. *The Great Tradition of the American Churches.* New York: Harper and Brothers, 1953.

Hutson, James H. *Church and State in America: The First Two Centuries.* New York: Cambridge University Press, 2008.

———. "Thomas Jefferson's Letter to the Danbury Baptists: A Controversy Rejoined." *The William and Mary Quarterly* 56 (October 1999): 775–90.

Ivers, Gregg. *To Build a Wall: American Jews and the Separation of Church and State.* Charlottesville: University Press of Virginia, 1995.

Jones, Robert P. *The End of White Christian America.* New York: Simon and Shuster, 2016.

Katz, Wilbur. "Freedom of Religion and State Neutrality." *University of Chicago Law Review* 20 (1953): 426–40.

Kauper, Paul G. "*Church, State, and Freedom*: A Review." *Michigan Law Review* 52 (April 1954): 829–48.

Kelley, Dean M. *Why Churches Should Not Pay Taxes*. New York: Harper and Row, 1977.

Kraft, Stephanie Russell. "The Right to Abortion and Religious Freedom." *The Atlantic* March 3, 2016.

Kruse, Kevin M. *One Nation Under God: How Corporate America Invented Christian America*. New York: Basic Books, 2015.

Kurland, Philip B. *Religion and the Law of Church and State and the Supreme Court*. Chicago: Aldine Publishing Co., 1962.

Lambert, Frank. *The Founding Fathers and the Place of Religion in America*. Princeton, NJ: Princeton University Press, 2006.

Larson, Edward J. *Summer for the Gods: The Scopes Trial and America's Continuing Debate over Science and Religion*. New York: Basic Books, 2006.

Laubach, John H. *School Prayers: Congress, the Courts, and the Public*. Washington, DC: Public Affairs Press, 1969.

Laycock, Douglas. "Nonpreferential Aid to Religion: A False Claim about Original Intent." *William and Mary Law Review* 27 (1985–1986): 875–923.

———. "The Remnants of Free Exercise." *The Supreme Court Review* (1990): 1–68.

Leo Pfeffer Papers. George Arendts Research Library, Syracuse University, Syracuse, New York.

Levy, Leonard W. *The Establishment Clause: Religion and the First Amendment*. 2nd ed., rev. Chapel Hill: University of North Carolina Press, 1994.

Littell, Franklin H. *From State Church to Pluralism: A Protestant Interpretation of Religion in American History*. New York: Macmillan Co., 1971.

Long, Emma. *The Church-State Debate: Religion, Education and the Establishment Clause in Post War America*. London: Bloomsbury Academic, 2012.

———. "Yet Another Threat to Religious Freedom?: Continuity and Change in the Church-State Debate." *Journal of Church and State* 60 (Winter 2018): 1–21.

Macleod, Colin. *Have a Little Faith: Religion, Democracy, and the American Public School*. Chicago: University of Chicago Press, 2016.

Malbin, Michael J. *Religion and Politics: The Intentions of the Authors of the First Amendment*. Washington, DC: American Enterprise Institute for Public Policy Research, 1978.

Manis, Andrew M. "Regionalism and a Baptist Perspective on Church and State." *American Baptist Quarterly* 3 (September 1983): 213–27.

Manwaring, David R. *Render Unto Caesar: The Flag Salute Controversy*. Chicago: University of Chicago Press, 1962.

Martin, William. *With God on Our Side: The Rise of the Religious Right in America*. New York: Bantam Doubleday, 1996.

McCluskey, Neil G. *Catholic Education in America*. New York: Teachers College, Columbia University, 1964.

McCollum, Vashti C. *One Woman's Fight*. Boston, MA: Beacon Press, 1951.

McConnell, Michael W. "Accommodation of Religion." *Supreme Court Review* (1985): 1–59.

———. "The Origins and Historical Understanding of the Free Exercise of Religion." *Harvard Law Review* 103 (May 1990): 1410–1517.

McCoy, Thomas and Gary Kurtz. "A Unifying Theory for the Religion Clauses of the First Amendment." *Vanderbilt Law Review* 39 (1986): 249–74.

McGloughlin, William G. "Isaac Backus and the Separation of Church and State in America." *American Historical Review* 73 (June 1968): 1393–413.

McLeod, Hugh. *The Religious Crisis of the 1960s*. New York: Oxford University Press, 2007.

Michaelson, Robert. *Piety in the Public School: Trends and Issues in Relationship Between Religion and the Public Schools in the United States*. New York: Macmillan Co., 1970.

Miller, Nicholas P. *The Religious Roots of the First Amendment: Dissenting Protestants and the Separation of Church and State*. New York: Oxford University Press, 2012.

Miller, Robert T. and Ronald B. Flowers. *Toward Benevolent Neutrality: Church, State, and the Supreme Court*. 2 vols. 5th ed. Waco, TX.: Baylor University Press, 1996.

Miller, William Lee. *The First Liberty: Religion and the American Republic*. New York: Paragon House, 1985.

———. *Piety Along the Potomac: Notes on Politics and Morals in the Fifties*. Boston, MA: Houghton Mifflin Co., 1964.

Mittleman, Alan et al., eds. *Jews and the American Public Square: Debating Religion and Republic*. Lanham, MD: Rowman and Littlefield Publishers, Inc., 2002.

———. "Toward a Postseparationist Public Philosophy: A Jewish Contribution." *This World* 25 (1989): 87–101.

Morgan, Edmund S. *Roger Williams: The Church and the State*. New York: Harcourt, Brace and World, 1967.

Murray, John Courtney. "Law and Preposessions." *Law and Contemporary Problems* 14 (Winter 1949): 23–43.

Neem, Johann N. *Democracy's Schools: The Rise of Public Education in America*. Baltimore, MD: Johns Hopkins University Press, 2017.

Neuhaus, Richard John. "Contending for the Future: Overcoming the Pfefferian Inversion." *Journal of Law and Religion* 8 (1990): 115–29.

———. "Genuine Pluralism and the Pfefferian Inversion." *This World* 25 (1989): 69–98.

———, ed. *Jews in Unsecular America*. Grand Rapids, MI: William B. Eerdmans Publishing Company, 1987.

———. *The Naked Public Square: Religion and Democracy in America*. Grand Rapids, MI: William B. Eerdmans Publishing Co., 1984.

———. "The Pfefferian Inversion." *National Review* (May 13, 1988): 44.

Newton, Merlin Owen. *Armed With the Constitution: Jehovah's Witnesses in Alabama and the U.S. Supreme Court, 1939–1946*. Tuscaloosa: University of Alabama Press, 2002.

Oaks, Dallin H., ed. *The Wall Between Church and State*. Chicago: University of Chicago Press, 1963.

Olitzky, Kerry M. *In Celebration: An American Jewish Perspective on the Bicentennial of the United States Constitution*. Lanham, MD: University Press of America; Cincinnati, OH: American-Jewish Archives, 1989.

O'Neill, James M. "Nonpreferential Aid to Religion is Not an Establishment of Religion." *Buffalo Law Review* 2 (Spring 1953): 18–52.

———. *Religion and Education Under the Constitution.* New York: Harper and Brothers, 1949.

Paulsen, Michael A. "Religion, Equality, and the Constitution: An Equal Protection Approach to Establishment Clause Adjudication." *Notre Dame Law Review* 61 (1986): 311–71.

Pekelis, Alexander H. "Full Equality in a Free Society: A Program for Jewish Action." In *Law and Social Action: Selected Essays of Alexander H. Pekelis*, ed. Milton R. Konvitz. Ithaca, NY: Cornell University Press, 1950.

Peters, Shawn Francis. *The Yoder Case: Religious Freedom, Education, and Parental Rights.* Lawrence: University of Kansas Press, 2003.

Peterson, Merrill D. and Robert C. Vaughan, eds. *The Virginia Statute for Religious Freedom: Its Evolution and Consequences in American History.* Cambridge: Cambridge University Press, 1988.

Pfeffer, Leo. "Aid to Elementary and Secondary Education (H.R. 2361 and 2362)." Testimony at Hearings of General Subcommittee on Education, U.S. House Committee on Education and Labor, Washington, DC, 2 February 1965.

———. "Abortion and Religious Freedom." *Congress Monthly* 43 (June 1976): 9–12.

———. "Aid to Parochial Schools: A Chess Game with the Constitution." *Reform Judaism* 1 (October 1972): 5.

———. "Amici in Church-State Litigation." *Law and Contemporary Problems* 44 (Winter 1984): 83–110.

———. "An Analysis of Federal Aid to Parochial Schools." *Journal of Church and State* 3 (November 1961): 137–48.

———. "The Becker Amendment." *Journal of Church and State* 6 (Autumn 1964): 344–51.

———. "Blasphemy on the Potomac." *The Christian Register* 134 (March 1955): 11–13.

———. Brief for Appellant, *Heisler v. Board of Review* 102 N.E. 2d 601 (1951) (No. 18093).

———. Brief for Appellants, *Meek v. Pittenger*, 421 U.S. 349 (1975) (No. 73-1765).

———. Brief for Appellants, *PEARL v. Nyquist*, 413 U.S. 756 (1973) (No. 72-694).

———. Brief for Appellants, *PEARL v. Regan*, 444 U.S. 646 (1980) (No. 78-1369).

———. Brief for Appellants, *Tilton v. Richardson*, 403 U.S. 672 (1971) (No. 153).

———. Brief for Appellant, *Torcaso v. Watkins*, 367 U.S. 488 (1961) (No. 373).

———. Brief for Appellant, *Zorach v. Clauson*, 343 U.S. 306 (1952) (No. 431).

———. Brief for Synagogue Counsel of America and National Community Relations Advisory Counsel as Amici Curiae Supporting Petitioners, *Abington v. Schempp*, 374 U.S. 203 (1963) (Nos. 142 & 149).

———. Brief for American Jewish as Amicus Curiae Supporting Appellants, *Board of Education v. Allen*, 392 U.S. 236 (1968) (No. 660).

———. Brief of Amicus Curiae, *Earley v. DiCenso,* 403 U.S. 602 (1971) (No. 569).

———. Brief for Synagogue Counsel of America and National Community Relations Advisory Counsel as Amici Curiae Supporting Petitioners, *Engel v. Vitale*, 370 U.S. 421 (1962) (No. 468).

———. Brief for American Civil Liberties Union, et al. as Amici Curiae, *Epperson v. Arkansas*, 393 U.S. 97 (1968) (No. 7).

———. Brief for Synagogue Counsel of America and National Community Relations Advisory Counsel as Amici Curiae Supporting Appellees, *Gallagher v. Crown Kosher Super Market*, 366 U.S. 617 (1961) (Nos. 11, 67).

———. Brief for American Ethical Union et al. as Amici Curiae Supporting Appellee, *Harris v. McRae*, 448 U.S. 297 (1980) (No. 79-1268).

———. Brief for American Association of School Administrators, et al. of Amici Curiae in Support of Appellants, *Lemon v. Kurtzman*, 403 U.S. 602 (1971) (No. 89).

———. Brief for Synagogue Council for America, et al. as Amici Curiae Supporting Appellants, *McCollum v. Board of Education*, 333 U.S. 203 (1948) (No. 90).

———. Brief as Amici Curiae Supporting Petitioner, *Moon v. U.S.*, 466 U.S. 971 (1984) (No. 83-1242).

———. Brief of Amicus Curiae, *Mueller v. Allen*, 463 U.S. 388 (1983) (No. 82-195).

———. Pfeffer, Leo, Brief for Synagogue Counsel of America and National Community Relations Advisory Counsel as Amici Curiae Supporting Appellant, *Sherbert v. Verner*, 374 U.S. 398 (1963) (No. 526).

———. Brief for Synagogue Counsel of America and National Community Relations Advisory Counsel as Amici Curiae Supporting Appellee, *Stainbeck v. Mo Hock Ke Lok Po*, 336 U.S. 368 (1949) (Nos. 52, 474).

———. Brief for the American Civil Liberties Union of Amicus Curiae Supporting the Appellees, *TransWorld Airlines v. Hardison*, 432 U.S. 63 (1977) (No. 75-1126).

———. Brief for the American Jewish Congress of Amicus Curiae Supporting the Appellee, *U.S. v. Seeger*, 380 U.S. 163 (1965) (No. 50).

———. Brief for Synagogue Counsel of America and its Constituents as Amici Curiae Supporting Appellee, *Walz v. Tax Commission*, 397 U.S. 664 (1970) (No. 135).

———. Brief for Synagogue Counsel of America and its Constituents as Amici Curiae Supporting Respondents, *Wisonsin v. Yoder*, 406 U.S. 205 (1972) (No. 70-110).

———. Brief for PEARL of Amicus Curiae Supporting Appellant, *Wolman v. Walter*, 433 U.S. 229 (1977) (76-496).

———. Brief as Amici Curiae Supporting Petitioner, *Worldwide Church of God v. State of California*, 446 U.S. 987 (1980) (No. 79-1348).

———. "The Case Against Parochiaid." *Church and State* 30 (April 1977): 14–17.

———. "The 'Child-Benefit' Theory: A Legal Fiction." *Church and State* 19 (April 1966): 6–7.

Pfeffer, Leo and Anson Phelps Stokes. *Church and State in the United States*. New York: Harper and Row, 1964.

———. "Church and State: Something Less than Separation." *University of Chicago Law Review* 19 (Autumn 1951): 1–29.

———. "Church, State, and American Jewry." In *A Reader in Jewish Community Relations*, ed. Ann G. Wolfe, 179–85. New York: KTAV, 1975.

———. *Church, State, and Freedom.* Boston, MA: Beacon Press, 1953; rev. ed. 1967.

———. "Commentary on Bellah's Essay: Civil Religion in America." In *The Religious Situation*, ed. Donald R. Cutler, 360–65. Boston, MA: Beacon Press, 1968.

———. "Counterreflections on Church and State." *Midstream* 8 (December 1962): 15–23.

———. "Court, Constitution, and Prayer." *Rutgers Law Review* 16 (Summer 1962): 735–52.

———. *Creeds in Competition: A Creative Force in American Culture*. New York: Harper and Row, 1958.

———. "The Current State of the Law in the United States and the Separationist Agenda." *The Annals of the American Academy of Political and Social Science* 446 (November 1979): 1–9.

———. "Equal Protection for Unpopular Sects." *New York University Review of Law and Social Change* 9 (1979–80): 9–15.

———. "The Establishment Clause: An Absolutist's Defense." *Notre Dame Journal of Law, Ethics and Public Policy* 4 (1990): 699–729.

———. "Fair Employment for Sabbath Observers." *Congress Monthly* 44 (May 1977): 10.

———. "Federal Funds for Parochial Schools? No." *Notre Dame Lawyer* 37 (March 1962): 309–22.

———. "The First Amendment to the United States Constitution with Respect to Bible Reading and Prayers in Public Schools (H.J. Res. 693)." Statement and Testimony submitted to U.S. House Committee on the Judiciary, Washington, DC (30 April 1964).

———. "Freedom and/or Separation." *University of Minnesota Law Review* 64 (March 1980): 561–84.

———. "Freedom and Separation: America's Contribution to Civilization." *Journal of Church and State* 2 (November 1960): 100–11.

———. "Freedom of Religion and Separation of Church and State." Statement submitted to Subcommittee on Constitutional Rights, U.S. Senate Committee on the Judiciary, Washington, DC, 30 October 1955.

———. "From Religious Monism to Pluralism in the United States." *Congress Bi-Weekly* 31 (February 10, 1964): 7–8, 13.

———. "The Future of First Amendment Provisions Regarding Church-State Relations." In *The Future of Our Liberties: Perspectives on the Bill of Rights*, ed. Stephen C. Halpern, 11–29. Westport, CT: Greenwood Press, 1982.

———. "The Gideons' March on the Schools." *Congress Weekly* 20 (October 5, 1953): 7–9.

———. *God, Caesar, and the Constitution: The Court as Referee of Church-State Confrontation*. Boston, MA: Beacon Press, 1974.

———. "Issues that Divide: The Triumph of Secular Humanism." *Journal of Church and State* 19 (Spring 1977): 203–16.

———. Jurisdictional Statement, *Chamberlin v. Dade County Board of Public Instruction*, 377 U.S. 402 (1964).

———. Jurisdictional Statement, *Horace Mann League v. Board of Public Works of Maryland*, 385 U.S. 97 (1966).

———. "Legal and Constitutional Aspects of Released Time." Paper presented at Conference on Religious Instruction and the Public School, National Jewish Community Relations Advisory Council and Synagogue Council of America, New York City, 11 November 1946.

———. "The Legitimation of Marginal Religions in the United States." In *Religious Movements in Contemporary America*, eds. Irving I. Zaretsky and Mark P. Leone, 9–26. Princeton, NJ: Princeton University Press, 1974.

———. *The Liberties of an American: The Supreme Court Speaks.* 2nd ed. enl. Boston, MA: Beacon Press, 1963.

———. "The Meaning of the First Amendment." *Liberty* 44 (Second Quarter 1949): 5–10.

———. "A Momentous Year in Church and State." *Journal of Church and State* 6 (Winter 1964): 36–43.

———. "No Law Respecting an Establishment of Religion." *Buffalo Law Review* 2 (Spring 1953): 1–17.

———. "Parochiaid: The Courts, the Legislature, and the Executive." Paper presented at the National Conference on School Finance, National Education Association, New York City, 27 March 1972.

———. "The Price We Pay for Federal Aid." *Midstream* 11 (March 1965): 38–42.

———. "Public School Sectarianism and the Jewish Child: A Report of Experiences." Paper prepared for the Commission on Law and Social Action of the American Jewish Congress, May 1957.

———. "Released Time and Religious Liberty: A Reply." *Michigan Law Review* 53 (November 1954): 91–98.

———. "Religion-Blind Government." *Stanford Law Review* 15 (March 1963): 389–406.

———. "Religion, Education, and the Constitution." *Lawyers Guild Review* 8 (May–June 1948): 387–400.

———. "Religion, the Public Schools, and the Jewish Community: A Thirteen Year Review." Paper presented at Conference of Synagogue Council of America and National Jewish Community Relations Advisory Council, New York City, 13 December 1959.

———. *Religion, State, and the Burger Court.* Buffalo, N.Y.: Prometheus, 1984.

———. "Religious Freedom and the American Community." *Judaism* 28 (Spring 1979): 137–46.

———. Review of *The Garden and the Wilderness: Religion and Government in American Constitutional History*, by Mark DeWolfe Howe. *Political Science Quarterly* 81 (December 1966): 655–56.

———. "Review: Secularization: A Case Study." *Texas Law Review* (August 1972): 1288–91.

———. "Some Current Issues in Church and State." *Case Western Reserve Law Review* 17 (December 1961): 9–33.

———. "The Special Constitutional Status of Religion." In *Taxation and the Free Exercise of Religion*, ed. John W. Baker, 7–10. Washington, DC: Baptist Joint Committee on Public Affairs, 1977.

———. "State Sponsored Prayer." *Commonweal* 76 (July 27, 1962): 417–19.

———. "Sunday Law and Sabbath Observance." *Congress Weekly* 17 (February 3, 1950): 9–11.

———. "The Supremacy of Free Exercise." *Georgetown Law Journal* 61 (May 1973): 1115–42.

———. "The Supreme Court as Protector of Civil Rights: Freedom of Religion." *The Annals of the American Academy of Political and Social Science* 275 (May 1951): 75–85.

———. "Uneasy Trinity: Church, State, and Constitution." *Civil Liberties Review* 2 (Winter 1975): 138–61.

———. "The Unity of the First Amendment Religion Clauses." In *The First Freedom: Religion and the Bill of Rights*, ed. James E. Wood, Jr., 133–66. Waco, TX: J. M. Dawson Institute of Church-State Studies, Baylor University, 1990.

———. "Worker's Sabbath: Religious Belief and Employment." *The Civil Liberties Review* 4 (November/December 1977): 52–56.

Pickus, Noah. "Before I Built a Wall – Jews, Religion, and American Public Life." *This World* 15 (1986): 28–43.

Preville, Joseph R. "Catholic Colleges, the Courts, and the Constitution: A Tale of Two Cases." *Church History* 58 (June 1989): 197–210.

———. "Catholic Colleges and the Supreme Court: The Case of *Tilton v. Richardson*." *Journal of Church and State* 30 (Spring 1988): 291–307.

———. "Leo Pfeffer and the American Church-State Debate: A Confrontation with Catholicism." *Journal of Church and State* 33 (Winter 1991): 37–53.

Powell, H. Jefferson. "The Original Understanding of Original Intent." *Harvard Law Review* 98 (March 1985): 885–948.

Ragosta, John A. *Wellspring of Liberty: How Virginia's Religious Dissenters Helped Win the American Revolution and Secured Religious Liberty*. New York: Oxford University Press, 2010.

Redlich, Norman. "Separation of Church and State: The Burger Court's Tortuous Journey." *Notre Dame Law Review* 60 (1985): 1094–149.

Reichley, A. James. *Religion in American Public Life*. Washington, DC: The Brookings Institution, 1985.

Rogers, Melissa. *Faith in American Public Life*. Waco, TX: Baylor University Press, 2019.

Rohr, John A. *Prophets Without Honor: Public Policy and the Selective Conscientious Objector*. Nashville: Abingdon Press, 1971.

Robbins, Thomas, William C. Shepherd, and James McBride, eds. *Cults, Culture, and the Law: Perspectives on New Religious Movements*. Chico, CA: Scholars Press, 1985.

Sarna, Jonathan. *American Jews and Church-State Relations: The Search for "Equal Footing."* New York: American Jewish Committee, Institute of Human Relations, 1989.

——— and David G. Dalin, eds. *Religion and State in the American Jewish Experience.* South Bend, IN: The University of Notre Dame Press, 1997.

Shapiro, Edward S. *A Time for Healing: American Jewry Since World War II.* Vol. 5 *The Jewish People in America.* Baltimore, MD: The Johns Hopkins University Press, 1992.

Singleton, Marvin K. "Colonial Virginia as First Amendment Matrix: Henry, Madison, and the Establishment Clause." *Journal of Church and State* 8 (Autumn 1966): 344–64.

Smith, Steven D. *Foreordained Failure: The Quest for a Constitutional Principle of Religious Freedom.* New York: Oxford University Press, 1995.

Sorauf, Frank. *The Wall of Separation: The Constitutional Politics of Church and State.* Princeton, NJ: Princeton University Press, 1976.

Stokes, Anson Phelps. *Church and State in the United States.* 3 vols. New York: Harper and Brothers, 1950.

Stone, Geoffrey, Richard A. Epstein, and Cass R. Sunstein, eds. *The Bill of Rights in the Modern State.* Chicago: University of Chicago Press, 1992.

Sullivan, Kathleen. "Religion and Liberal Democracy." *University of Chicago Law Review* 59 (1992).

Swatos, Jr., William H. and James K. Wellman, Jr., eds. *The Power of Religious Publics: Staking Claims in American Society.* Westport, CT: Praeger, 1999.

Sweet, William W. *The Story of Religion in America.* New York: Harper and Row, 1950.

Thiemann, Ronald F. *Religion in Public Life: A Dilemma for Democracy.* Washington, DC: Georgetown University Press, 1996.

Thorndike, Jonathan L. *Epperson v. Arkansas: The Evolution-Creationism Debate.* Berkeley Heights, NJ: Enslow Publishers, 1999.

Walch, Timothy. *Parish School: American Catholic Parochial School Education From Colonial Times to the Present.* 2nd ed. Washington, DC: The National Catholic Education Association, 2016.

Wenz, Peter S. *Abortion Rights as Religious Freedom.* Philadelphia, PA: Temple University Press, 1992.

West, Ellis. "The Case Against the Right to Religion-Based Exemptions." *Notre Dame Journal of Law, Ethics, and Public Policy* 4 (1990): 567–90.

White, Ronald C. and Albright G. Zimmerman, eds. *An Unsettled Arena: Religion and the Bill of Rights.* Grand Rapids, MI: W.B. Eerdmans Pub. Co., 1990.

Whitfield, Stephen J. *Voices of Jacob, Hands of Esau: Jews in American Life and Thought.* Hamden, CT: Archon Books, 1984.

Williams, Daniel K. *God's Own Party: The Making of the Christian Right.* New York: Oxford University Press, 2012.

Witte, John, Jr. and Joel A. Nichols. *Religion and the American Constitutional Experiment.* 4th ed. New York: Oxford University Press, 2016.

Wood, Gordon S. *The Creation of the American Republic, 1776–1787*. New York: W.W. Norton and Company, 1969.

Wood, James E., Jr. *The First Freedom: Religion and the Bill of Rights*. Waco, TX: J.M. Dawson Institute of Church-State Studies, Baylor University, 1990.

———. "A Tribute to Leo Pfeffer (1909–1993)." *Journal of Church and State* 35 (Summer 1993): 605–06.

———, Jr. *Religion and the State: Essays in Honor of Leo Pfeffer*, ed. James E. Wood, Jr. Waco, TX: Baylor University Press, 1984.

———, ed. *Religion, the State, and Education*. Waco, TX: Baylor University Press, 1984.

Wood, James E., Jr. and Derek Davis, eds. *The Role of Government in Monitoring and Regulating Religion in Public Life*. Waco, TX: J.M. Dawson Institute of Church-State Studies, 1993.

Worthing, Sharon L. "The State Takes Over a Church." *Annals of the American Academy of Political and Social Science* 446 (November 1979): 136–48.

Wuthnow, Robert. *The Restructuring of American Religion*. Princeton, NJ: Princeton University Press, 1988.

LIST OF CASES

Abington Township School District v. Schempp, 374 U.S. 203 (1963).
Aguilar v. Felton, 473 U.S. 402 (1985).
Agostini v. Felton, 521 U.S. 203 (1997).
Board of Education v. Allen, 392 U.S. 236 (1968).
Braunfeld v. Brown, 366 U.S. 599 (1961).
Burwell v. Hobby Lobby Stores, Inc., 573 U.S. 682 (2014).
Cantwell v. Connecticut, 310 U.S. 296 (1940).
Chamberlin v. Dade County, 307 U.S. 402 (1964).
Church of Jesus Christ of Latter-Day Saints v. U.S., 136 U.S. 1 (1890).
Church of the Holy Trinity v. United States, 143 U.S. 457 (1892).
City of Boerne v. Flores, 521 U.S. 507 (1997).
Cochran v. Louisiana State Board of Education, 281 U.S. 370 (1930).
Committee for Public Education and Religious Liberty v. Nyquist, 413 U.S. 756 (1973).
Committee for Public Education and Religious Liberty v. Regan, 444 U.S. 646 (1980).
Cutter v. Wilkinson, 544 U.S. 709 (2005).
Davis v. Beason, 133 U.S. 333 (1890).
Doremus v. Board of Education, 342 U.S. 429 (1952).
Earley v. DiCenso, 403 U.S. 602 (1971).
Edwards v. Aguillard, 482 U.S. 578 (1987).
Engel v. Vitale, 370 U.S. 421 (1962).
Epperson v. Arkansas, 393 U.S. 97 (1968).
Everson v. Board of Education, 330 U.S. 1 (1947).
Flast v. Cohen, 392 U.S. 83 (1968).

Friedman v. New York, 341 U.S. 907 (1981).
Frothingham v. Mellon, 262 U.S. 447 (1923).
Gallagher v. Crown Kosher Super Market, 366 U.S. 617 (1961).
Gitlow v. New York, 268 U.S. 652 (1925).
Goldman v. Weinberger, 475 U.S. 503 (1986).
Hamilton v. Board of Regents of the University of California, 293 U.S. 245 (1934).
Harris v. McRae, 448 U.S. 297 (1980).
Hein v. Freedom from Religion Foundation, 551 U.S. 587 (2007).
Heisler v. Board of Review, 343 U.S. 939 (1952).
Holt v. Hobbs, 574 U.S. 352 (2015).
Holy Trinity v. United States, 143 U.S. 457 (1892).
Horace Mann League v. Board of Public Works, 385 U.S. 97 (1966).
Hunt v. McNair, 413 U.S. 678 (1978).
In re Summers, 325 U.S. 561 (1945).
Jimmy Swaggart v. Board of Equalization of California, 493 U.S. 378 (1990).
Kitzmiller v. Dover Area School District, 400 F. Supp. 2d 707 (M.D. Pa. 2005).
Lee v. Weisman, 505 U.S. 577 (1992).
Lemon v. Kurtzman, 403 U.S. 602 (1971).
Levitt v. Committee for Public Education and Religious Liberty, 413 U.S. 472 (1973).
Locke v. Davey, 540 U.S. 712 (2004).
Lynch v. Donnelly, 465 U.S. 668 (1984).
Marsh v. Chambers, 463 U.S. 783 (1983).
McCollum v. Board of Education, 333 U.S. 203 (1948).
McGowan v. Maryland, 366 U.S. 420 (1961).
Meek v. Pittenger, 421 U.S. 349 (1975).
Minersville School District v. Gobitis, 310 U.S. 586 (1940).
Missouri Church of Scientology v. State Tax Commission, 439 U.S. 803 (1978).
Mitchell v. Helms, 530 U.S. 793 (2000).
Mueller v. Allen, 463 U.S. 388 (1983).
National Labor Relations Board v. The Catholic Bishop of Chicago, 440 U.S. 490 (1979).
Oregon v. Smith, 493 U.S. 378 (1990).
Pierce v. Society of Sisters, 269 U.S. 510 (1925).
Prince v. Massachusetts, 321 U.S. 158 (1949).
Reynolds v. United States, 98 U.S. 145 (1878).
Roemer v. Board of Public Works of Maryland, 426 U.S. 736 (1976).
Rosenberger v. Rector and Visitors of the University of Virginia, 515 U.S. 819 (1995).
Santa Fe Independent School District v. Doe, 530 U.S. 290 (2000).
Sherbert v. Verner, 374 U.S. 398 (1963).
Sloan v. Lemon, 413 U.S. 825 (1973).
Tilton v. Richardson, 403 U.S. 672 (1971).
Torcaso v. Watkins, 367 U.S. 488 (1961).
Town of Greece v. Galloway, 572 U.S. 565 (2014).
Trans World Airlines v. Hardison, 432 U.S. 63 (1977).
Trinity Lutheran Church of Columbia, Inc. v. Comer, 327 S. Ct. 2012 (2017).

Tudor v. Board of Education, 348 U.S. 816 (1954).
United States v. Macintosh, 283 U.S. 605 (1931).
United States v. Schwimmer, 279 U.S. 644 (1929).
United States v. Seeger, 380 U.S. 163 (1965).
Van Orden v. Perry, 545 U.S. 677 (2005).
Wallace v. Jaffree, 472 U.S. 38 (1985).
Watson v. Jones, 13 Wall. 679 (1872).
Walz v. Tax Commission of the City of New York, 397 U.S. 644 (1970).
West Virginia v. Barnette, 319 U.S. 624 (1942).
Wisconsin v. Yoder, 406 U.S. 205 (1972).
Witters v. Washington Department of Services for the Blind, 474 U.S. 481 (1986).
Wolman v. Walter, 433 U.S. 229 (1977).
Worldwide Church of God v. State of California, 446 U.S. 987 (1980).
Zelman v. Simmons-Harris, 536 U.S. 639 (2002).
Zobrest v. Catalina Foothills School District, 509 U.S. 1 (1993).
Zorach v. Clauson, 343 U.S. 306 (1952).

Index

About the Author

Dr. J. David Holcomb is professor of history and political science and director of the honors program at the University of Mary Hardin-Baylor. He received a BA in history and philosophy from William Jewell College and an MA and PhD in church-state studies from Baylor University. Holcomb's publications include articles in the *Journal of Law and Religion* and the *Journal of Church and State*.

www.ingramcontent.com/pod-product-compliance
Ingram Content Group UK Ltd.
Pitfield, Milton Keynes, MK11 3LW, UK
UKHW041842031026
15587UKWH00002B/950

9 780739 14901